D0857056

LC 212.2 .S22
C2

00714

3 1735 005 243 484

Sex Equity Handbook for Schools

UNIVERSITY
OF PITTSBURGH

LIBRARIES

Sex Equity
Handbook for Schools

TBC

Sex Equity
Handbook for Schools

Myra Pollack Sadker
David Miller Sadker

LC212.2
S22
c.2

Longman
New York & London

Sex Equity Handbook for Schools

Longman Inc., 19 West 44th Street, New York, N.Y. 10036
Associated companies, branches, and representatives
throughout the world.

Copyright © 1982 by Longman Inc.

All rights reserved. No part of this publication may be
reproduced, stored in a retrieval system, or transmitted
in any form or by any means, electronic, mechanical,
photocopying, recording, or otherwise, without the prior
permission of the publisher.

Developmental Editor: Lane Akers
Editorial and Design Supervisor: Diane Perlmuth
Interior Design: Pencils Portfolio, Inc.
Manufacturing and Production Supervisor: Anne Musso
Composition: Kingsport Press
Printing and Binding: Fairfield Graphics

Library of Congress Cataloging in Publication Data

Sadker, Myra.
  Sex equity handbook for schools.

  Bibliography: p.
  Includes index.
  1. Sex discrimination in education—United States.
I. Sadker, David Miller, 1942–   II. Title.
LC212.2.S22   370.19'345   81–8213
ISBN 0-582-28260-8 (cased)   AACR2
ISBN 0-582-28261-6 (pbk.)

Manufactured in the United States of America
9 8 7 6 5 4 3 2 1

Acknowledgments

The authors and publisher gratefully acknowledge permission to reprint the following material:

From *The House that Jill and Jack Built,* Berkeley Unified School District, Berkeley, California. Reprinted by permission of Berkeley Unified School District.

From *The Yellow, Blue, and Red Book* by Project Equality, John D. Ross and LaRae Glennon, Directors, 1977. Reprinted by permission of Project Equality, Seattle, Washington.

From *How High the Sky? How Far the Moon?* by Sharon Menard, 1980. Developed by the Non-Sexist Child Development Project, Women's Educational Equity Act Program, U.S. Department of Health, Education and Welfare. Reprinted by permission of the U.S. Department of Education.

From *Career Development: Education for Living* © 1974 by J. C. Penny Company, Inc., Consumer Affairs Department. Used by permission.

From *Classroom Activities to Combat Stereotyping in Career Choice* by American Institutes of Research, April 1980. American Institutes of Research, Palo Alto, California. Reprinted by permission of Learning Corporation of America.

From *Choices: Learning About Changing Sex Roles* by Sherri Wagner, 1977. Reprinted by permission of Sherri Wagner, Minneapolis, Minnesota.

From *Today's Changing Roles: An Approach to Non-Sexist Teaching,* developed by Educational Challenges, Inc., Alexandria, Virginia, 1974. Resource Center for Sex Roles in Education, The National Foundation for the Improvement of Education. Reprinted by permission of Educational Challenges, Inc. and Resource Center for Sex Roles in Education.

The authors and publisher gratefully acknowledge permission to adapt and reprint the following monographs:

Being a Man by David Sadker, 1979. Resource Center on Sex Roles in Education, National Foundation for the Improvment of Education, U.S. Department of Health, Education and Welfare. Reprinted by permission of the U.S. Department of Education.

Sexism in Education by Rita Bornstein, 1980. Non-Sexist Teacher Education Project, Myra and David Sadker, Project Directors, Women's Educational Equity Act Program, U.S. Department of Education. Reprinted by permission of the U.S. Department of Education.

Beyond the Dick and Jane Syndrome: Confronting Sex Bias in Instructional Materials by Donna Gollnick, 1980. Non-Sexist Teacher Education Project, Myra and David Sadker, Project Directors, Women's Educational Equity Act Program, U.S. Department of Education. Reprinted by permission of the U.S. Department of Education.

Between Teacher and Student: Overcoming Sex Bias in Classroom Interaction by Myra and David Sadker, 1980. Non-Sexist Teacher Education Project, Myra and David Sadker, 1980. Non-Sexist Teacher Education Project, Myra and David Sadker, Project Directors, Women's Educational Equity Act Program, U.S. Department of Education. Reprinted by permission of U.S. Department of Education.

Contents

Preface

Not much more than a decade ago, sex equity was an unknown term in most educational circles. When there was a rare presentation at conventions or meetings, people would get the term mixed up with sex education. But as consciousness grew, so did activity, excitement, commitment. Articles were written about bias in books. Research studies documented the harmful impact of sex bias in school and society. Grants were awarded to develop nonbiased materials and educational programs. And Title IX of the Education Amendments of 1972 provided a much needed legal tool to combat discrimination in schools.

This book could not have been written without the progress achieved during the past decade. The *Sex Equity Handbook for Schools* provides an overview of the critical areas of sex equity in schools, as well as practical strategies for the elimination of sex bias in education. Lesson plans and units are included along with a synopsis of the relevant research and a narrative of the nature of sex bias in today's classrooms. This *Handbook* is intended to inform; it is also designed for practical classroom application.

There is a tendency to perceive sex equity as a women's issue; this *Handbook* assumes a broader perspective. Although the research documents the significant and damaging impact of sex bias on females, sex stereotyping also harms males. This *Handbook* considers the impact of sex stereotyping on boys as well as girls, on men as well as women.

Some of the chapters in this book were developed by the authors through the support of a Women's Educational Equity Act (WEEA) grant to develop a Nonsexist Teacher Education curriculum. These chapters were field tested in 10 colleges and universities across the nation, and then revised based on the evaluation results. Our thanks go to Leslie Wolfe, Director of the Women's Educational Equity Act Program, and to John Fiegel, our project officer, for their help in this endeavor. Several of the lesson plans and unit activities were also developed as a result of various WEEA grants. In our opinion, they represent the many excellent strategies that are now available for teachers to use in their class-rooms.

Other materials were developed by the authors through the support of Title IV of the 1964 Civil Rights Act. Special appreciation is extended to Shirley McCune, Deputy Assistant Secretary for Equal Educational Opportunity Programs. Dr. McCune has been a source of constant support for so many who are working for sex equity in education.

We want to thank many other individuals—Barbara Gordon and Susan Shaffer for their careful compilation of the Resource Directory; Rita Bornstein and Donna Gollnick for developing two of the chapters in this book; Tom Hicks for his innovative suggestions and diligent proofreading. But most of all we offer our appreciation and admiration to educators across the country who are working to make sex equity a reality. Schools and children are better off for their efforts.

Myra Pollack Sadker
David Miller Sadker

This book is dedicated
to our parents

Shirley and Louis Pollack
Evelyn and Jerome Sadker

Sex Equity
Handbook for Schools

1

Cost of Sex Bias in Schools:
The Report Card

Objective

- To become aware of how sex bias affects girls and boys in school

The first chapter of this book is a report card. You will not find it in any elementary or secondary school classrooms. Nevertheless, it is an important evaluation. It reflects the loss that both girls and boys suffer because of sex bias in society and in our schools. Years after the passage of Title IX of the Education Amendments of 1972, sex bias and discrimination still permeate school life.

GIRLS	BOYS

Academic

GIRLS	BOYS
• Girls start out ahead of boys in speaking, reading, and counting. In the early grades, their academic performance is equal to boys in math and science. However, as they progress through school, their achievement test scores show significant decline. The scores of boys, on the other hand, continue to rise and eventually reach and surpass those of their female counterparts, particularly in the areas of math and science.[1]	• Boys are more likely to be scolded and reprimanded in classrooms, even when the observed conduct and behavior of boys and girls does not differ. Also, boys are more likely to be referred to school authorities for disciplinary action than are girls.[6]
• In spite of performance decline on standardized achievement tests, girls frequently receive better grades in school. This may be one of the rewards they get for being more quiet and docile in the classroom. However, this may be at the cost of independence and self-reliance.[2]	• Boys are far more likely to be identified as exhibiting learning disabilities, reading problems, and mental retardation.[7]
• Girls are more likely to be invisible members of classrooms. They receive fewer academic contacts, less praise, fewer complex and abstract questions, and less instruction on how to do things for themselves.[3]	• Not only are boys identified as having learning and reading disabilities; they also receive lower grades, are more likely to be grade repeaters, and are less likely to complete high school.[8]

GIRLS	BOYS

Academic

- Girls who are gifted in mathematics are far less likely to be identified than are gifted boys. Those girls who are identified as gifted, are far less likely to participate in special or accelerated math classes to develop this special talent.[4]
- Girls who suffer from learning disabilities are also less likely to be identified or to participate in special education programs than are learning-disabled boys.[5]

Psychological and Physical

- Although women achieve better grades than men, they are less likely to believe that they can do college work. In fact, of the brightest high school graduates who do not go on to college, 70 to 90 percent are women.[9]
- Learned helplessness exists when failure is perceived as insurmountable. Girls are more likely than boys to exhibit this pattern. They attribute failure to internal factors, such as ability, rather than to external factors, such as luck or effort. Girls who exhibit learned helplessness avoid failure situations—they stop trying. Research indicates that teacher interaction patterns may contribute to the learned helplessness exhibited by female students.[10]
- By high school, young women demonstrate a decline in career commitment. This decline is related to their feeling that boys disapprove of a woman using her intelligence.[11]
- Tests reveal that the majority of female and male college students report that the characteristics traditionally associated with masculinity are more valuable and more socially desirable than those characteristics associated with femininity.[12]
- In athletics, females also suffer from sex bias. For example, women's athletic budgets in the nation's colleges are equal to approximately 18 percent of the men's budgets.[13]

- Society socializes boys into an active, independent, and aggressive role. But such behavior is incongruent with school norms and rituals that stress quiet behavior and docility. This results in a pattern of role conflict for boys, particularly during the elementary years.[14]
- Hyperactivity is estimated to be nine times more prevalent in boys than in girls. Boys are more likely to be identified as having emotional problems, and statistics indicate a higher male suicide rate.[15]
- Boys are taught stereotyped behaviors earlier and more harshly than girls; there is a 20 percent greater probability that such stereotyped behavior will stay with them for life.[16]
- Conforming to the male sex role stereotype takes a psychological toll. Boys who score high on sex-appropriate behavior tests also score highest on anxiety tests.[17]
- Males are less likely than females to be close friends with one another. When asked, most males identify females as their closest friends.[18]
- The strain and anxiety associated with conforming to the male sex stereotype also affects boys physically. Males are more likely to succumb to serious disease and to be victims of accidents or violence. The average life expectancy of men is eight years shorter than of women.[19]

GIRLS	BOYS

Careers and Family Relationships

- When elementary school girls are asked to describe what they want to do when they grow up, they are able to identify only a limited number of career options, and even these fit stereotypic patterns. The majority identify only two careers, teaching and nursing. Boys, on the other hand, are able to identify many more potential occupations.[20]
- The majority of girls enter college without completing four years of high school mathematics. This lack of preparation in math serves as a "critical filter," inhibiting or preventing girls from many science, math, and technologically related careers.[21]
- The preparation and counseling girls receive in school contribute to the economic penalties that they encounter in the workplace. Although over 90 percent of the girls in our classrooms will work in the paid labor force for all or part of their lives, the following statistics reveal the cost of the bias that they encounter:[22]
- More than a third of families headed by women live below the poverty level.
- A woman with a college degree will typically earn less than a male who is a high school dropout.
- The typical working woman will earn 59 cents for every dollar earned by a male worker.
- Minority women earn even less, averaging only 50 percent of the wages earned by white males.
- Women are 79 percent of all clerical workers, but only 5 percent of all craft workers.
- Women must work nine days to earn what men get paid for five days of work.
- In contrast to the popular belief that things are getting better for female workers, since 1954 the gap between the wages earned by men and women has not gotten smaller.
- A majority of women work not for "extra" cash, but because of economic necessity.

- Teachers and counselors advise boys to enter sex stereotyped careers and limit their potential in occupations like kindergarten teacher, nurse, or secretary.[23]
- Many boys build career expectations that are higher than their abilities. This results in later compromise, disappointment, and frustration.[24]
- Both at school and at home, boys are taught to hide or suppress their emotions; as men they may find it difficult or impossible to show feelings towards their family and friends.[25]
- Boys are actively discouraged from playing with dolls (except those that play sports or wage war). Few schools provide programs that encourage boys to learn about the skills of parenting. Many men, through absence and apathy, become not so much parents as "transparents." In fact, the typical father spends only 12 minutes a day interacting with his children.[26]
- Men and women differ in their beliefs of the important aspects of a father's role. Men emphasize the need for the father to earn a good income and to provide solutions to family problems. Women, on the other hand, stress the need for fathers to assist in caring for children and responding to the emotional needs of the family. These differing perceptions of fatherhood lead to family strain and anxiety.[27]

GIRLS	BOYS

Careers and Family Relationships

Nearly two-thirds of all women in the labor force are single, widowed, divorced, or separated, or are married to spouses earning less than $10,000 a year.

THE CHANGING REPORT CARD [28]

We sat solemnly in our seats as the roll was called. It seemed as though the day's lessons would never end. For some of us, the walk home after school was long and lonely as we explored potential alibis and excuses. The real impact of "Report Card Day" was yet to be felt.

If you have ever experienced being on the receiving end of a poor report card, then you may recall that mixture of fear and remorse as you explained your unsatisfactory grades to your parents. Your litany of excuses seemed weak in the face of the school's official evaluation. Perhaps the only effective weapon in your arsenal was the promise to mend your ways, to do better next time.

That same response can also be offered in terms of this report card on the cost of sex bias. As grim as these statistics and research findings are, they are not etched in stone. There will be other report cards, other opportunities to create an educational system that is more equitable in its treatment of both girls and boys. Change is not only possible. It is already taking place. Consider the following:

- Formerly studies indicated that as children progressed through school, their opinion of boys became higher and their opinion of girls became lower. Recent research indicates that girls now ascribe a more positive value to their own sex. This more positive self-image may reflect society's greater sensitivity to sexism and a more positive perception of the role of women.[29]
- One-third of the women participating in a recent survey indicated a preference for a nontraditional, androgynous parenting role.[30]
- In the report card, we reported that women's athletic budgets in 1978–1979 were only 18 percent of men's budgets. But seen in perspective, a positive trend is apparent. In 1974, this figure was only 2 percent. Moreover, the number of females participating in athletics has increased 570 percent between 1970 and 1980.[31]
- In 1958, the labor force participation rate of women stood at 33 percent; by 1980 it had reached 50 percent. Although most

women are still overrepresented in low-paying jobs, barriers are falling as some women are entering higher level positions previously held only by men.[32]

These new findings are encouraging, but many barriers still exist. For example, as far back as 1946,[33] studies documented the extensive sex bias in textbooks. Women were frequently omitted, and when included, were portrayed in stereotypic roles. In response to these studies and to the voices of criticism, the publishing companies issued guidelines designed to help authors and editors avoid sexist portrayals. But recent analysis of school textbooks has disclosed that the number of male-centered stories has *increased* rather than decreased. Minority females remain almost nonexistent. Language is not so blatantly masculine, fewer women are pictured wearing aprons; but schoolbooks are still telling stories in which few women find a place.[34]

Change seldom comes easy or fast. There are few quick and dirty tricks that will break down barriers that have existed for centuries. Identifying the problem is only the first step. In many ways, it is the easiest step to take. The real challenge and opportunity belong to teachers.

The chapters that follow describe the problems and provide resources to solve them. When teachers become aware of the nature and cost of sex bias in schools, they can make an important difference in the lives of their students. Teachers can change the report card or even make it obsolete. They can make sex equity become a reality for children in our schools. Then tomorrow's children, boys and girls, need not suffer from the limiting impact of sex-role stereotyping.

ENDNOTES

[1] Eleanor Maccoby and Carol Jacklin, *The Psychology of Sex Differences* (Stanford, Calif.: Stanford University Press, 1974).

[2] Ibid.
Ina Mullis, *Educational Achievement and Sex Discrimination* (Denver: National Assessment of Educational Progress, 1975).

[3] T. Jeana Wirtenberg, "Expanding Girls Occupational Potential: A Case Study of the Implementation of Title IX's Anti-Segregation Provision in Seventh Grade Practical Arts" (unpublished doctoral dissertation, University of California, 1979).

H. Felsenthal, "Sex Differences in Expressive Thought of Gifted Children in the Classroom," American Educational Research Association, ERIC, Ed. 039–106, 1970.

G. Leinhardt, A. Seewald, and M. Engel, "Learning What's Taught: Sex Differences in Instruction," *Journal of Educational Psychology* 71 (1979).

W. Casper, "An Analysis of Sex Differences in Teacher-Student Interaction as Manifest in Verbal and Nonverbal Cues," (unpublished doctoral dissertation, University of Tennessee, 1970).

Lisa Serbin and D. O'Leary, "How Nursery Schools Teach Girls to Shut Up," *Psychology Today* 9 (1975).

[4] Lynn H. Fox, "The Effects of Sex Role Socialization on Mathematics Participation and Achievement," in Lynn H. Fox, Elizabeth Fennema, and Julia Sherman, *Women and Mathematics: Research Perspectives for Change*, NIE Papers in Education and Work, No. 8 (Washington, D.C.: National Institute of Education, 1977).

[5] William E. Davis, "A Comparison of Teacher Referral and Pupil Self-Referral Measures Relative to Perceived School Adjustment," *Psychology in the Schools* 15 (January 1978).

Jeremy Lietz and Mary Gregory, "Pupil Race and Sex Determinants of Office and Exceptional Educational Referrals," *Education Research Quarterly* 3 (Summer 1978).

Paula Caplan, "Sex, Age, Behavior, and School Subject as Determinants of Report of Learning Problems," *Journal of Learning Disabilities* 10 (May 1977).

[6] D. L. Duke, "Who Misbehaves? A High School Studies Its Discipline Problems," *Educational Administration Quarterly* 12 (1976).

Claire Etaugh and Heidi Harlow, "Behaviors of Male and Female Teachers as Related to Behaviors and Attitudes of Elementary School Children," *The Journal of Genetic Psychology* 127 (1975).

Thomas Good and Jere Brophy, "Questioned Equality for Grade One Boys and Girls," *Reading Teacher* 4 (1971).

[7] Maccoby and Jacklin, *The Psychology of Sex Differences.*

Davis, "A Comparison of Teacher Referral and Pupil Self-Referral Measures Relative to Perceived School Adjustment."

National Assessment of Educational Progress, *Reading Change, 1970–75: Summary Volume*, Reading Report No. 06-R-21 (Denver: NAEP, 1978).

Patricia Gillespie and Albert H. Fink, "The Influence of Sexism on the Education of Handicapped Children," *Exceptional Children* 41 (1974).

[8] Jere Brophy and Thomas Good, "Feminization of American Elementary Schools," *Phi Delta Kappan* 54 (April 1973).

[9] *Facts About Women in Education*, WEAL Washington, D.C., 1976.

[10] Carol Dweck and N. Reppucci, "Learned Helplessness and Reinforcement Responsibility in Children," *Journal of Personality and Social Psychology* 25 (1973).

J. Nicholls, "Causal Attributions and Other Achievement-Related Cognitions: Effects of Task Outcomes, Attainment Value, and Sex," *Journal of Personality and Social Psychology* 31 (1975).

Carol Dweck and D. Gilliard, "Expectancy Statements as Determinants of Reactions to Failure: Sex Differences in Persistence and Expectancy Change," *Journal of Personality and Social Psychology* 32 (1975).

[11] Peggy Hawley, "What Women Think Men Think," *Journal of Counseling Psychology* 18 (Autumn 1971).

[12] I. K. Broverman, S. R. Vogel, D. M. Broverman, F. E. Clarkson, and P. S. Rosenkranz, "Sex-Role Stereotypes: A Current Appraisal," *Journal of Social Issues* 28 (1972).

[13] *AIAW School Year Summary, 1978–79,* The Association for Intercollegiate Athletics for Women, Washington, D.C. 1979.

[14] Nancy Frazier and Myra Sadker, *Sexism in School and Society* (New York: Harper & Row, 1973).

William Goldman and Anne May, "Males: A Minority Group in the Classroom," *Journal of Learning Disabilities* 3 (May 1970).

[15] Frances Bentzen, "Sex Ratios in Learning and Behavior Disorders," *The National Elementary Principal* 46 (1966).

Diane McGuiness, "How Schools Discriminate Against Boys," *Human Nature* (1979).

[16] S. Fling and M. Manosevitz, "Sex Typing in Nursery School Children's Play Interests," *Developmental Psychology* 7 (1972).

Ruth Hartley, "Sex Role Pressures and the Socialization of the Male Child," *Psychological Reports* 5 (1979).

[17] I. Waldron, "Why Do Women Live Longer than Men?" *Journal of Human Stress* 2 (1976).

S. L. Bem, "The Measurement of Psychological Adrogyny," *Journal of Consulting and Clinical Psychology* 42 (1974).

S. L. Bem, "Sex Role Adaptability: One Consequence of Psychological Adrogyny," *Journal of Personality and Social Psychology* 31 (1975).

[18] M. Komarovsky, "Patterns of Self-Disclosure of Male Undergraduates," *Journal of Marriage and the Family* 36 (1974).

Joseph Pleck, "Male-Male Friendship: Is Brotherhood Possible?" in M. Glazer (ed.) *Old Family/New Family: Interpersonal Relationships* (New York: Van Nostrand Reinhold, 1975).

[19] Waldron, "Why Do Women Live Longer than Men?"

[20] W. R. Looft, "Sex Differences in the Expression of Vocational Aspirations by Elementary School Children," *Developmental Psychology* 5 (1971).

[21] Lucy Sells, "High School Mathematics as the Critical Filter in the Job Market," in *Developing Opportunities for Minorities in Graduate Education,* proceedings of the Conference on Minority Graduate Education at the University of California, Berkeley, 1973.

[22] These statistics have been compiled from *The Earnings Gap Between Men and Women,* U.S. Department of Labor, Women's Bureau, GPO (1979); *Twenty Facts on Working Women,* U.S. Department of Labor, Women's Bureau, GPO (1978).

[23] Looft, "Sex Differences in the Expression of Vocational Aspirations by Elementary School Children."

Frazier and Sadker, *Sexism in School and Society.*

Joseph Pleck and Robert Brannon (eds.), "Male Roles and the Male Experience," *Journal of Social Issues* 34 (1978).

[24] Pleck and Brannon (eds.), "Male Roles and the Male Experience."

[25] S. Jourard, *The Transparent Self* (New York: Van Nostrand, 1976).

M. Komarovsky, *Dilemmas of Masculinity: A Study of College Youth* (New York: Norton, 1976).

Herb Goldberg, *The Hazards of Being Male* (New York: Nash, 1976).

[26] Philip Stone, "Child Care in Twelve Counties," in Alexander Szalai (ed.) *The Use of Time* (The Hague: Mouton, 1972).

[27] Deanna Eversoll, "The Changing Father Role: Implications for Parent Education Programs for Today's Youth," *Adolescence* XIV (Fall 1979).

[28] The report card on sex bias in schools was adapted from a handout developed by Myra and David Sadker for the Mid-Atlantic Center for Sex Equity at The American University.

[29] Nancy Olsen and Eleanor Willemsen, "Studying Sex Prejudice in Children," *The Journal of Genetic Psychology* 133 (1978).

Deanna Kuhn, Sharon Nash, and Laura Bricken, "Sex Role Concepts of Two- and Three-Year-Olds," *Child Development* 49 (1978).

S. Smith, "Age and Sex Differences in Children's Opinion Concerning Sex Differences," *Journal of Genetic Psychology* 54 (March 1939).

[30] Eversoll, "The Changing Father Role: Implications for Parent Education Programs for Today's Youth."

[31] AIAW School Year Summary, 1978–79.

More Hurdles to Clear, U.S. Commission on Civil Rights, Washington, D.C., 1980.

[32] *More Hurdles to Clear.*

[33] I. Child, E. Potter, and E. Levine, "Children's Textbooks and Personality Development: An Explanation in the Social Psychology of Education," *Psychological Monographs* 60 (1946).

[34] Gwyneth Britton and Margaret Lumpkin, *A Consumer's Guide to Sex, Race and Career Bias in Public School Textbooks* (Corvallis, OR: Britton and Assoc., 1977).

2

Sexism in Education*

Rita Bornstein

Objectives

- To analyze commonly held assumptions about sex-appropriate roles, jobs, and behavior
- To describe the differential treatment of female and male students
- To evaluate the effects of sex bias on females and males
- To describe the status of women in the paid labor force
- To explain the rationale and requirements of Title IX
- To speculate about the ideal nonsexist teaching environment

ANATOMY AS DESTINY

Members of a New Guinea tribe studied by anthropologist Margaret Mead in the early 1930s believed that only a baby born with its umbilical cord wrapped around its neck would grow up to be an artist. Astoundingly, such babies did grow up to become artists. And no matter how hard and long other tribe members practiced, they never became accomplished artists.[1] Social expectations for adult development in this tribe had clearly limited the achievement possible for individual tribe members.

Is it possible that in enlightened twentieth-century America we limit individual achievement in the same way by marking out roles, jobs, and behavior for people based on other arbitrary factors such as sex, race, and social class? Educators, parents, and politicians claim that they want every individual to have access to all opportunities afforded by this society. But beneath this professed philosophy there seems to run a deeper current of assumptions that the capacities, interests, and talents of people are related to their class, color, and sex. Much like the accidental placement of the umbilical cord, these factors subtly influence an individual's possibilities for adult achievement.

This difference between our stated philosophies of education and our actual expectations for student achievement accounts for the mixed messages children receive in school. They are told they can be anything

---

* This chapter is adapted from Rita Bornstein, *Sexism in Education* (U.S. Dept of Education, Women's Educational Equity Act Program, 1980).

they want to be and that all opportunities, careers, and life styles will be available to them as adults.

In practice, however, subtle factors work to result in the sorting, grouping, and tracking of minority and female students in stereotyped patterns that prepare them to accept traditional roles and jobs in adult life, rather than to explore all options and opportunities according to their individual talents and interests.

These subtle influences on students are part of the unplanned, unofficial learning that children absorb as they move through school— often called the hidden curriculum—in contrast to the official planned curriculum. This hidden curriculum includes: the messages children receive about themselves and others of their sex and race through the illustrations, language, and content of textbooks, films, and visual displays; the ways in which administrators, teachers, and other students interact with them; the part they play in important school rituals; and the extent to which they come in contact with influential role models of their own sex and race.

Thus, poor, minority, and female students learn very early that social expectations for their development limit them to traditional educational and career patterns. On the other hand, affluent, nonminority, male students find that society has high expectations for their performance and achievement and that anything less represents failure. Fortunately, our educational and social system is flexible enough to allow people to try out and succeed in nontraditional paths. We all know many persons who have surmounted the handicaps of arbitrary and limiting social expectations.

As educators, your role is to ensure that your students break out of group stereotypes to explore and pursue a wide variety of school and life options. You will be strengthening individual students to resist the continuous bombardment of messages they receive regarding sex-, race-, and class-appropriate roles, jobs, and behavior.

You have the opportunity to break the vicious circle that may otherwise imprison your students for the rest of their lives. This vicious circle is a web of attitudes and behavior that severely constricts options for human development. In prescribing what is appropriate and natural for people based on their class, sex, and race, it functions as a self-fulfilling prophecy.

The vicious circle of sexism begins with commonly accepted stereotyped assumptions regarding sex differences. These assumptions manifest themselves in different expectations for and treatment of girls and boys in school. When students undergo different experiences, training, and opportunities based on their sex, they lose their individual academic, occupational, and personality potential. As adults, these well-rehearsed students take up traditional functions at home, at work, and in the community. The perpetuation of these traditions reinforces stereotyped assumptions people hold about what is appropriate and natural for women and men, and the circle of sexism continues.

In this chapter we will explore the implications of this vicious circle of sexism for the education of women and men. We will examine common assumptions about people based on their sex, the differential treatment of female and male students, and the negative outcomes of this treatment. Finally, we will discuss the potential of Title IX, the federal law prohibiting sex discrimination in schools, for equalizing student treatment, thus changing the destinies of women and men, and, in the long run, changing our basic assumptions about female and male behavior.

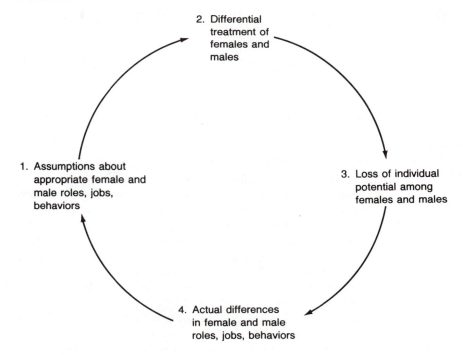

SEX DISCRIMINATION TODAY? DON'T BE RIDICULOUS!

It is a matter of history that in early American society women were not considered the equals of men. They were not sent to school or permitted to vote, had no legal control over their property or children, could not initiate a divorce, and could not smoke or drink in public. These facts sound like ancient historical curiosities—as outdated as pantaloons and powdered wigs. Few people think there is any difference between the way women and men are treated in today's world, especially in schools.

Certainly, most teachers, counselors, and principals do not want to be guilty of sex or race discrimination or of discrimination based on a person's physical or emotional handicaps. They want to treat students as unique individuals.

But regardless of well-stated philosophies of education, people act on the basis of deep-rooted assumptions that differentiate between the appropriate behavior, roles, and jobs for women and men. These assumptions may not even be conscious, but they result in subtle differences in the way we treat people—what we expect from them, how we think they should act, what we think they should look like, and how we think they should respond to us.

Let us explore some of these assumptions about women. Rate the following statements true or false according to your own beliefs.

QUESTIONNAIRE ON WOMEN

True False

1. A woman's primary role in life is raising children and taking care of her husband. Any career she has should fit around those responsibilities.

2. A woman should work only if her husband cannot support her, if she has no children, or if she is single.

3. Women make better elementary school teachers than men because they are more patient with young children.

4. A woman who appears intelligent, aggressive, and demanding will probably have trouble finding a husband.

5. Girls who engage in competitive athletics run the risk of becoming muscular and unfeminine.

6. Unattractive women are more in need of job skills than attractive women.

7. A girl should never play better tennis than her boyfriend because it is bad for his ego.

8. Men convey the authority and leadership necessary for school administration better than women do.

9. Tomboyish behavior is unbecoming in a teenage girl.

10. Women are too emotional to inspire confidence as brain surgeons, criminal lawyers, corporate executives, or military commanders.

11. The fact that there have been so few women political leaders, artists, explorers, and scientists indicates that they do not have the creative and intellectual ability of men.

12. A man should stand when a woman enters a room, give a woman his seat in a crowded bus, and hold the door open for a woman to enter first.

____ ____ 13. It is more unbecoming for a woman to be intoxicated than for a man.

____ ____ 14. There are still many jobs in which men should be given preference over women in hiring and promotion.

____ ____ 15. Menstruating women should not engage in strenuous physical activity or in important decision making.

____ ____ 16. While men can be expected to tell dirty jokes occasionally, women should never do so.

____ ____ 17. A woman will never be truly satisfied unless she has been a wife and a mother.

____ ____ 18. If a family has limited finances, it is more important to send a son to college than to send a daughter.

____ ____ 19. There are some jobs that will never be suitable for women, such as automobile repair, bricklaying, and long-distance trucking.

____ ____ 20. In the ideal family, the father works and the mother stays home and raises the children.

How did you answer the 20 items in this questionnaire? What evidence can you present to support your point of view?

These statements can be grouped under three basic assumptions that run like an undercurrent through American life, and are reflected in all of our social institutions. Each of these assumptions carries with it many implications for the education of women.

ASSUMPTION 1: Women's Place Is in the Home

Conventional wisdom: Many people today believe that a woman should have job skills to fall back on in case she must work. Her primary prescribed role, however, is in the home; if in the paid work force, it should be as that of nurturer, helper, and supporter.

Implications for schooling: If women are to orient themselves around the home rather than around civic or economic affairs, then they must be reinforced with domestic images and goals. If women are to be mothers, elementary school teachers, secretaries, nurses, hairdressers, maids, and social workers, then they do not need training in calculus, physics, chemistry, auto mechanics, or welding. If a young woman is to concentrate on catching a husband, then it is not necessary to plan seriously for college or a career.

ASSUMPTION 2: Women Are Physically, Emotionally, and Intellectually Inferior to Men

Conventional wisdom: Human history as recorded in history books subtly communicates the idea that women have contributed little to society besides babies. They have not been hunters, builders, explorers, artists, leaders, scholars, or philosophers. This is evidence to many people of the inferior physical, emotional, and intellectual makeup of women. A tradition of protection has arisen for this supposedly poorly endowed but necessary group—protection from strenuous physical exertion, protection from stress, protection from unpleasantness, protection from fiscal matters, protection from decision making, protection from competition, and protection from intellectual challenge.

Implications for schooling: If strenuous activity, physical exertion, and competition are not appropriate for women, then rigious physical education programs and interscholastic team sports are not essential. If women are emotionally fragile, then they ought not be given leadership responsibilities in classes or clubs. If women are not intellectual, then it isn't essential that they master highly complex information—particularly in areas of politics, science, and technology.

ASSUMPTION 3: Women Should Cultivate Traditionally Feminine Characteristics

Conventional wisdom: Many people find women who are ambitious, decisive, challenging, independent, or intellectual to be unfeminine and offensive. They want women to develop their talents but to remain typically feminine—deferential, accommodating, restrained, and accepting. Women who adopt conventionally male modes of behavior are often mocked, scorned, or pitied.

Implications for schooling: If women are to exhibit typically feminine behaviors, then they must be reinforced for being attractive, sweet, quiet, attentive, and neat; not for being scholarly, questioning, argumentative, or independent. Inappropriate behavior such as physical and intellectual assertiveness can be discouraged through ridicule, lack of attention, or punishment.

IF AMELIA EARHART HAD BEEN A LADY, SHE WOULDN'T HAVE HAD WINGS

As a child, Amelia Earhart, the well-known aviator who made a solo flight across the Atlantic a year after Lindbergh, was encouraged to experiment, to build things, to run free and explore the outdoors along with her brothers. Her husband, in his biography of her, traces her "masculine" spirit of adventure to this "deviant" upbringing.[2] Many outstanding women remember being tomboys as children.

Successful adults in our society, men and women both, exhibit the so-called masculine characteristics of independence, assertiveness, leadership ability, self-reliance, and emotional stability. Are schools nurturing these traits in female students?

In the nineteenth century, those families who could afford it sent their daughters to female academies where they learned the skills necessary to make a good marriage: foreign languages, piano, handwriting, embroidery, religious reading. Girls and boys in today's schools are not assigned a separate curriculum; they have exposure to the same experiences and training. Is it possible that despite this progress toward equal education we are still subtly preparing girls primarily for marriage and motherhood and a few traditional career goals? Are we driving into the future while looking backward through the rearview mirror instead of at the road ahead? Alvin Toffler writes in *Future Shock*, ". . . our schools face backward toward a dying system rather than forward to the emerging new society." [3] Is the nineteenth-century view of women still with us?

VEHICLES OF DIFFERENTIAL TREATMENT

Certain traditional vehicles exist through which educators transmit the information, skills, and experiences believed necessary for students. These vehicles include: textbooks and other instructional materials, the curriculum, teacher behavior, counseling materials and techniques, physical activity, extracurricular activities.

As these traditional educational vehicles prepare students for adult life in this society, they also communicate subtle but powerful messages about appropriate female and male roles, jobs, and behavior.

1. Textbooks and Instructional Materials

Can you imagine school without textbooks? Was there ever a year you did not have a stack of those heavy, hard-covered books with the slick paper from which classroom lessons were conducted and homework assigned? Probably you carried them around, did your assignments, read aloud from them in class, without ever consciously noticing the sex, race, ethnic and class biases they reflected. From those books you learned reading, mathematics, history, literature, science and psychology.

While you were learning the cognitive information conveyed in those books, you were also assimilating stereotypic values and roles. Textbooks appear to be authoritative, and are treated with reverence by many teachers. Thus we tend to absorb without questioning the subtle messages they convey—through language, illustrations and content— what information is omitted, what is included, and how it is arranged.

The hidden messages in textbooks have been analyzed by a number of researchers. Their findings are startling and unsettling to us because we have grown up so oblivious to these subtle but pervasive messages.

One major study conducted in 1972, *Dick and Jane as Victims,* analyzed 2760 stories in 134 elementary school readers published by 14 major United States publishing companies and reported the following ratios: [4]

Boy-centered to girl-centered stories	5:2
Adult male to adult female main characters	3:1
Male to female biographies	6:1
Male to female animal stories	2:1
Male to female folk or fantasy stories	4:1

This study also found that the males portrayed in these stories demonstrated the traits of ingenuity, creativity, bravery, perseverance, achievement, adventurousness, curiosity, sportsmanship, helpfulness, acquisition of skills, competitiveness, use of power, autonomy, self-respect, friendship. These males also displayed the attitude that anything associated with femininity is unmanly and to be avoided at all costs.

Girls in these stories demonstrated the traits of dependency, passivity, incompetence, fearfulness, concern about their physical appearance, obedience, domesticity.

> Little girls endlessly play with dolls, cry over dolls, give tea parties, look on helplessly or passively or admiringly while boys take action. . . . They look on while boys play cowboy, look on while boys make carts, look on while boys rescue animals, look on while boys save the day.[5]

In a study of illustrations in science, math, reading, and social studies textbooks published between 1967 and 1972, females comprised only 31 percent of the total illustrations (although they are 51 percent of the population) and as the grade level increased, pictures of females decreased. Minority women were pictured only half as often as minority men, who were themselves inadequately portrayed.[6]

A 1971 study of women in over 12 of the most popular high school United States history textbooks found that women were omitted from the topics discussed and, when portrayed at all, were in a passive role.[7] Male figures were featured and quoted almost exclusively. Male pronouns ("he," "his") were used to refer both to men and to women, implying that all historical activities were carried on by men. The texts surveyed found that the contributions made by American women to Colonial life, the Civil War, frontier life, and the world wars were overlooked. Also omitted were women's work on pioneer farms, the role of women in the earlier days of the labor movement, the development of birth control and its impact on the American family, and the issues of sex discrimination in society.

Sex stereotyping and bias have also been found to be pervasive in other instructional materials on which teachers depend: audiovisuals of all types, paperback books, individualized learning kits, curriculum units, and tests.

In response to pressures for change, many publishers have developed nonsexist guidelines for their authors. However, although some changes are evident in more recently published texts, bias remains. A review of more recent studies (1975, 1976, 1977), some of them replications of earlier studies, on sexism in children's reading materials concludes that progress is slow toward nonsexist books. For example, a 1972 study found 84 percent of the women shown in homemaking roles and 17 percent in professional roles. In the 1975 replication study, 68 percent of the women were in homemaking roles and 32 percent in professional roles.[8] Although change has occurred, the books are still biased.

A recent study reports similar findings regarding university texts. An analysis of the 24 most widely used teacher education texts found that: [9]

Twenty-three give less than 1 percent of space to the issue of sexism.

One-third do not mention the issue of sexism at all. Most of the texts guilty of this oversight are in math and science—the areas where girls are most likely to have achievement difficulties.

Not a single text provides future teachers with curricular resources and instructional strategies to counteract sexism in the classroom and its harmful impact on children.

2. Curriculum

When we speak of the curriculum of a school we refer to the plan of study for the students in that school during their enrollment there. This includes the courses they take, the description and content of those courses, and the methods by which they are taught. It also includes the educational tracks students follow—general, academic, business, vocational.

Until recently there were a variety of single-sex courses offered in high schools around the country: powder-puff football, bachelor cooking, girls' and boys' physical education. Some classes were required of each sex for graduation, such as home economics for girls and shop for boys. Course descriptions, language, and content have often made it abundantly clear that no students of the other sex were welcome: "This course in sewing is for the student who would like to make some of *her* own clothes."

Course content and methodology frequently make it difficult for students of one sex to relate to the subject matter. Sex-biased language, assignments, activities, and tests perpetuate traditional stereotypes. We forget that tests teach as well as assess. For example, a test question might read: "In the United States, voters do not directly choose the *man* they wish to be president." This, of course, reinforces the notion that women are not suited for the presidency.

The contributions of women and minorities are frequently ignored or treated superficially no matter what the subject. This conveys the impression that the only worthwhile contributions to our history and culture have been made by white males.

Course prerequisites may be discriminatory if one sex has been discouraged or prevented from taking required courses or training. Discrimination also exists when students must choose between sex-stereotyped units or classes such as modern dance and basketball.

Students enter educational tracks—general, academic, business, vocational—based on counseling, teacher recommendation, vocational and achievement testing, peer and parental pressure, personal interest, and tradition. Curriculum ghettoes exist in many schools as students continue to make choices based to a great extent on race, sex, and class expectations. These choices will have enormous impact on their adult lives. For example, white girls predominate in typing and shorthand classes; thus it is unlikely that boys or minority girls will get clerical or secretarial jobs. Since white boys predominate in trade courses, girls and minority boys are not prepared for jobs in welding, carpentry, and auto mechanics.

The courses students take in secondary school influence and limit subsequent college and career choices. Most girls, for example, do not go on for advanced science and mathematics classes even if they do well in those subjects. Although there is little difference in the ability of males and females to do mathematics, there is an enormous gap in the numbers that study mathematics. Lacking four years of college-preparatory math, young women find themselves eliminated from many college majors, including astronomy, civil engineering, biochemistry, physics, mathematics, medicine, forestry, economics, and computer science. Thus, they generally find themselves in education, social work, nursing, and the humanities—fields that offer much in the way of social worth, but comparatively less pay.

Nor is it that boys like mathematics better than girls. In a study of secondary school students, one researcher found no differences in the degree to which female and male students liked mathematics relative to other subjects.[10] The greater participation by males in math is related instead to their understanding that math may be a necessary prerequisite for their subsequent careers.

Although black girls are more likely to have to work than white girls, 58 percent of black high school girls as compared with 44 percent of white high school girls enroll in the general curriculum, which offers little skill training, rather than a vocational, college preparatory, or commercial program. Among young black women out of school, those who had enrolled in the general curriculum experienced the most unemployment.[11]

Vocational education is a training ground for the world of work. However, nearly half of all the girls enrolled in vocational education are in consumer and homemaking courses, which do not prepare them for paying jobs. Moreover, the courses of study that do train for employment—and in which girls predominate—offer training in only 33 different occupations. In contrast, courses of study in which boys predominate offer training for paid employment in 95 different occupations. When girls do enroll in programs leading to paid employment, it is most often in areas such as office education or health services, which offer relatively poor pay and relatively poor prospects for advancement.[12] Minority females seem to be disproportionately concentrated in those areas of training for which anticipated pay is lowest.

Boys tend to enroll in agriculture and skilled trades, girls in home economics, child care, fashion merchandising, office occupations, and cosmetology. Since 1972, there has been an increase of 10 percent more boys studying home economics, but less than 1 percent more girls in trade and industrial programs.

3. Teacher Behavior

As you think back over your school experiences, you may remember one or two teachers who made a difference in your life. Why were those teachers significant to you? Was it that they made you feel good about yourself, special, important, worthwhile? Was it that they pushed you to study and learn, believing in your ability to master the subject matter? Was it that they found out what you were good at and rewarded it?

Many children do not receive that kind of support and encouragement from any of their teachers. The basic assumptions that teachers hold about people influence the messages they convey to their students. Teachers in mixed school settings interact more with high achieving, white, male students. When questioned, most teachers prove to be unaware of such bias in their behavior and appalled at the idea of it. However, research indicates that teachers do have a different set of expectations, behavior standards, rewards, and punishments for female and male students, minority and nonminority students, high and low achievers. Other manifestations of teacher bias can be found in classroom assignments, course content, materials, activities, language, tests, displays, and class groupings based on sex and race.

From the moment boys enter school, most teachers expect that they will be noisy, aggressive, sloppy, poor at reading, and good at mathematics. Teachers also tend to expect that girls will be well behaved, quiet, neat, good at reading, and poor at mathematics. One researcher investigated the effect of teachers' beliefs on pupil achievement and concluded that if teachers believe that first-grade boys will do as well in reading as girls do, then this will happen. Conversely, if teachers do not expect boys to do as well as girls, then their reading performance will be lower.[13] Although in our nation's schools boys more often than girls demonstrate reading and other learning difficulties, this is not true in other countries where such problems are not sex-linked and teachers expect boys to be good readers.[14]

In a study of junior high school teachers' expectations for their students, they were asked to select adjectives that they felt would describe good female and good male students.[15] Their responses follow:

Good Female Students		*Good Male Students*	
appreciative	sensitive	active	energetic
calm	dependable	adventurous	enterprising
conscientious	efficient	aggressive	frank
considerate	mature	assertive	independent
cooperative	obliging	curious	inventive
mannerly	thorough		
poised			

Other studies indicate that many teachers have lower expectations for black students than for whites and give less attention to black students.[16]

Research with elementary school teachers indicates that they interact far more with boys than with girls. Boys are not only reprimanded more, but they also receive more praise, and more direct instruction; they are listened to more frequently, and are rewarded more for creative behavior.[17]

The kinds of tasks and groupings assigned by teachers are often based on stereotyped notions about appropriate female and male behavior. Boys are asked to carry books, move furniture, operate audiovisual equipment; girls are asked to carry messages and erase the board. Girls in elementary school are frequently bigger and stronger than boys, but they are protected from such arduous chores as carrying books. Because of their assumed mechanical ineptitude, they do not have opportunities to operate complicated machinery like film projectors.

Many teachers continually reinforce what they perceive to be innate, appropriate, and irreversible sex differences. This creates animosity and competition between female and male students. Spelling bees and debates pit girls against boys. Girls and boys are grouped separately for projects. A girl who shoots spitballs might be shamed by the teacher who says, "That's not ladylike behavior. I am ashamed of you!" Boys who misbehave are often punished and humiliated by being sent to sit with the girls. In addition, for similar kinds of misbehavior, boys are more often physically punished than girls. And, minority students are subjected to more frequent disciplinary action than nonminority students.

4. Counseling and Guidance

Students may be influenced by a variety of school personnel regarding course and career decisions—teachers, counselors, administrators, secretaries, custodians. Guidance counselors, of course, do more formal course and career counseling than other school personnel. They are also responsible for most of the following activities: scheduling of classes; selection and interpretation of achievement, personality, and interest measurement tests; selection, display, and distribution of career guidance material; writing references; referring students to jobs.

These counseling activities play a primary role in sorting, classifying, and tracking students to fill socially prescribed occupational roles. Counselors, like teachers, often have different career expectations for females and males. Students can be greatly influenced by counselor attitudes in educational, career, and life choices. Two studies illustrate the point:

> When female and male high school counselors were asked to listen to audio taped self-descriptions of high school girls with either traditionally feminine or traditionally masculine goals, counselors of both sexes indicated that "feminine" goals were more appropriate for female students and those girls with "masculine" goals as more in need of counseling services.[18]

> When asked to invent backgrounds and interests for college-bound and noncollege-bound women, male counselors portrayed college-bound women as interested in traditionally "female" occupations at the semiskilled level, while female counselors portrayed them as interested in occupations requiring college education. In addition, male counselors did not consider any traditionally "male careers for women." [19]

Girls and boys today need counseling that is free from stereotyped expectations. For example, although 97 percent of high school girls report that they expect to have careers, they are generally more interested in the arrival of Prince Charming and tend to underplan for their educational and occupational goals.[20]

This vague, dreamy approach to their adult lives goes unchallenged by many counselors who fail to guide girls toward serious academic and career planning. Counselors, like other adults in education, are operating from the basic assumption that a girl's career will be her husband and not her work. These assumptions do not recognize that nine out of ten young women in today's high schools will work outside the home for a major part of their adult lives.

In general, tests and materials used by counselors to help students make academic and career choices also reflect traditional biases. Achievement tests use more references to men than to women, and show women primarily as homemakers or in pursuit of hobbies. Career interest inventories offer a wider variety of career choices for males than for females and more careers at higher status and income. Materials describing careers depict mostly men in challenging professional or managerial positions. Technical and trade brochures portray only males at work. And college catalogs portray female and male students in stereotyped classes and roles.

5. Physical Activity

Physical education classes and athletic programs offer students opportunities to develop strength, coordination, skills, good health habits, leisure time pursuits, and teamwork. Physical development and fitness has a positive influence on intellectual and social development as well as self-concept. Control over one's body in acts of skill promotes "the growth of an individual's sense of personal worth, self-reliance, personal freedom, and increases his [sic] worth as a social being." [21] Recently, researchers have confirmed that both male and female athletes are "less depressed, more stable and have higher psychological vigor than the general public." [22]

Despite the knowledge that physical activity is good for people and despite the fundamental role sport plays in American culture, physical education and athletic programs from kindergarten through college minimize the importance of physical development for females. Girls have been treated as second-class citizens or worse in physical activities, relegated to separate and inferior classes, and to a few sports that receive nowhere near the kind of equipment, facilities, staff, benefits, publicity, and money that boys' sports receive.

Physical ability varies more among individuals of the same sex than between the sexes, so segregation of students by sex for purposes of participating in physical activity is not an educationally sound method of grouping. Many girls are stronger, more skilled, and have more endurance than many boys. The girls who are good athletes are praised by being compared to boys, as in "She throws just like a boy." Boys, on the other hand, are derogatorily compared to girls when they do badly, as in "Look at him, he runs like a girl!" As a result of segregated classes and sports programs, which reflect different expectations and treatment based on sex, girls learn to view themselves as weaker than boys, more easily hurt, and they deduce from this that they are therefore inferior. Physical education has been called "the only sex-identified body of knowledge in the school curriculum." [23] (Imagine girls' Social Studies, or boys' English!)

From the time girls enter elementary school, they are discouraged from engaging in rowdy play or physical movement which is not "ladylike." Throughout their school years, girls get a clear message about the value placed on their acquisition of skills and strength. They are protected from strain or injury and prevented from developing skills and experiencing teamwork. Traditional feminine traits of delicacy and physical weakness are reinforced, and girls are not encouraged to participate in athletics. Dancing, cheerleading, and pep squad have been the most acceptable outlets for them. Studies indicate that vigorous athletic programs and training are in no way injurious to females but, on the contrary, overprotectiveness inhibits the full development of their physical powers.

Are women interested in sports when given encouragement and opportunity? Between 1970 and 1979, the percentage of high school athletes who were girls rose from 7 percent to over 30 percent. In some school districts, the number of girls participating in interscholastic athletics has risen over 600 percent since 1974.

The sex stereotyping that interferes with the development of girls works in the reverse for boys. If girls are not expected to enjoy and be good in sports, all boys are expected to love and excel in athletics. Boys who do not are considered "sissies." All boys are encouraged, often forced, to participate in athletics from an early age. Continuous pressure on boys to compete and to win is very stressful, but athletic prowess brings prestige with peers and adult approval. The low- and average-ability male athlete is frequently overlooked by win-oriented sports programs.

Minority males and females face special problems related to athletics. Black male students sometimes find acceptance and status through sports and dream of professional careers. Only a tiny percentage achieve their dreams, and since schools fail to emphasize academic as well as athletic performance for black males, most find themselves with few career options.

Black females, on the other hand, are not rewarded for athletic participation. Opportunities and prestige at the high school are limited, and colleges offer far fewer athletic scholarships to women than to men. Minority female athletes who need financial aid to attend college are less likely than men to get it.

Sociologists point out that American business has been "socialized" by sport.[24] "The road to the boardroom leads through the locker room," where boys learn loyalty, brotherhood, persistance, initiative, and sportsmanship. If women were allowed greater participation in competitive team sports, they would have more opportunities for developing leadership and teamwork skills that are needed for managerial jobs.

6. Extracurricular Activities

Extracurricular activities have provided experience and skills that reinforce basic assumptions about appropriate female and male roles, jobs, and behavior. Until recently this meant separate activities. Boys' activities have been oriented to the development of creativity, leadership, and physical prowess. Males have traditionally dominated activities like inter-scholastic athletics, science clubs and competitions, aviation, photography, and chess clubs, marching bands, jazz bands, and student government. In the past, many of these creative, intellectually stimulating, character and leadership building activities were virtually off limits to girls.

Girls' activities, on the other hand, were designed to develop domestic skills and focused on helping or serving others. Girls have been involved in cheerleading, pep squads, and future-teachers, future-homemakers, and service clubs. Until about 1975, a visitor to any high school in the United States would very likely have found the following classic division of activities: boys playing football and girls cheering; boys serving as student council president, girls as treasurer or secretary; boys in Future Farmers of America, girls in Future Homemakers; boys in Key Club meeting important community leaders, girls as candy stripers helping out in local hospitals.

Many of these divisions have begun to break down and students have learned to work in mixed groups. This interaction and shared responsibility may overcome some of the awkwardness that arises when boys and girls begin dating after years of separation and hostility.

We have seen how the traditional vehicles of education—instructional materials, curriculum, teacher behavior, counseling, physical activity, extracurricular activities—are used to reinforce biased assumptions. What are the cumulative effects on girls and women of continuous bombardment by such messages? Are girls and boys being educated to cope with the realities of their adult lives? We will take a look at the girls first, and see what the situation is for boys later on.

ASSESSING THE DAMAGE

The characteristics we cultivate in women are dependency, passivity, deference, sweetness, helplessness, agreeableness, weakness. Women tend to be: low in self-esteem, ambivalent about success, power, and achievement; intellectually underdeveloped; unassertive; overeducated for the jobs they hold; underprepared for traditionally male career options; and at the bottom of the ladder in employment, status, pay, and opportunities for advancement. These are generalizations about women as a group, of course, and do not apply to the many examples of successful, proud, strong, assertive, independent women who have confounded the stereotypes.

The story of Emma Green follows. Everything that happens to Emma is true, through Emma is not a real person but a composite of many women. Her story may read like a soap opera, but it is based on research on the rearing and education of girls. The story of Emma is told from a middle-class perspective because, unfortunately, most research on sex bias deals with middle-class subjects, most of them white. Many girls, however, those in the minority as well as the majority, lower-class as well as middle-class, are to some degree captives of the same fairy tale. They believe that if they look pretty enough, smell good enough, and act sweet enough, they can catch a man who will protect and shelter them happily ever after.

Although 97 percent of high school girls today say they plan for salaried work, this is peripheral to their lives. They believe their real rewards will come through their husbands and children. The Cinderella myth keeps girls from seriously planning educational and occupational goals. As you read this story, notice the messages Emma receives from her parents, teachers, counselors, and peers about appropriate female roles, jobs, and behavior. Notice that sometimes those messages come directly from the words and behavior of others, and sometimes indirectly. Note also how these messages affect Emma.

THE STORY OF EMMA

Emma's parents would have preferred a son to carry on her father's family name; however, they soon adjusted to her arrival because she was a cute little girl. Her mother was rather pleased with a daughter. She felt that girls were neater, sweeter, and cleaner than boys—and more obedient. Girls, her mother knew, were helpful around the house because they could do chores and take care of younger brothers and sisters. As Emma grew up, she had dolls to play with, and tea sets, and doll houses; and girl friends her age with whom to share these.

Once, when she was about to shinny up a tree, her father said: "No, Emma, don't do that. You might fall down and hurt yourself." The boys on her block were playing ball almost as soon as they could walk, and Emma used to watch them. Once or twice, she asked to play, but the boys said, "Ah, girls can't play ball. Go play with your dolls."

Within a few years Emma had a younger brother, Tom. Emma's father was proud to have a boy, and tossed him up in the air, and called him "Tiger." Tom was allowed to run and jump and play ball and climb trees. Emma watched him.

Emma and Tom watched television together. They followed the adventures of Superman, Batman, Spiderman, the Hardy Boys, and the Cosby Kids. They saw boys and men save lives, help people, and swing between buildings. The men appeared to be very brave, adventuresome, courageous, and independent. Tom could dream of being like these male heroes someday. But Emma could not because women in these shows were usually helpless, and they did not do exciting things.

At nursery school, Emma played in the doll corner similar to the one she had at home. There was a block corner and a truck corner, but the teacher, who was a very nice woman, never went to the block corner or the truck corner herself, so it did not seem like a thing that women did, and Emma never went to play with the blocks or the trucks.

When she entered first grade, Emma felt good. She could read a little and knew her numbers. But the teacher praised Emma's clothes and her polite behavior. And when Emma turned her papers in, the teacher did not say much about her work, except to comment on how neatly she had written her assignments.

Emma loved to read. Besides her textbooks, Emma read books from the library. The books had few pictures of girls or women; they were mostly about boys and men doing important things. Her math and science books had no pictures of girls at all. Emma decided that was because math and science were subjects meant for boys. She thought that if she were smart she could probably be a teacher when she grew up.

One thing Emma hated was taking tests. She got very nervous because she was afraid she wouldn't do well. Sometimes when she got a good grade, the kids teased her and called her "Smartypants." She wasn't sure she liked being smart.

In junior high school Emma decided that she was ugly and no boy would ever look at her. She imagined she would never get married unless she did something about her appearance. She and her friends began experimenting with makeup and started to diet.

In high school, at last, a boy asked Emma to go out with him. Her mother gave her some advice: "Smile and listen to your date. Ask him questions about how he does all the things he does. Don't talk too much. Boys don't like girls who talk too much. And remember, be polite, sit with your legs together. Act like a lady."

As she progressed through high school, Emma made good grades. She was an A and B student, and liked school. Since junior high, however, she wasn't doing as well as she used to on the achievement tests, especially in math, science, and civics. She had been a good math student but dropped it because math was boring and didn't seem important to her career goals.

Emma wondered whether she should go to college. Even though she had a good grade point average and liked school, she wasn't sure that she would do well in college. But her parents encouraged her to go. For one thing, they said, she would meet some nice boys there.

After she had been in college for a year, Emma began to think seriously about what she ought to do for a career. She had heard that there were opportunities in engineering for women. When she went and asked a counselor about it, she found that because she had dropped out of math in high school so early, she would have to take two years of math just to make it up. She thought that would be a waste of time and decided that she might as well major in English because she was good at it, loved to read, and wrote well.

In college, she met Joe and fell in love with him. When they got married, Emma dropped out and went to work so that Joe could finish school. Emma took a job as a clerk in an office. She didn't have any typing or stenography skills, but she was bright and taught herself to type.

When Joe graduated, he took a job with a large company. Emma soon gave birth to a boy and later two girls. Emma was completely involved with her husband and family, but she was bothered because sometimes Joe seemed more interested in his work than he was in her.

Whem Emma was 39 and Joe was 40, Joe divorced Emma. Emma was at a loss. She wondered how she had failed Joe and what she had done wrong in her marriage. For a while Joe paid alimony and child support, but then he remarried and started a new family. Soon after, the money stopped.

Emma realized she would have to get a regular job. She had worked on and off as a part-time clerk, but had no skills with which to build a career. She had not even learned stenography. She went to an employment agency and they sent her to work as a file clerk, back to a job like the one she had 20 years ago when she dropped out of college.

Did you recognize any of Emma's experiences? Have they happened to anyone you know? To what extent do you believe her experiences to be typical for women in this society? What differences are there in the messages received by women with different racial, ethnic, and class backgrounds?

Let us look at some of the research on which Emma's story is based.

Research on Women

Sex preference: In a study of 1,500 young married women and 375 of their husbands, twice as many women expressed a preference for boy children and their husbands preferred boys to girls by as much as three or four to one.[25]

Play: Children spend 65 percent of their free time playing. Girls tend to play indoor games, while boys play in "larger, more open spaces further from home [which] contributes to greater physical development and training for independence. Complicated rules and strategies for team sports prepare boys for competition in work situations and survival in bureaucratic organizations, while girls' play develops interpersonal relationships and empathetic skills." [26]

Tomboys: According to one researcher, for a girl to develop into an intellectual person, she must be a tomboy at some point in her childhood.[27]

Television: Women are underrepresented in television programming and news, and minority women are nearly invisible. When portrayed, women are shown in stereotyped roles.[28]

Nursery school: Teachers act and react in quite different ways to boys and girls. While they encourage aggression in boys, they encourage dependency in girls.[29]

Teacher interactions: Teachers praise and scold girls and boys for very different kinds of behavior. Boys are reprimanded for misbehavior and praised for academic performance. Girls are more likely to be criticised for their academic performance, and praised for nonacademic qualities such as appearance, neatness, politeness.[30]

Achievement tests: At the age of nine, female and male performance on achievement tests in mathematics, science, social studies, and citizenship is nearly equal, while females outperform males in reading, literature, writing, and music. However, by the age of 13, females begin a decline in achievement, which continues through age 17 and into adulthood. By adulthood, males outperform females in everything but writing and music.[31]

Grades: Girls make much better high school grades than boys, in part because they follow the rules, are better behaved and neater. Despite their good grades, girls are less likely than boys to believe that they have the ability to do college work.[32]

Mathematics: Fifty-seven percent of male students entering the University of California at Berkeley in 1973 had four years of high school mathematics. Only 8 percent of the entering female students had four years of math. Because 5 of the 20 majors at Berkeley require calculus or statistics, 92 percent of the entering females were not even eligible to take these courses. They were limited to the traditional women's fields: humanities, music, social work, elementary education, guidance, and counseling.[33]

Self-esteem: Fewer high school girls than boys rate themselves above average on leadership, popularity in general, popularity with the opposite sex, and intellectual as well as social self-confidence.[34]

Careers: Although more elementary school girls today are beginning to consider a variety of careers, they are unable to specifically describe what having a career would be like. Boys, in contrast, are able to describe in detail the activities that might comprise their chosen careers.[35]

Career commitment: Decline in career commitment has been found in girls of high school age. This decline was related to their feelings that male classmates disapproved of a woman's using her intelligence.[36]

Career planning: Females tend to underplan their future occupational and educational goals in terms of their academic ability compared to boys. For example, girls who anticipate working in the lowest-status occupations earn a higher grade point average than do boys who anticipate working in medium-status occupations.[37]

Jobs: Of the women in the work force in March, 1978, nearly 80 percent were in clerical, sales, service, factory, or plant jobs. In professional jobs, 60 percent of the women are noncollege teachers or nurses, while men tend to be lawyers, doctors, or college professors.[38]

Alimony and child support: Alimony awards are made in only 14 percent of all divorces, with only half collected regularly. Forty-four percent of divorced mothers get child support awards, which typically cover less than one-half the support costs of the children and are also very difficult to collect.[39]

These findings raise serious questions about the rearing and education of women. If the overt and covert messages with which women are bombarded confine them to nineteenth-century roles and jobs and make the female achiever into an object of fear, scorn, or ridicule, then we are out of step with the demands on adult women in twentieth-century America.

WHAT ARE TWENTIETH-CENTURY WOMEN DOING?

Society has changed radically in the past century. Economist Eli Ginsberg calls the entry by women into the work force "the single most outstanding phenomenon of our century." [40] A British news magazine cited the change in the position and status of women in society as the most significant world event in 135 years, even over Freud's psychoanalytical theory, Darwin's theory of the origin of species, the Communist Manifesto, the end of slavery, the invention of the automobile and the airplane, and the development of electricity.[41]

Have schools kept pace with the significant changes in the lives of women by providing them the skills, training, and experiences they need to fulfill their responsibilities?

To what extent are you in touch with the changes that have taken place? You can find out by taking the following quiz that tests your knowledge about the lives of women in contemporary American society. Check your responses with the answer key at the end of the chapter.

QUIZ ON WOMEN IN THE WORLD OF WORK

1. What percentage of American women are in the labor force?

    a. 20 percent
    b. 35 percent
    c. 55 percent
    d. 75 percent

2. On an average, women in the labor force earn

    a. roughly the same as men
    b. more than men do

    c. 86 cents for every dollar earned by men
    d. 59 cents for every dollar earned by men

3. What percentage of working women are in managerial or professional jobs?

    a. 19 percent
    b. 30 percent
    c. 45 percent
    d. 70 percent

4. Why do most women work?

    a. to get out of the house
    b. they need the money
    c. to buy extras
    d. to develop careers

5. What percentage of working women are married and living with their husbands?

    a. 80 percent
    b. 10 percent
    c. 50 percent
    d. 20 percent

6. What percentage of women with children between 6 and 17 years of age are employed?

    a. 50 percent
    b. 10 percent
    c. 80 percent
    d. 15 percent

7. The average married woman is likely to work outside the home for

    a. 3 years
    b. 5 years
    c. 15 years
    d. 25 years

8. The average unmarried woman is likely to work for

    a. 45 years
    b. 30 years
    c. 60 years
    d. 25 years

9. Which of the following groups is most likely to be unemployed though looking for work?

    a. minority teenage men
    b. minority teenage women
    c. minority adult men
    d. minority adult women

10. What portion of girls in high school today can expect to be part of the labor force?

    a. 70 percent
    b. 90 percent
    c. 60 percent
    d. 50 percent

11. What percentage of 17-year-old girls list "housewife" as their first choice for a career?

    a. 28 percent
    b. 73 percent
    c. 18 percent
    d.   3 percent

12. Roughly what percentage of American families today consist of a father who works and a mother who stays home to raise the children?

    a. 87 percent
    b.   7 percent
    c. 67 percent
    d. 27 percent

13. By what percentage did the number of women in the workforce increase between 1950 and 1978?

    a.   50 percent
    b. 100 percent
    c.   80 percent
    d. 130 percent

14. If current trends continue, what percentage of the labor force will be female in the year 2000?

    a. 50 percent
    b. 85 percent
    c. 25 percent
    d. 35 percent

The lives of women in the twentieth century are dramatically different from the lives of their mothers and grandmothers. The majority of American women today work for pay outside the home. By the year 2000, well over half of the labor force will be female. Most women workers are single, divorced, widowed, separated, or have husbands earning under $7,000 a year. They earn three-fifths of what men earn for the same work, and minority women are most likely to be underpaid and underemployed.

Our educational system has responded very slowly to these contemporary social realities. Our schools have always had dual, somewhat contradictory functions to perform. They are supposed to be conservers of the status quo and also harbingers of change. It has been easier to keep the status quo than to change, and our schools do not yet seem to be ready to educate young people for the future that awaits them. Although we should be training girls for lives of paid work, for leadership, to manage money and power, we have not quite eliminated the image of the nineteenth-century Victorian woman—the quiet, delicate, and passive woman who "knows her place."

In the course of Emma Green's development, there were many points at which understanding adults could have encouraged her full physical and intellectual flowering, increased her self-confidence, and oriented her toward realistic and satisfying academic and career goals. As an educator, you have the opportunity to nurture the Amelia Earhart in every girl, for it is there. Encourage girls to be assertive, brave, daring, athletic, intellectual, independent, creative, and strong. Then they will be better able to deal with life as it is for women in the world today.

IF MEN ARE IN CHARGE, CAN THEY BE IN TROUBLE?

Many people resent the recent emphasis on bias and discrimination against girls and women. They point out that boys and men also suffer damaging consequences from differential treatment. Others believe that since males (white males) run the world and are in power, we should not feel sorry for them. They point to the differential treatment of white males as providing them the skills, knowledge, and characteristics necessary to get and keep power, and to ensure a certain level of income and status.

Let's explore some basic assumptions people hold about men. Rate the following statements true or false, according to your own beliefs.

QUESTIONNAIRE ON MEN

True False

——— ——   1. A man's primary responsibility in life is to support his family.

___ ___ 2. To be respected, a man should be strong and self-reliant at all times.

___ ___ 3. Physical strength and athletic prowess are the essence of masculinity.

___ ___ 4. It is inappropriate for a man to show fear.

___ ___ 5. It is embarrassing to see a male nurse, secretary, or flight attendant.

___ ___ 6. Most men are too rough and insensitive to work with young children.

___ ___ 7. A man who maintains the home and cares for his children while his wife works probably feels inadequate.

___ ___ 8. In order to survive in a cutthroat world a man must be competitive and ambitious.

___ ___ 9. It is more appropriate for a man to engage in extramarital affairs than for a woman.

___ ___ 10. Liberated women sometimes make unreasonable demands on men.

___ ___ 11. A male elementary teacher is probably preparing himself to become a principal.

___ ___ 12. Women are not attracted to men who are yielding, sensitive, and unambitious.

___ ___ 13. Boys should be discouraged from choosing careers in dancing in order to avoid ridicule.

___ ___ 14. Little boys should not be given dolls to play with unless they are masculine adventure dolls.

___ ___ 15. A man should not marry a woman smarter than he is.

___ ___ 16. It would be inappropriate for a business executive to have a male secretary.

___ ___ 17. There is nothing wrong with a male college student expecting his girl friend to type his papers, do his laundry, or cook for him if he reciprocates by taking her out.

___ ___ 18. A man should not expect his date to pay for her own dinner.

___ ___ 19. After dealing with the stress and pressure of the workplace all day, a man has the right to expect his wife to cater to him when he comes home.

___ ___ 20. A man's life must revolve around his work first and his family second.

How did you answer the 20 items in this questionnaire? What evidence can you present to support your point of view?

These statements can be grouped under three basic assumptions about attitudes, roles, jobs, and behavior society considers appropriate for men. And each of these assumptions carries with it many implications for how boys should be educated.

ASSUMPTION 1: Men Must Participate Directly and Lead in the Civic, Political, and Economic Affairs of the Society

Conventional wisdom: More and more men are assuming some of the responsibility for home and child care, often because their wives are working. But prevailing sentiment still assigns the "important" work of the world to men. Men must support families, run businesses and factories, provide vital professional services, and govern the community and the nation. Men are under continuing pressure to advance themselves: the senator to become president, the teacher to become principal, the auto mechanic to own the shop, the factory worker to become the foreman or the shop steward.

Implications for schooling: Clearly, if men are to enter the job market at the best level they can and advance to the highest point they can, they must be bombarded with images of men at work, dominant and successful. They must be well grounded in academics so as to be prepared for a wide range of career choices, or they must be taught marketable vocational skills. Men must be encouraged to accept responsibility for leadership, decision making, and risk taking as they progress through school.

ASSUMPTION 2: Men Are Physically, Emotionally, and Intellectually Superior to Women

Conventional wisdom: Men are generally thought to be stronger, wiser, and emotionally more stable than women. All a man needs to achieve success is training, drive, and opportunity. His status is heightened by the acquisition of an attractive, supportive, dependent wife.

Implications for schooling: If men are to run the world, then their minds and bodies must be fully developed to meet the challenges of adult life. If a strong, healthy body, competitive spirit, and ability to work cooperatively within a team are vital to a man's success in life, then as many boys as possible should participate in team sports. If men are to make discoveries, invent things, and write great novels, then intellectual curiosity and creativity must be valued and encouraged. If they are to work in the paid labor force for all of their adult lives, they must be given marketable job skills or a strong academic background and encouraged and reinforced through class and school division of responsibilities.

ASSUMPTION 3: Men Should Cultivate Traditionally Masculine Characteristics

Conventional wisdom: Boys learn early that all things associated with femininity are to be shunned, lest they be called "sissy," "fag," "queer," or "gay." Accepting roles and jobs that are conventionally feminine is thought to demean men, and only men who have already proven their masculinity through sports, business, or military success can relax and step out of character occasionally. Rosie Grier, the football player, can do needlepoint because nobody would dare laugh at him. Although contemporary male heroes in movies, television, and novels are increasingly sensitive, tender, and gentle, they are also without question strong, brave, decisive, and dominant.

Implications for schooling: If men are to shun feminine qualities and develop masculine characteristics, they must be reinforced only for "manly" behavior. Emotional control must be encouraged, which means that fear, anxiety, distress, even great joy, must be contained and not expressed. Aggression and fighting are to be expected as natural expressions of masculinity.

THE PRICE

When females and males are treated differently in schools, the results are bad for both. The pressure on men to compete and succeed results in frustration and stress. Traits of tenderness, sensitivity, and emotionality are underdeveloped in males along with skills in child rearing and homemaking. Unrestrained aggressive behavior causes serious problems in schools and in society.

While it is true that the images, models, and experiences of leadership and success to which boys are exposed do provide many of them the strength, self-esteem, motivation, and skills to achieve mastery of their environment, the cost is high. Most men work constantly to build and preserve their "masculinity." This superman fixation includes sexual virility, personal bravery, adventuresomeness, physical strength, skill in sports, aggressiveness, exercise of power, control, and dominance. Since the performance of most boys can never match all of these superhuman expectations, many become maladjusted, low achievers, truants, delinquents, inattentive, and rebellious.

This is the story of Joe Green, Jr., the man Emma married. Like the story of Emma it may seem melodramatic. Remember that Joe is a composite of research findings about the negative outcomes of traditional role expectations for men. As you read the story, notice the direct and indirect messages Joe receives from his parents, teachers, counselors, and peers about appropriate male roles, jobs, and behavior. Note, too, the effects of those messages.

THE STORY OF JOE

Joe, Jr. was the third child of the Greens. His father was overjoyed when, after two girls, a namesake was born. The proud father gave out cigars and invited his friends over to see the sturdy-looking baby wrapped in blue blankets. "Mary, wake up the baby and carry him out here so my friends can get a good look at him," Joe, Sr., would command.

Joe grew up playing with cars and trucks and blocks. He learned very early that his parents did not approve when he played dolls and house with his sisters. His mother teased him and sent him back to his own toys.

As he grew older, Joe played cops and robbers, space explorers, and football with other boys his age. Sometimes, Joe wanted to stay home alone and read, but his mother pushed him outside to play with the boys. If Joe came home crying after he had fallen off his bike or been hit with a ball, his parents told him not to be a crybaby and sent him back outside.

Joe hated to fight, but the guys called him "sissy" and "queer" so he did, but he was always afraid he would get hurt. If Joe's father heard that he had backed away from a fight, he would get angry and lecture him on being a man and standing up to bullies. Joe was sure that his father would have preferred a different kind of boy—tougher, braver, stronger.

Joe saw very little of his father who came home late and tired in the evening. On weekends his dad wanted to do his own chores and then relax, but once in a while they fished or played ball together. Those were special times for Joe. One summer, Joe's father built him a treehouse, which the boys promptly made off limits to all girls including Joe's sisters. Joe and his friends teased his sisters, called them names, and made fun of the way they walked and talked.

From the time Joe entered school, he was a behavior problem. Teachers liked him, but he was always talking, fooling around, or daydreaming. He was frequently scolded and punished. It made him feel bad, but he was not able to change his behavior. He found school boring.

Joe made many friends at school, all of them boys. He felt that, like his sisters, the girls were strange and different. They played silly games, giggled, whispered, and were always combing their hair. They didn't tell jokes, or play sports, and were always goody-goodys in class. Joe could see that his teachers liked girls a lot better than boys. For one thing, Joe imagined that girls were smarter because they always won the spelling bees against the boys. Joe hated it when he was punished for rowdy behavior by having to sit with the girls at lunch. Even his best friends teased him.

In junior high school there was a lot of pressure to have a girl friend. Joe was shy. He liked a quiet girl named Donna. He liked her for a whole year without ever talking to her except once to offer her a piece of gum—which she refused. He went to some school dances and hung around with a group of his friends. They rated all the girls. Joe planned and rehearsed a good opener: "Hi, would you like to dance?"

But he did not approach anyone. He was afraid they would refuse him, because he wasn't tall and muscular like Dave, a terrific dancer like Harold, or funny like Jackson.

The only class Joe liked was physical education. He was not an outstanding athlete; he was too small and too fearful of getting hurt to really be a competitor, but he enjoyed sports anyway. The coach and the kids were angry when Joe fumbled a move, but generally he did all right.

When he got to tenth grade, a counselor asked him about his career plans. "Oh," he said, "I'm going to be a lawyer." "Not with these grades, you're not," he was told. Joe was told to shape up and to take a language, plenty of math, history, and English.

Joe was afraid he would not even do well enough to get into college. It was hard for him to discuss his fear of being a failure with anyone. He did not want his counselor to think he couldn't do the work. And he did not want to disappoint his parents. None of his friends seemed to worry very much about school work, so he did not feel comfortable talking about it.

Joe began to get pains in his stomach and lost his appetite, but he was too ashamed to tell his parents. It was his mother who finally found out and sent him to a doctor. The doctor warned him that if he didn't relax he would have an ulcer by the time he was 21. He also told him that liquor would aggravate his stomach. Joe was embarrassed and wondered how the doctor had guessed that he was drinking.

Joe did all right in his high school classes—at least well enough to get into college. There was never any question about his going to college and preparing for a career. Joe's father often stressed the importance of earning a good living in order to support a wife and family.

In college he continued a pattern he had begun during his last year of high school. He dated many different girls to avoid serious involvement. His friends began to call him a Romeo, and he didn't mind at all. It made him feel masculine and successful.

In his junior year, Joe began a serious relationship with Emma. He felt a tremendous sense of release because he could talk to her in a way he had never talked to anyone. When he and Emma got married, he strongly believed that his role was to protect and care for her. It made him uncomfortable when she took a job to support him through college, and he vowed that he would be so successful in his career that she would never have to work again.

After graduation Joe accepted a job with a large company because he thought it was a good opportunity. He worked hard to prove himself so that he could get ahead. This meant long hours, intense concentration, figuring out the politics of the firm, cultivating the right associates. It was a strain, and Joe's stomach pains recurred. He knew he should slow down, but did not want to appear unsociable or unambitious.

Joe had little time for his family. He and Emma had three children, but he began to drift apart from them. He found himself more and more involved in his job, and eventually he had an affair with a woman he met at work.

After his divorce from Emma, that relationship ended also and Joe found himself alone and without a sense of purpose. He hadn't received a promotion in several years, and felt that he was a failure at business as well as in his personal life. He was bored with his work, and often dreamed of what it might have been like to be a successful lawyer. With his financial obligations, he realized it was foolish even to think about a career change. Joe struggled with moods of severe depression, but eventually forced himself to focus on his work. After a while, he married again. He and his new wife had a baby and Joe found little time, money, or energy for his other family.

The story of Joe may read like a soap opera, but it is based on research about men's lives. Perhaps you know men who have gone through some of Joe's experiences. Do the men you know talk about their personal problems, anxieties, and failures? How relevant is Joe's story to the experiences of men with differing racial, ethnic, and class backgrounds?

Let us look at some research and information that underlies Joe's story.

Research on Men

Toys: Parents can tolerate girls playing with boys' toys but both mothers and fathers strongly discourage boys from playing with girls' toys or doing "girlish" things.[42]

Fathers and sons: Fathers spend relatively little time with their sons and the relations between them are less good than those between girls and their mothers or fathers. Fathers are perceived as punishing or controlling agents.[43]

Aggression: Boys are encouraged to be aggressive by parents while girls are not. In addition, almost all the models on television that encourage aggression are men, thereby encouraging boys to continue the aggression they learn from their parents.[44]

Teacher discipline: Boys receive eight to ten times as many prohibitory control messages from teachers as do girls. In addition, when teachers criticize boys, they are more likely to use harsh or angry tones than when reprimanding girls.[45]

Grades: Among boys and girls of comparable I.Q., boys are more likely to receive lower grades than girls. Even boys who score as well or better than girls on achievement tests are more likely to get lower grades in school.[47]

Maladjustment: Far more boys than girls are maladjusted, low achievers, truants, delinquents, inattentive, and rebellious. National delinquency rates are five times higher among boys than girls.[48]

Athletics: Athletes learn toughness, independence, nonemotionality, insensitivity, blocking of pain, and to focus on the concrete details and goals of winning. In high school, these masculine characteristics are valued and bring success in dating, but in college women prefer other personality traits—greater openness, sharing of feelings, more verbal communication, and sensitivity to moods.

Nonathletes experience feelings of failure, of inadequacy, inferiority and nonmembership in the world of their male peers.[49]

Male friendships: Although men may report more same-sex friendships than women do, these friendships are not close or intimate. Self-disclosure is either very low or utterly lacking between males.[50]

Role strain: Over 80 percent of male college seniors experience some form of role strain (mild to severe) in fulfilling role obligations.[51]

Life and death: In comparison to females, males experience a higher accident rate, higher alcohol and drug abuse rate, higher suicide rate, and higher general mortality rate. One researcher asserts that "attempts to fulfill [male] role requirements result in anxiety, emotional difficulty, a sense of failure, compensatory behavior which is potentially dangerous and destructive, and stress which results in physical illness and premature death."[52]

The research and information on which the story of Joe Green is based raise serious concerns about the effects of rigid sex-role expectations on men in our society. What is the loss in human potential to each man as well as to society as a whole?

THERE'S A LAW, YOU KNOW

Title IX of the 1972 Education Amendments was passed by Congress because of strong evidence that American schools were indeed guilty of differential, stereotyped, and discriminatory treatment of students based on their sex.

Title IX states that

> No person shall, on the basis of sex, be excluded from participation in, be denied the benefits of, or be subjected to discrimination under any education program or activity receiving federal financial assistance.

While the basic assumptions and attitudes people hold about appropriate female and male roles, jobs, and behaviors cannot be changed by law, rights, privileges, opportunities, and treatment can be equalized.

Equal treatment of male and female students from kindergarten through university will increase fulfillment of individual potential. As individuals explore new opportunities to express their talents, the traditional stereotypes will break down and eventually change basic assumptions about sex-appropriate roles, jobs, and behaviors. A graphic representation of this change follows. Compare it to the vicious circle of sexism presented at the beginning of this chapter.

Note that interference with one element of the circle will completely change the course of events. The self-fulfilling prophecy becomes a positive one in that students are limited by nothing but their own interests and abilities.

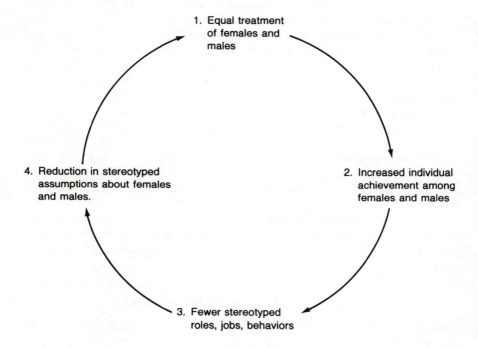

1. Equal treatment of females and males
2. Increased individual achievement among females and males
3. Fewer stereotyped roles, jobs, behaviors
4. Reduction in stereotyped assumptions about females and males.

What's Your Line on Title IX?

How much accurate information do you have regarding the rights of teachers and students under Title IX? The following brief true/false quiz is designed to provide some instant feedback on your level of information—or misinformation.

True False

_____ _____ 1. Title IX requires that a girl be allowed to play on the football team if she is good enough.

_____ _____ 2. Title IX requires that all classes have both females and males in them.

____ ____ 3. Title IX requires that when there is a disproportionately small number of women principals, that women be promoted before men.

____ ____ 4. Title IX encourages special programs for pregnant girls.

____ ____ 5. Title IX permits the use of separate vocational interest tests for females and males, which provide occupational choices geared to the special interests of each sex.

____ ____ 6. Title IX requires that there be female coaches for girls' sports.

____ ____ 7. Title IX requires that as much money be spent on girls' as on boys' athletics.

____ ____ 8. Title IX prohibits the use of sex-biased textbooks.

____ ____ 9. Title IX requires that all clubs and extracurricular activities be coeducational.

____ ____ 10. Title IX requires that resolution of sex-discrimination grievances must be attempted within the school district before a grievance is filed with the federal government.

Misinformation Quotient

How many of the above statements did you think were false? They are all false! Therefore you may consider yourself *completely misinformed* if you thought they were all true, *poorly informed* if you thought six or more were true, and *well informed* if you knew that at least seven were false.

Should you be well informed about Title IX? Part of the legal obligation of all the schools you have attended since 1975 was to inform you of your rights under this law, as well as of available procedures for filing a grievance if you think your rights have been violated. Following are some questions and answers designed to provide an overview of Title IX.

What Is Title IX?

In response to public pressure for sex equity in schools, Congress passed a law known as Title IX of the Education Amendments of 1972. The law was then sent to the Department of Health, Education, and Welfare's Office for Civil Rights to draw up specific guidelines for its implementation in schools. There was considerable public controversy over what Title IX should cover. Feminist groups wanted extensive coverage. The National Collegiate Athletic Association wanted minimal coverage. Ten thousand written comments were received by the government. Because the issue was complex and controversial, the Office for Civil Rights took three years to develop those regulations. The final Title IX implementing regulation, true to American tradition, represented a compromise among the varying public interests and was signed into law by

President Ford on July 21, 1975. For a copy of the Title IX Regulation, write to the Office for Civil Rights, Department of Education, 330 Independence Avenue, S.W., Room 1656, Washington, D.C., 20201.

Was Title IX Necessary?

The information and research on sex-differentiated treatment of students and its negative outcomes, which we have already reviewed, provide the best argument for Title IX. When the United States Congress was deliberating on the new law in 1971 and 1972, numerous individuals and organizations from around the country testified to existing conditions, which they believed made the passage of such a law necessary. Highlights of this testimony follow:

Item—Girls were often denied the opportunity to enroll in traditionally male courses such as industrial arts, and boys were often denied the opportunity to enroll in home economics.

Item—Girls and boys were counseled to enroll in traditionally female or male career development courses.

Item—Girls' physical education programs were generally inferior to boys' programs.

Item—Top female athletes frequently were denied access to coaching and other athletic opportunities and even opportunities to play if no team existed.

Item—In 1970–1971, while women were 67 percent of all school teachers, they were only 15 percent of all principals, and 0.6 percent of all superintendents.

Item—Women college faculty members received average salaries almost $2,500 less than their male counterparts.

Item—9.7 percent of female faculty members had achieved the rank of professor compared to 25.5 percent of males.

Which Institutions Are Covered by Title IX?

All educational institutions that receive federal financial assistance are covered by the law. This includes virtually all 16,000 public school systems and 2,700 post-secondary institutions in the United States. The penalty for failure to comply with the provisions of Title IX is the loss of all federal money coming into a school district. Generally, this is a substantial amount of money enabling a school district to carry out a number of special programs ranging from free lunch to education of the handicapped, from career education to bilingual education. Clearly, the loss of federal aid would bring down the quality of education in most school districts.

What Did Title IX Require of Educational Institutions During Its First Year?

The Title IX Regulation required five procedural steps to be implemented by school districts and post-secondary institutions by July 21, 1976. These procedures should still be used to monitor compliance with Title IX, and be reviewed and updated regularly.

A. *Self-evaluation.* All policies and practices were to have been carefully evaluated for compliance with the Title IX requirement, modifications made where they were out of compliance, and remedial steps taken to eliminate the effects of past sex discrimination. Was a self-evaluation conducted at your school? How could you find out?

B. *Designation of Title IX Coordinator.* At least one employee was to have been designated to coordinate efforts to comply with Title IX and to investigate Title IX complaints. Do you know who this person is at your school?

C. *Grievance procedures.* Internal grievance procedures were to have been adopted and published for the "prompt and equitable" resolution of sex-discrimination complaints. Would you know how to file a grievance if you felt that you were being discriminated against because of your sex?

D. *Dissemination of policy.* All employees, students, parents of elementary and secondary students, sources of referral for job applicants, and labor organizations were to have been notified that the school district or institution adheres to the requirements of Title IX and does not discriminate on the basis of sex. Such a policy statement must appear regularly on all official documents, such as job announcements, course announcements, student and faculty handbooks, job applications. Have you noticed such a policy statement in your institution's materials?

E. *Assurance of compliance.* An assurance form indicating compliance with Title IX was required of all districts and institutions receiving federal funds. This is an ongoing responsibility.

What General Areas Does Title IX Cover?

A. *Admission of students.* This section applies primarily to post-secondary institutions and not to public school districts with the exception of vocational education institutions.

B. *Treatment of students.* This section covers all students at every education institution receiving federal funds once they have been admitted. We will focus on this part of the regulation as it applies to students in kindergarten through twelfth grade.

C.   *Employment.* As this book is being written, the courts are deciding whether sex discrimination in employment is covered under Title IX. Even if the courts determine that employment is not covered under Title IX, other federal and many state laws prohibit sex discrimination in this area.

What Constitutes Equal Treatment of Students?

The Title IX Regulation *requires* that:

> . . . no person shall, on the basis of sex, be *excluded* from participation in, be *denied* the benefits of, or be subjected to *discrimination* under any academic, extracurricular, research, occupational training or any other education program or activity operated by the recipient. [*emphasis added*]

The Title IX Regulation *prohibits:*

> provision of DIFFERENT aid, benefits, or services on the basis of sex;
> DENIAL of such aid, benefits, or services to persons of either sex;
> SEPARATE or DIFFERENT rules of behavior, punishments, or other treatment, on the basis of sex;
> LIMITATION of any right, privilege, advantage, or opportunity on the basis of sex.

The language of Title IX clearly makes it illegal to treat students differently or separately on the basis of what sex they happen to be. All programs, activities, and opportunities offered by a school district must be equally available to all students. In addition, school districts are required to remedy the effects of past discriminatory practices with affirmative measures when necessary. This could mean actively recruiting girls for competitive athletics and counseling students to explore nontraditional course and career options. Without such affirmative steps, equal access often produces little real change because past conditioning has been so strong.

The Title IX Regulation prohibits discrimination, denial, exclusion, limitation, or separation in any school-sponsored or assisted program or activity. This covers all of the traditional vehicles for educating students with some exceptions permitted in athletics. The regulation covers in detail the following areas that relate to elementary and secondary students: course offerings, physical education, athletics, counseling, employment assistance, financial assistance, health and insurance benefits, marital and parental status, extracurricular activities, and facilities.

Course Offerings

No courses or education activities may be provided separately on the basis of sex. All courses must be open to all students. Participation in classes may not be required or refused on the basis of sex. This includes health, physical, industrial, business, vocational, technical, home economics, music, and adult education.

Course titles and descriptions should not contain language or illustrations that exclude one sex.

Course requirements, prerequisites, or selection procedures may not have a discriminatory or differential result based on sex.

Students may not be separated for instruction in a course—with the following exceptions:

- Portions of classes dealing exclusively with human sexuality may (not must) be conducted separately for females and males.
- Choruses of one or predominantly one sex that result from tryouts based on vocal range (as opposed to the establishment of "boys" and "girls" chorus, which is prohibited).
- Although physical education classes must be completely coeducational, students may be grouped by ability for each sport and may (not must) be separated during participation in contact sports.

Textbooks and Other Curricular Materials

The Title IX Regulation does not specifically prohibit the use of biased books and materials. The government decided that such restrictions might violate free-expression guarantees of the First Amendment.

However, the regulation acknowledges that "sex-role stereotyping and other sex bias in textbooks and curriculum materials are serious problems" and *assumes* "that local education agencies will deal with the problem of sex bias in curriculum materials in the exercise of their general authority and control over course content."

Counseling and Counseling Materials

Counseling services may not differ on the basis of sex. This prohibits:

- biased course or career guidance (to remedy past discriminatory practices it may be necessary to periodically apprise students of the advantages of nontraditional opportunities that are now available to them);
- use of biased achievement, ability, or interest tests;
- use of college and career materials that are biased in content, language, or illustration.

A school district has two additional responsibilities in the counseling area.

- It must develop and use internal procedures to ensure that appraisal and counseling materials do not discriminate on the basis of sex.

● If certain classes contain a substantially disproportionate number of students of one sex, it must ensure that such imbalance is not the result of sex discrimination in counseling or appraisal materials.

Employment Assistance

A school district may not assist any business or individual in employing students if the request is for a student of a particular sex.

Financial Assistance

A school district may not discriminate in the type or amount of financial assistance provided or in the eligibility or criteria for receipt of such aid.

Health and Insurance Benefits

Medical, hospital, accident, or life insurance benefits, services, policies, or plans that are available to students may not discriminate on the basis of sex.

Marital and Parental Status

No rules regarding a student's actual or potential, familial, or marital status may be applied if it results in treating students differently on the basis of sex.

Pregnant students may not be discriminated against or excluded from any education program or activity, including compulsory participation in or exclusion from any class or extracurricular activity.

Extracurricular Activities

Single-sex clubs and other activities are prohibited, with certain exceptions. These exceptions include: YWCA, YMCA, Girl Scouts, Boy Scouts, Camp Fire Girls, Boys' State, Girls' State, Key clubs and other voluntary and tax-exempt youth service organizations that have been traditionally single sex with membership limited to persons 19 years or younger.

Organizations and activities such as crossing guards, hall monitors, Future Farmers of America, Future Homemakers of America, honor societies, vocational, interest, and professional clubs must be open to students of both sexes.

Assistance to such organizations and activities must not be discriminatory in such matters as meeting times, facilities, assignments of faculty, advisors, and the like.

Conduct and Honors

Rules of behavior and punishments for violation of those rules must be the same for students of both sexes.

Honors and awards given by a school or by a community organization through the school may not designate the sex of the student as one criterion for the award, for example, outstanding girl or boy. Awards for similar achievement should be comparable for both sexes.

Athletics

Intramural, club, or interscholastic sports must be coeducational with two major exceptions:

- when selection for teams is based upon competitive skill
- when the activity is a contact sport

In these two exceptions, separate teams are permitted but not required. Decisions about whether separate or coeducational teams should be established in specific sports must be based on what best accommodates the interests and abilities of both sexes.

Intramural teams in noncontact sports must be coeducational.

Although Title IX does not require the expenditure of equal dollar amounts on girls' and boys' athletic programs, the funds necessary to ensure equality of opportunity must be provided. Factors that affect equality of opportunity include:

- equipment and supplies provided
- travel and per diem allowances
- practice and game schedules
- locker rooms, practice, and competitive facilities
- medical and training facilities and services
- publicity

Title IX is more complex than this overview indicates, but this general summary should provide enough basic information for you to identify some of the more obvious violations that may exist in schools. Following are some brief situations. Test your knowledge by indicating whether or not a Title IX violation is involved in each case, and give reasons for your decisions. If there is time, you may want to discuss your choices and reasons with your classmates, then check your responses with the answer key at the end of the chapter.

IS THERE A VIOLATION OF TITLE IX?

Yes No 1. George and Sonia have been brought to the principal by their fifth-grade teacher because they have been fighting, screaming, cursing, throwing erasers, and turning over desks. The principal calls Sonia's mother for an appointment to discuss the child's behavior, and sends George to the assistant principal for paddling.

Reasons for your decision:

_____

_____

_____

Yes No 2. Laurie is six-months pregnant and her counselor tells her she must transfer to the adult education program at night where she can get an excellent education without feeling embarrassed by her condition.

Reasons for your decision:

_____

_____

_____

Yes No 3. Mr. Steers, the diesel mechanics instructor, asks a guidance counselor to transfer Georgine Williams out of his class. He explains that the girl's long hair might get caught in a machine and that she seems to be very nervous in the shop area.

Reasons for your decision:

_____

_____

_____

Yes No 4. Bob wants to sign up for the girls' volleyball team since there is none for boys. The coach explains that in general there are many more opportunities for boys in athletics at the school, so this team is reserved for girls.

Reasons for your decision:

_____

_____

_____

Yes No 5. Sheila is an outstanding athlete and plays basketball, volley-ball, and softball. This year she wants to try out for the boys' baseball team but the coach refuses because the girls' softball team needs her and he's afraid that the boys would tease her and refuse to play ball with her.
Reasons for your decision:

_____

_____

_____

Yes No 6. Rose Ann decides to sign up for auto mechanics with her boyfriend Clifton. She finds out that she cannot take the course because she has not taken Small Motor Repairs, which is a prerequisite. Clifton took it last year when it was for boys only.
Reasons for your decision:

_____

_____

_____

Yes No 7. Louis signs up for Bachelor Cooking.
Reasons for your decision:

_____

_____

_____

Yes No 8. A sign is posted in the work-study office: "Girls interested in grocery check-out jobs see Mr. Dobbs at Thrifty Supermarket."
Reasons for your decision:

_____

_____

_____

Yes No   9. Jackson receives the award for outstanding all-around tenth- grade male student.
Reasons for your decision:

_____

_____

_____

Yes No   10. Lucille and Henry receive awards for outstanding contributions to their school's athletic program. Lucille receives a certificate of merit, which she plans to frame in her room. Henry receives a sweater, which he promptly gives his girlfriend to wear.
Reasons for your decision:

_____

_____

_____

Yes No   11. The Compton High School girls' basketball team plays its games on Wednesday nights. Although the boys play on Friday nights, the girls do not mind since they do not attract much of an audience yet.
Reasons for your decision:

_____

_____

_____

Yes No   12. Cindy complains to her middle school principal that the mathematics book she is using has no pictures or examples of girls or women.
Reasons for your decision:

_____

_____

_____

Yes No 13. Although Sam is embarrassed, his parents have urged him to ask his guidance counselor for information on nursing as a career. He sheepishly approaches Mr. Ellis who says that nursing is now available to men as well as women. Mr. Ellis also says that Sam might be uncomfortable working with so many women and under the supervision of a woman. Reasons for your decision:

_____

_____

_____

Yes No 14. Mr. Collins always separates girls and boys in his third-grade physical education classes because he knows that at this age students do not like to play in mixed-sex teams. Reasons for your decision:

_____

_____

_____

Yes No 15. Geneva goes to her counselor to find out what to do about being refused admission to the Future Farmers of America. Her counselor tells her that there is nothing that can be done but to try and work it out with the club members and their advisor. Reasons for your decision:

_____

_____

_____

Yes No 16. The Albertson County School District has allocated $15,000 for its interscholastic athletic program this year. Two-thirds of the funds will be spent on the boys' program. Reasons for your decision:

_____

_____

_____

Yes No   17. Mr. and Mrs. Stoner have just found out that while their son's basketball uniform and traveling expenses to away games are provided by the high school, their daughter's are not.

Reasons for your decision:

_____

_____

_____

Yes No   18. Hillside Elementary School has a 25-year-old tradition of holding an annual schoolwide spelling bee—girls against the boys. The competition begins in each classroom and culminates before a big assembly with parent and community interest and trophies for the winners.

Reasons for your decision:

_____

_____

_____

How Is Title IX Enforced?

The Office for Civil Rights (OCR) of the Department of Education is empowered by Congress to enforce Title IX. OCR conducts on-site inspections of school districts around the country to determine if the rights of students and employees are being protected. At stake is all of the federal money received for any purpose by the school district.

If an individual believes she or he has been discriminated against on the basis of sex, several options for relief are available.

A.   File a grievance using the internal grievance process of the school district, which is supposed to operate fairly and within a reasonable period of time.

B.   File a complaint with the Office for Civil Rights in Washington, D.C., or a regional branch. This may be done at the same time as a local grievance is filed, or if the local grievance fails to work quickly and fairly, or in place of filing a local grievance. The Office for Civil Rights must respond to the complaint within 15 days, and, within 180 days, it must make a determination about whether sex discrimination exists. Complaints must be filed within 80 days of the alleged grievance.

C.   File a suit in court. The United States Supreme Court ruled in

Cannon v. *The University of Chicago,* in May, 1979, that an individual has the right to file a private lawsuit under Title IX.

Is Title IX Here to Stay?

Title IX should be viewed as a process for change rather than a set of specific answers to the problems created by sexism in our schools. Typically, American laws and regulations are responsive to political and social concerns and conditions. From the time the Title IX Regulation was first issued by the Department of Health, Education, and Welfare, various special interest groups have pressured for changes. And, in fact, interpretations and compliance activities by the federal government have changed in response to some of those pressures.

Many unresolved Title IX sex equity issues remain. In the coming years educators, the general public, the Department of Education, the U.S. Congress, and the courts will be grappling with some of the following problems. What do you think?

- Title IX permits separate athletic teams for females and males. Several recent court decisions, however, indicate that outstanding female athletes must be allowed to play on male teams, even in contact sports.
- Title IX does not cover biased textbooks but many people believe that the use of biased instructional materials should be prohibited altogether or supplemented with nonbiased materials and techniques.
- Title IX permits school districts to spend unequal amounts of money on girls' and boys' athletics, but many think expenditures should be equal.
- Some single-sex clubs such as Girl Scouts and Boy Scouts have been exempted from the Title IX requirement that all extracurricular activities must be coeducational. Many people think that these clubs should also be coeducational.
- Will mixed-sex sports, clubs, and activities reduce opportunities for girls to gain experience in leadership positions since they tend to defer to boys?

These and other Title IX issues will be discussed for a long time. Although it is frustrating not to have all the answers, Title IX is part of a new frontier in educational equity. As an educator, you will be a pioneer on that frontier.

Among the important factors that will affect the achievement of sex equity in our schools are: congressional support for educational equity and Title IX; the degree of modification and enforcement of Title IX by the Office for Civil Rights; relevant court decisions; the level of commitment of educators. Now that you have some background and information about this important but still controversial law, watch the news media and educational journals for developments.

WHAT YOU CAN DO

In this chapter, we have looked into the classrooms, corridors, and gyms of American schools to uncover the ways in which students are treated differently based on their sex. We have examined the negative outcomes of sex-differentiated treatment on both women and men and the potential of Title IX for equalizing treatment and freeing human beings to be all that they can be.

Here is a brief summary of the major points made in this chapter:

- Social expectations for people based on their sex limit the development of their full potential.
- Despite the fact that many people deny the existence of sex bias and discrimination in schools, children are bombarded with overt and covert messages about what they can be and do based on what sex they are.
- Girls and boys need encouragement to explore nontraditional as well as traditional options.
- The vehicles of education (instructional materials, curriculum, counseling, physical activity, extracurricular activities) convey information to students about appropriate female and male roles, jobs, and behavior.
- Negative effects of differential treatment on women include: lowered self-esteem, limited educational and career goals, inadequate vocational and career training, physical and intellectual underdevelopment, ambivalence about success and leadership.
- Negative effects of differential treatment on men include: stress arising from rigid sex-role orientation, underachievement, behavioral and psychological problems, uncontrolled aggression, alcohol and drug abuse, a high mortality rate, alienation from children and friends, and limited career and leisure options.
- Title IX prohibits sex discrimination in schools and will help change traditional practices based on limiting stereotypes. Equal educational opportunities should lead to more and better options for both female and male students.

Keep in mind the information we have examined that indicates that an individual's developmental potential may be limited by rigid sex-role stereotypes. Traditionally defined female and male roles may not suit the realities of contemporary society. In today's complex and changing society, a healthy adult must be self-reliant and assertive as well as caring and sensitive. Both men and women will find it increasingly necessary to express the full range of human behavior instead of being restricted to that which is stereotypically feminine or masculine.

In an ideal world Emma and Joe Green would have been encouraged to explore a wide range of behavior and experience. They would both have played with blocks and trucks as well as with dolls; they would have climbed trees, and played football, jumprope, and space explorers. Joe would have been encouraged to play with girls as well as boys; he would have been given a doll to hold so that he could express tenderness and also prepare for the possibility of parenthood. Emma's teachers would have paid more attention to the quality of her work and less to her appearance, while Joe's teachers would have given him more support for sensitive and nurturing behavior.

Emma's counselors would have presented the realities of adult life to her, and would have helped her with careful educational and career planning. Joe's counselors would have encouraged him to express his doubts and anxieties, and they would have helped him to determine what his real interests and talents were.

And, perhaps, in our ideal world, Emma and Joe would come to their marriage as two fully developed human beings. Neither would be a burden on the other, each would be confident and independent yet at times vulnerable and dependent. They would be equally satisfied with female or male children and would share home and child-rearing responsibilities.

As an educator, you can take some specific steps toward this ideal world now.

- Examine your own attitudes and behavior continuously for sex bias and stereotyping.
- Help sensitize others to these issues by sharing information and exchanging ideas.
- Don't let biased or discriminatory behaviors go unchallenged.
- Inform others about their rights.
- Continue to inform yourself about the issue of sexism in education by reading the latest news, reports, and research findings in this field.
- Challenge the years of habit and tradition that keep female and male students confined to prescribed roles.
- Keep in mind that you can be a leader in the process of change. You can help make this a better world for future Emmas and Joes.

You can make a real difference.

ANSWER KEY: Quiz on Women in the World of Work

1.	c	8.	a
2.	d	9.	b
3.	a	10.	b
4.	b	11.	d
5.	c	12.	b
6.	a	13.	d
7.	d	14.	a

Give yourself ten points for every correct answer.

A score of 120–140 points shows that you are exceptionally knowledgeable (or that you have a job collecting statistics about women).

A score of 70 to 110 is still pretty good, and you are observant and well informed about what's going on around you.

A score of 60 or less is poor. You need to wake up and get into the mainstream of a world that is changing every minute.

ANSWER KEY: Is There a Violation of Title IX?

1. Yes. The principal is disciplining a girl and boy differently for the same behavior.

2. Yes. The pregnant student has a right to remain in the regular school program if she wants to.

3. Yes. Proper safety measures should be enforced and the female student encouraged to relax and learn the rules, but she has a right to be in the class.

4. No. If boys have more opportunities than girls to participate in athletics in the school then they need not be allowed on girls teams.

5. Yes. A girl must be allowed to try out for a team in a noncontact sport if there is no team in that sport for girls. (Baseball and softball are different sports.)

6. Yes. If a girl has not had access to a course, making it a prerequisite to another course is discriminatory.

7. Yes. No courses may be for one sex only.

8. Yes. Schools may only deal with employers who do not discriminate in hiring their students.

9. Yes. Awards may not be sex biased.

10. Yes. Awards for comparable achievements should be comparable in value.

11. Yes. Despite the attitude of the girls themselves, they must have equal opportunities with boys to play before prime-time audiences.

12. No. Bias in textbooks is not covered by the regulation. The principal and teacher should supplement biased materials and raise the issue as a social problem with the students.

13. Yes. Counselors must provide unbiased counseling and guidance to students and encourage them to explore all career options.

14. Yes. Physical education classes at all grade levels must be completely coeducational except for ability grouping and competition in contact sports.

15. Yes. Every school district is required to have a grievance procedure for sex-discrimination complaints. In fact there are two violations here. Refusing to admit a female student into Future Farmers of America is sex discriminatory.

16. No. Equal financial expenditures on athletics for girls and boys are not required.

17. Yes. Necessary funds must be provided to support girls' teams.

18. Yes. Students may not be grouped separately based on their sex. Girl-boy spelling bees and other such activities have no more educational validity than blacks opposing whites, or Chicanos opposing Asians.

ENDNOTES

[1] Margaret Mead, *Sex and Temperament in Three Primitive Societies* (New York: Dell, 1935).

[2] Cited in Lois W. Banner, *Women in Modern America: A Brief History* (New York: Harcourt, Brace, 1974).

[3] Alvin Toffler, *Future Shock* (New York: Random House, 1970).

[4] Women on Words and Images, *Dick and Jane as Victims: Sex Stereotyping in Children's Readers* (Washington, D.C.: Resource Center on Sex Roles in Education, 1974).

[5] Women on Words and Images, "Look Jane Look. See Sex Stereotypes," in Judith Stacey et al. (eds.), *And Jill Came Tumbling After: Sexism in American Education* (New York: Dell, 1974).

[6] Lenore Weitzman and Diane Rizzo, *Biased Textbooks* (Washington, D.C.: Resource Center on Sex Roles in Education, 1974).

[7] Janice Law Trecker, "Women in U.S. History High-School Textbooks," in Judith Stacey et al. (eds.), *And Jill Came Tumbling After: Sexism in American Education* (New York: Dell, 1974).

[8] Sylvia-Lee Tibbetts, "Sex-Role Stereotyping in Children's Reading Material: Update," *Journal of the National Association for Woman Deans, Administrators, and Counselors* 42 (1979).

[9] Myra Sadker and David Sadker, *Beyond Pictures and Pronouns: Sexism in Teacher Education Textbooks* (Washington, D.C.: Dept. of Education, Women's Educational Equity Act Program, 1980).

[10] Karen Rappaport, "Sexual Roles and Mathematical Expectations," *The Math Journal* 19 (Fall 1978).

[11] Gloria Stevenson, "Counseling Black Teenage Girls," *Occupational Outlook Quarterly* 19 (Summer 1974).

[12] Mary Ellen Verheyden-Hilliard, *Cracking the Glass Slipper: PEER's Guide to Ending Sex Bias in Your Schools* (Washington, D.C.: Project on Equal Educational Rights, 1977).

[13] Michael Parlady, "For Johnny's Reading Sake," *Reading Teacher* 22 (May 1969).

[14] Jere E. Brophy and Thomas L. Good, "Feminization of American Elementary Schools," *Phi Delta Kappan* 54 (April 1973).

[15] B. J. Kemer, "A Study of the Relationship Between the Sex of the Student and the Assignment of Marks by Secondary School Teachers" (Ph.D. dissertation, Michigan State University, 1965).

[16] P. Rubovitz and M. Maehr, "Pygmalion Analyzed: Toward an Explanation of the Rosenthal-Jacobson Findings," *Journal of Personality and Social Psychology* 25 (1973). *See also* E. Leacock, *Teaching and Learning in City Schools* (New York: Basic Books, 1969).

[17] Pauline S. Sears and David H. Feldman, "Teacher Interactions with Boys and with Girls," in Judith Stacey et al. (eds.), *And Jill Came Tumbling After: Sexism in American Education* (New York: Dell, 1974).

[18] Arthur Thomas and Norman Stewart, "Counselor Response to Female Clients with Deviate and Conforming Career Goals," *Journal of Counseling Psychology* 18 (1971).

[19] N. W. Friedersdorf, "A Comparative Study of Counselor Attitudes Toward the Further Educational and Vocational Plans of High School Girls," unpublished study (Lafayette, Indiana: Purdue University, 1969) cited in *Implementing Title IX and Attaining Sex Equity—The Counselor's Role* (Washington, D.C.: Resource Center on Sex Roles in Education, 1977).

[20] National Assessment of Educational Progress, "Essay Task: A Woman's Place Is (Where?)," *NAEP Newsletter* X (June 1977).

[21] Harvey Edwards, *The Sociology of Sport* (Homewood, Ill.: Dorsey Press, 1973).

[22] William Morgan, University of Arizona Sports Psychology Laboratory, quoted in *Time* (June 26, 1978).

[23] Celeste Ulrich, "Schools and Physical Survival," *Non-Sexist Education for Survival* (Washington, D.C.: National Education Association, 1973).

[24] David Riesmen, Harvard Sociologist, quoted in *Time* (June 26, 1978).

[25] "It's a Boy!" *The Miami Herald* (January 25, 1978).

[26] "Child's Play: What Every Parent Needs to Know," *Ms* (February 1977).

[27] Eleanor Maccoby, "Woman's Intellect," in Farber and Wilson (eds.), *The Potential of Women* (New York: McGraw-Hill, 1963).

[28] *Window Dressing on the Set: Women and Minorities in Television. A Report of the U.S. Commission on Civil Rights* (Washington, D.C.: U.S. Commission on Civil Rights, 1977).

[29] Lisa A. Serbin and K. Daniel O'Leary, "How Nursery Schools Teach Girls to Shut Up," *Psychology Today* (December 1975).

[30] C. A. Dweck, "Sex Differences in the Meaning of Negative Evaluation Situations: Determinants and Consequences" (paper presented at the annual meeting of the Society for Research in Child Development, Denver, Colo., 1975).

[31] National Assessment of Educational Progress, "Males Dominate in Educational Success," *NAEP Newsletter* VIII (October 1975).

[32] Patricia Cross, "College Women: A Research Description," *Journal of National Association of Women Deans and Counselors* 32 (Autumn 1968).

[33] Lucy Sells, "Mathematics—A Critical Filter," *The Science Teacher* 45 (February 1978).

[34] Cross, "College Women: A Research Description."

[35] Lynne B. Iglitzin, "A Child's Eye View of Sex Roles," *Sex Role Stereotyping in the Schools* (Washington, D.C.: National Education Association, 1973).

[36] Peggy Hawley, "What Women Think Men Think," *Journal of Counseling Psychology* 18 (Autumn 1971).

[37] Elizabeth Douban and Anne Locksley, "Teenaged Boys and Girls Suffer Different—But Equally Serious Psychological Problems," *ISR Newsletter* 5 (Summer 1977).

[38] U.S. Department of Labor Statistics, cited in "An Overview of Women in the Workforce," (Washington, D.C.: National Commission on Working Women, Center for Women and Work, September 1978).

[39] International Women's Year Commission Study, cited in "Wives Get Short Shrift," *The Miami Herald* (October 31, 1977).

[40] "Women Entering Job Market at an Extraordinary Pace," *New York Times* (September, 1976) cited in *Implementing Title IX and Attaining Sex Equity—Generic Session One* (Washington, D.C.: Resource Center on Sex Roles in Education, 1977).

[41] *The Economist,* cited in Sylvia Porter, "You've Come the Longest Way, Baby," *The Miami Herald* (November 27, 1978).

[42] L. M. Lansky, "The Family Structure also Affects the Model: Sex-Role Attitudes in Parents of Pre-School Children," *Merrill-Palmer Quarterly* 13 (1967); and S. Fling and M. Manosevitz, "Sex Typing in Nursery School Children's Play Interests," *Developmental Psychology* 7 (1972).

[43] Ruth E. Hartley, "Sex-Role Pressures and the Socialization of the Male Child," in Judith Stacey et al. (eds.), *And Jill Came Tumbling After: Sexism in American Education* (New York: Dell, 1974).

[44] Warren Farrell, *The Liberated Man* (New York: Random House, 1975).

[45] William Meyer and George Thompson, "Teacher Interactions with Boys, as Contrasted with Girls," in Raymond Kuhlens and George Thompson (eds.), *Psychological Studies of Human Development* (New York: Appleton-Century-Crofts, 1963).

[46] P. Rosenkrantz, H. Bee, S. Vogel, I. Broverman, and D. Broverman, "Sex-Role Stereotypes and Self-Concepts in College Students," *Journal of Consulting and Clinical Psychology* 32 (1968).

[47] Gary Peltier, "Sex Differences in the School: Problem and Proposed Solution," *Phi Delta Kappan* 50 (November 1968).

[48] Patricia Cayo Sexton, "Schools Are Emasculating Our Boys," in Judith Stacey et al. (eds.) *And Jill Came Tumbling After: Sexism in American Education* (New York: Dell, 1974).

[49] Peter J. Stein and Steven Hoffman, "Sports and Role Strain," *Journal of Social Issues* 34 (1978).

[50] M. Komarovsky, *Dilemmas of Masculinity* (New York: Norton, 1976), cited in Stein and Hoffman, "Sports and Role Strain."

[51] Robert A. Lewis, "Emotional Intimacy Among Men," *Journal of Social Issues* 34 (1978).

[52] James Harrison, "Warning: The Male Sex Role May Be Dangerous to Your Health," *Journal of Social Issues* 34 (1978).

3

Beyond the Dick and Jane Syndrome:

Confronting Sex Bias in Instructional Materials *

Donna Gollnick, Myra Sadker and David Sadker

Objectives

- To describe the role of the teacher in combating sex bias in instructional materials
- To identify six forms of sex bias that often exist in textbooks and other instructional materials, and to examine how these types of bias affect student attitudes and behaviors
- To examine what publishers and educators have done and still must do to bring about the development of nonsexist materials
- To develop strategies for counteracting sex bias in instructional materials

Give yourself five minutes for this quick creativity quiz. How many different kinds of instructional materials can you name? Take a few moments to generate your own list.

The National Education Association lists 24 different kinds of materials.[1] Compare your list to theirs, which is on pp. 61-62. Don't be surprised if you couldn't name every available type of teaching aid. Categories keep growing, and the total number of learning materials now available to teachers is astonishing. There are over half a million different materials available for classroom use! Over 20,000 titles of textbooks are mentioned in the 1977 edition of *El-Hi Textbooks in Print*. Another 500,000 nonprint titles are listed by the National Information Center for Education Media.[2] Instructional materials are the base of most classroom teaching with the main focus on textbooks. Research has shown that 95 percent of all teaching time is spent on the use of some type

---

* This chapter is adapted from Donna Gollnick, Myra Sadker, and David Sadker, *Beyond the Dick and Jane Syndrome: Confronting Sex Bias in Instructional Materials* (U.S. Dept. of Education, Women's Educational Equity Act Program, 1980).

of instructional materials, while 62.5 percent of students' classroom time is structured around print materials alone.[3]

Because instructional materials are used so frequently in classrooms, their selection is critical to effective teaching. At the same time it is difficult for teachers to determine which materials might be best for their schools and classrooms because the number of available items is so large. Consequently, publishers, researchers, and users (i.e., teachers and students) are concerned with the development of criteria for selecting materials. There is general agreement that the following four general criteria should be considered:[4]

1. *Desirability.* Do the materials meet a need? Are they appropriate for the students who will use them? Do they adhere to local social, moral, and instructional values?

2. *Practicality.* What are the instructional advantages and disadvantages of the materials? Are they affordable, available, easily used, and adaptable to different classrooms?

3. *Intrinsic Quality.* Do the materials reflect equity? Are their presentations balanced in terms of sex, race, ethnicity, age, and socioeconomic level? Is the content accurate and current? Are the instructional and technical qualities adequate? Are the materials attractive and appealing to students?

4. *Product Development.* How were the materials developed? What are the qualifications of the authors? Have the materials been evaluated? If so, how?

All of these criteria are important in the selection of instructional materials. However, this chapter will focus on only one aspect of textbook selection criteria: Do instructional materials reflect equity in their representation and portrayal of females and males? Although the emphasis here is on sex bias, it is important to be aware that many instructional materials reflect similar biases concerning racial and ethnic groups. Also, textbooks may exhibit bias against individuals or groups because of socioeconomic level, age, religion, or mental/physical handicap. The information on sex bias presented in this module can be adapted to examine and counteract bias against these other groups as well.

All of the following are classified as instructional materials by the National Education Association:

textbooks	supplementary books
workbooks	paperbacks
pamphlets	programmed instructional systems
anthologies	dictionaries
encyclopedias	reference books
tests	classroom periodicals

newspapers	filmstrips
films	audio and video tapes
records and cassettes	slides
transparencies	globes
kits of realia	manipulative objects
learning games	graphic items (cards, posters, maps, photographs)

YOUR ROLE AS INSTRUCTIONAL DECISION MAKER

As instructional decision maker in your classroom, you are faced with a multitude of decisions ranging from instructional style to grading policies, from methods of discipline to the physical organization of your classroom. Some of the most important decisions you make will be concerned with instructional materials. As a teacher, you may have some role in selecting the texts for your classroom, or they may be distributed to you as one of the instructional "givens" of your teaching assignment. In most cases you will be able to decide how much you wish to rely on the textbooks assigned to you. You also are likely to have a good deal of latitude in selecting a variety of materials to supplement these texts. As instructional decision maker, you are in a very influential position. You have the opportunity to combat sexism in your classroom and to develop a curriculum that encourages all students to reach their full potential.

SIX FORMS OF BIAS IN INSTRUCTIONAL MATERIALS

Most of us have been conditioned to read information in textbooks as if it were unquestionably accurate. Consequently, it is difficult to begin reading critically, for the purpose of identifying sex or race bias. However, this is a necessary first step; in order to implement a nonsexist curriculum, you must first be able to recognize the biases that often exist in instructional materials.

In the following pages, we discuss six different forms of sex bias. As we've mentioned, these forms of bias may also apply to racial and ethnic groups; they exist not only in textbook materials, but also in children's literature, television, movies, and many other areas as well.

Susan B. Who? Invisibility in Instructional Materials

How much do you know about the contributions of women to the historical and contemporary development of this nation? Test your knowledge by completing the matching items in the following "Susan B. Who?" quiz.

SUSAN B. WHO?

_____ 1. Prudence Crandall

_____ 2. Mary Berry

_____ 3. Sor Juana Ines de la Cruz

_____ 4. Patricia Harris

_____ 5. Dixie Lee Ray

_____ 6. Harriet Tubman

_____ 7. Alice Paul

_____ 8. Lupe Anguiano

_____ 9. Susan B. Anthony

_____ 10. Betty Friedan

_____ 11. Maria Tallchief

_____ 12. Maria Goeppert-Mayer

_____ 13. Wilma Rudolph

_____ 14. Chien-Shiung Wu

_____ 15. Margaret Mead

a. An organizer of the Underground Railroad during the Civil War

b. First woman president of a major state university

c. Nuclear physicist

d. Winner of Nobel Prize for Physics in 1963

e. Established a school for black girls in Connecticut prior to the Civil War

f. Responsible for the creation of several Hispanic women's coalitions

g. Classic ballet dancer in the 1940s and 1950s

h. Author of a rationale for educating women in the fifteenth century

i. Governor of Washington, former head of Atomic Energy Commission

j. Anthropologist, psychologist, writer, lecturer, and teacher

k. Leader in the struggle for women's rights during the nineteenth century

l. U.S. runner who won three Olympic gold medals in 1960 for field and track

m. Militant suffragist who organized parades and demonstrations in the nation's capital

n. First black woman to be appointed an ambassador and later a member of the U.S. Cabinet

o. Author of *The Feminine Mystique* and one of the founders of the National Organization for Women (N.O.W.)

Although the women in this quiz have made significant contributions to the growth and development of this nation, few will appear in the texts that your students are assigned to read. If you were to list figures from your own study of U.S. history, how many would be women?

Some researchers have examined textbooks to determine the number of women included and how they are portrayed. After a careful analysis of the most widely used secondary school U.S. history texts, one researcher concluded:

> Women arrived in 1619. They held the Seneca Falls Convention on Women's Rights in 1848. During the rest of the nineteenth century, they participated in reform movements, chiefly temperance, and were exploited in factories. In 1920 they were given the vote. They joined the armed forces during the Second World War and thereafter have enjoyed the good life in America.[6]

Women suffer from such widespread omission in these texts that students typically must read over 500 pages before they find one page of information about women.[7] This form of sex bias, *invisibility*, characterizes not only history books, but texts in reading, language arts, mathematics, science, spelling, and vocational education as well.

You can examine your own textbooks for invisibility by counting the number of: (1) male-centered and female-centered examples—that is, stories or problems where the main character is male or female; (2) males and females in illustrations; (3) males and females in various occupations; and (4) male and female biographies. This was the technique used by researchers who analyzed 134 elementary readers and disclosed the following ratio: [8]

Boy-centered stories to girl-centered stories	7:2
Male illustrations to female illustrations	2:1
Male occupations to female occupations	3:1
Male biographies to female biographies	2:1

A 1972 study of science, math, reading, spelling, and social studies textbooks revealed that only 31 percent of all illustrations included females and that the percentage of females decreased as the grade level increased.[9] This same pattern was found for illustrations of minority persons. While minorities were 33 percent of the illustrations in first-grade textbooks, they were only 26 percent at the sixth-grade level. By sixth grade, only 15 percent of the illustrations in math books and 8 percent in science books reflected minority representation. The most invisible member of school texts was the minority female. Minority females appeared only half as often as minority males and they made up only 7 percent of all females in textbooks.

Research has demonstrated that children need strong positive role models for the development of self-esteem. When females and minorities are omitted from textbooks, a hidden curriculum is created, one that teaches children that minorities and females are less important and less significant in our society than are majority males.

Can't Girls Be Exciting too? Stereotyping in Instructional Materials

Many studies demonstrate that textbook children and adults are assigned rigid traits and roles based on their sex. This represents another form of bias—*stereotyping*—and it is prevalent in the narrative and illustrations of elementary and secondary textbooks.

Over and over again boys are portrayed as exhibiting one set of values, behaviors, and roles, and girls as exhibiting another and different set of attributes and characteristics. Here is the way researchers have found boys and girls portrayed in reading texts: [10]

Boys	Girls
ingenious	dependent
creative	passive
brave	incompetent
persevering	fearful
achieving	victims
adventurous	docile
curious	concerned with domesticities
autonomous	objects of scorn & ridicule
athletic	aimless
self-respecting	concerned about physical appearance
problem solver	spiritless

A quick glance at the lists above shows that the characteristics are based on rigid and blatant sex-role stereotypes. Furthermore, the traits assigned to boys are generally considered more desirable and positive than are those accorded to girls.

Textbook girls play with dolls, give tea parties, work in the kitchen, rarely conduct experiments, and are frightened of animals and loud noises. These girls ask advice of others and seek assistance in solving problems. In illustrations, girls often are spectators, usually watching boys who are busy and active in work and at play.[11]

Textbook boys, on the other hand, generally participate in important activities that prepare them for the careers to be pursued as adults. They save girls and women from danger. If there is a problem to solve, they are ingenious and creative enough to find the answer. Whether they are swimming, running, riding bicycles, winning ballgames, or solving mysteries, textbook boys are active and in charge.

Adult figures also suffer from sex-role stereotyping. Overwhelmingly, women are portrayed as mothers, and seldom do they work outside of the home. Textbook mothers always seem to be cooking or cleaning; in contrast, textbook fathers buy presents, take their children on trips, and in general, play with them.

Textbook occupations for women are very limited. Women are usually depicted as working in service occupations as baker, cafeteria worker, cashier, cleaning woman, cook, dressmaker, governess, housekeeper, librarian, recreational director, school crossing guard, nurse, teacher, or telephone operator. Once in a while, there is a female doctor. Men are found working in approximately six times as many different occupations as are women. In a major study of elementary readers, males were found in 147 different occupations while women were found in only 26.[12]

Although males appear to be blessed with more desirable characteristics, they also suffer from stereotyping. Many real-life males do not fit the confining stereotype of textbooks. They are expected to show emotions in real life, but in textbooks they are never allowed to cry. Although many real-life adult males change diapers, wash dishes, clean the house, and cook meals, they seldom do these things in textbooks. Some men today choose nonstereotyped careers such as nursing or preschool teaching—but not in textbooks.

In short, textbooks too often depict both males and females as sex-role stereotypes rather than as multidimensional human beings. Such stereotyping denies the reality of individual differences and prevents readers from understanding the complexity and the diversity that exists within groups.

What Struggle for Equality? Selectivity and Imbalance in Instructional Materials

Imagine this. You are an author who has collected 200 pages of notes on the second half of the nineteenth century, and this has to be reduced to one 35-page chapter for a U.S. history text. You must decide what is most important and should be included and what is of lesser significance and can be left out. Do you think wars and political decisions had the overwhelming influence on the development of society? Should the lives of "common people" be discussed and articulated? How much emphasis will you place on creative and artistic endeavors of the times? What reform movements deserve coverage in the 35 pages? As you, or any other author, make such choices, another form of bias may come into play. This form is known as *selectivity and imbalance*.

As textbook authors decide what information to include and emphasize, the contributions of one group of people may be highlighted while those of another group may be partially or even totally omitted. For example, when the emphasis in history texts is placed on wars, the textbook characters will be primarily male. When the emphasis is placed on the role of the family or labor, the textbook characters will include more women and minorities because their contributions in these areas have been profound. If the author emphasizes the continual struggle for equality, minorities and women who led and participated in such reform movements will be recognized.

Researchers who have analyzed history texts have found that imbalance in perspective has minimized women's roles and contributions. For example, Janice Trecker studied the most widely used history texts and found that there was more information on women's skirt lengths than on the suffrage movement. In fact, the typical amount of space allotted to the struggle for women's right to vote was only a few sentences. One high school history book actually devoted a column to the Gibson girl without mentioning the suffragists of the period. The Gibson girl was described as:

> . . . completely feminine, and it was clear that she could not, or would not, defeat her male companion at golf or tennis. In the event of a motoring emergency, she would quickly call upon his superior knowledge. . . .[13]

By emphasizing the Gibson girl and omitting suffragists, this text provides an imbalanced portrayal of women's roles and contributions. It also results in a historical presentation that lacks scholarly accuracy and comprehensiveness.

Many issues, situations, and events are complex and must be viewed from a variety of perspectives. Often authors of textbooks present only one aspect or perspective in their discussion of an event or topic. Think back to your high school history texts. Do you remember a cartoon depiction of Carrie Nation, an axe-carrying temperance movement leader? As a result of that caricature you may think of the temperance movement as ridiculous. While highlighting the activities of Carrie Nation, your text may not have stressed the reasons for the temperance movement. Families of men who were alcoholics suffered devastating abuse; wives had little recourse in such situations since divorces were difficult to obtain and economic opportunities for females were severely limited. To caricature the temperance movement without providing discussion of why it occurred represents only one aspect of a very serious problem. This is another example of bias through selectivity and imbalance.

This form of bias is harmful not only to the presentation of women, but to that of other minorities as well. History texts have focused primarily on the origins and heritage of European settlers in this nation. The voluntary and nonvoluntary immigration of other groups is given little attention. The relationships between the federal government and Native Americans are usually examined only from the government's perspective in terms of treaties and "protection"; a Native American perspective would also examine broken treaties and appropriation of native lands.

The selectivity and imbalance found in textbooks is unfair to students. It prevents females and minority group members from realizing that they have contributed significantly to the development of our society. It prevents all students from realizing the complexity of historical and contemporary situations and developments.

On the Sunny Side of the Page: Unreality in Instructional Materials

Think of ten women and ten men you know. What work do they do? Are they married? Do they have children. Complete the following charts with this information.

Look at the charts you have just completed and determine how many women work outside the home. How many men work outside the home? What does your chart reflect about the contemporary reality of women's and men's lives? Let's examine how these contemporary roles are reflected in textbooks.

Almost half of the nation's workforce is female, and 90 percent of all women will work outside the home at some time during their lives. Moreover, 35 percent of these working women have children under 18. Many working mothers travel on business trips and take the family on vacation. In reality, traditional roles of both females and males are in flux. Both men and women today work in a variety of careers and share many formerly sex-typed roles and activities. But this change is not reflected in most textbooks. Textbooks failure to reflect accurately the contemporary and changing nature of men's and women's roles represents another form of bias, that of *unreality*. Texts reflect unreality not only when they fail to recognize social change, but also when they gloss over or even completely ignore controversial and troublesome issues. Many of these changes and issues involve women and minorities.

For example, consider the textbook "housewife," a truly amazing character. Well groomed and protected by a spotless apron, she smoothly organizes her household world; she is invariably happy and calm. The realities of caring for children and husband, cleaning, cooking, shopping, doing laundry, repairing a leaky faucet, entertaining, chauffeuring, and bookkeeping are not presented. Nor is the difficult juggling act of combining a career and the care of home and children.

Let's broaden the focus a little to consider the typical textbook family—a mother, father, older son, younger daughter, and dog called Spot. In real life over 30 percent of the families in this nation are headed by a single parent, and one of every 17 American children lives in single-parent families. But these nontraditional families are rarely seen in textbooks, and the issue of divorce is seldom presented.

Textbooks also reflect unreality when they ignore controversial or unpleasant issues such as racism, sexism, prejudice, discrimination, and intergroup conflict. Contemporary problems of minorities and women are often glossed over. For example, textbooks typically provide only historical information on Native Americans. There is far less discussion of the devastating problems faced by this group today. There is also little discussion of sex and race bias in employment and salaries.

Obviously the achievements and successes of this nation should be presented in textbooks. But problems and difficulties must be analyzed as well. When controversial issues are not presented, students are denied the information they need to confront contemporary problems and work toward their resolution.

FEMALES

	Name	Occupation	Marital Status	Number of Children
1.				
2.				
3.				
4.				
5.				
6.				
7.				
8.				
9.				
10.				

MALES

	Name	Occupation	Marital Status	Number of Children
1.				
2.				
3.				
4.				
5.				
6.				
7.				
8.				
9.				
10.				

Woman in a Box: Fragmentation and Isolation in Instructional Materials

Have you ever opened a book and found a section that was set off from the regular text by different colored type or boxed-off lines? These sections may have had titles such as: "Ten Distinguished Black Americans" or "Susan B. Anthony: An Early Feminist." Such treatment results in another form of bias, one called *fragmentation and isolation.*

Texts reflect this form of bias when they isolate information pertaining to women and minorities from the main body of the narrative. Publishers often include these separate boxes, sections, or chapters in an attempt to update their books and incorporate previously omitted information. Obviously it's much easier to insert these "add-ons" than to integrate women and minorities throughout the main body of the text.

However, isolating information sends negative messages to students; it suggests that the experiences and contributions of women and minorities are merely an interesting diversion, but they are not integral to the mainstream of historical and contemporary developments in our society.

It probably sounds like an easy matter to spot fragmentation and isolation in texts—a simple check for a separate box or section on women. Actually, it's a bit more complex. You should be aware that if information on women and minorities is integrated throughout the text, then a separate section may actually serve to highlight their contributions. However, if pertinent information is not woven throughout the textbook, then a separate section or box does reflect this form of bias.

Fragmentation and isolation also occur when women and minority group members are depicted as interacting only among themselves and having little or no influence on society as a whole. For example, textbook discussions of feminism often talk about how women are affected by this contemporary movement; typically there is little analysis of the impact of the women's movement on other groups and social issues. Such treatment of women and minorities in textbooks implies that their history, their experiences, and their contributions are insignificant to the development of contemporary society.

Will People Replace Mankind? Linguistic Bias in Materials

It's time to change pace for a minute—get out your sketch pad (or use the box provided) and draw a picture of early caveman. Try to reflect in your drawing the kind of activities he was involved in, the type of implements he used, and what his life may have been like.

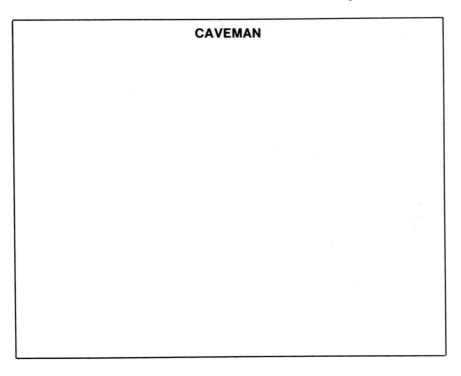

CAVEMAN

Let's examine what you drew. Is your early caveman male or female? What are the activities and implements you depicted?

Caveman is supposedly a generic term used to refer to all persons living during our earliest history. However, studies show that when elementary school children are asked to draw pictures of early cavemen, they do what they are told. They draw men. On the other hand, when they are asked to draw early cave people, they also do what they are told. They draw people—men, women, children, family groupings. In short, masculine nouns—*caveman, mankind, forefathers*—and masculine pronouns such as *he* and *his* are not as generic as we once thought. When children hear or read them, they may not form images of all people. Rather, they take the terms literally; when they read *he* and *man,* they think male.

A similar process occurs with occupational terms. When texts mention *policemen, firemen, salesmen,* or *businessmen,* children may not realize that these terms are supposed to include everyone. As a result, they may consider a wide range of occupational aspirations as inappropriate for girls.

NONSEXIST ALTERNATIVES FOR SOME COMMON WORDS AND PHRASES

mankind	humanity, human beings, human race, people
primitive man	primitive people, primitive men and women
manmade	artificial, synthetic, manufactured
congressman	member of Congress, representative
businessman	business executive, business manager
fireman	fire fighter
mailman	mail carrier, letter carrier
salesman	sales representative, salesperson, sales clerk
insurance man	insurance agent
statesman	leader, public servant
chairman	the presiding officer, the chair, head, leader, coordinator, chairperson, moderator
policeman	police officer

Another form of linguistic bias occurs when women are referred to as someone's wife or possession: "Phillip Lau took his wife to Chicago." Or, "The pioneer and his wife, children, and cattle moved West." When this is reworded, "The pioneer family moved West," all members of the family become associated with the traits of ingenuity, bravery, and courage—not just the pioneer male.

While language reflects the biases of society, it is probably the easiest form of bias to change in textbooks. Language is the area most frequently addressed by commercial publishers who have developed guidelines for improving the image of women in books. Changing language alone will not greatly alter the way women are perceived by readers, but such change is one positive way to begin. On the other hand, continued use of sexist terms and predominantly male references can only reinforce sex biases that exist in other forms.

Can you recognize the six forms of bias in instructional materials? Let's recap each form; then try your hand at the exercises that follow.

THE FORMS OF BIAS IN CURRICULAR MATERIALS [14]

INVISIBILITY: Certain groups are underrepresented in curricular materials. The significant omission of women and minority groups has become so great as to imply that these groups are of less value, importance, and significance in our society.

STEREOTYPING: By assigning traditional and rigid roles or attributes to a group, instructional materials stereotype and limit the abilities and potential of that group. Stereotyping denies students a knowledge of the diversity, complexity, and variation of any group of individuals. Children who see themselves portrayed only in stereotypic ways may internalize these stereotypes and fail to develop their own unique abilities, interests, and full potential.

IMBALANCE/SELECTIVITY: Textbooks perpetuate bias by presenting only one interpretation of an issue, situation, or group of people. This imbalanced account restricts the knowledge of students ragarding the varied perspectives that may apply to a particular situation. Through selective presentation of materials, textbooks distort reality and ignore complex and differing viewpoints. As a result, millions of students have been given limited perspective concerning the contributions, struggles, and participation of women and minorities in our society.

UNREALITY: Textbooks frequently present an unrealistic portrayal of our history and our contemporary life experience. Controversial topics are glossed over and discussions of discrimination and prejudice are avoided. This unrealistic coverage denies children the information they need to recognize, understand, and perhaps some day conquer the problems that plague our society.

FRAGMENTATION/ISOLATION: By separating issues related to minorities and women from the main body of the text, instructional materials imply that these issues are less important than and not a part of the cultural mainstream.

LINGUISTIC BIAS: Curricular materials reflect the discriminatory nature of our language. Masculine terms and pronouns, ranging from our *forefathers* to the generic *he,* deny the participation of women in our society. Further, occupations such as *mailman* are given masculine labels that deny the legitimacy of women working in these fields. Imbalance of word order and lack of parallel terms that refer to females and males are also forms of linguistic bias.

TEST YOUR RECOGNITION OF SEX BIAS IN TEXTS

Directions: Read each excerpt and determine if sex bias is present. If you find bias, indicate which form is present. By the way, as is the case in so many of our textbooks, you may come across more than just one form of bias in each excerpt. Finally, assume the role of author and rewrite the excerpt so that bias is no longer reflected. Check your answers with those in the answer key.

Case 1

The contemporary farmer is radically different from the frontiersman of the past. He is knowledgeable in a complex, scientific endeavor, and his livelihood is dependent upon his efficiency.[15]

Is sex bias present? _____

What form of sex bias is present? _____

Suggested revision: _____

_____

_____

_____

Case 2

Soon after John arrived home from school, he received a call from his father who said that he would be leaving the office later than usual. It was up to John to start dinner.

Is sex bias present? _____

What form of sex bias is present? _____

Suggested revision: _____

_____

_____

_____

Case 3

Sam led, and Helen went after him. Helen held his hand in a hard grip. She was timid in the darkness . . . Helen fell and Sam helped her get up.[16]

Is sex bias present? _____

What form of sex bias is present? _____

Suggested revision: _____

_____

_____

_____

Case 4

In a mathematics workbook there are 31 word problems showing males and females involved in the following activities:

Boys	*Girls*
1. buying a model car & plane	1. deciding whether to plant grass around a doghouse
2. painting (2 times)	
3. walking (4 times)	2. figuring out the living space
4. making a map	3. working for her father
5. doing an experiment	4. drinking
6. making a paper chain	5. working
7. losing weight	6. making a paper chain
8. riding a bicycle	7. gaining weight
9. running a race	8. growing taller
10. swimming	9. missing questions
11. using calories (2 times)	10. driving boys home
12. driving a delivery truck	
13. buying land (2 times)	

Is sex bias present? _____

What form of sex bias is present? _____

Suggested revision: _____

_____

_____

_____

Case 5

Father came home early and noticed Tommy had been crying. He put off starting dinner and took Tommy for a "walk talk." Starting junior high school certainly had its problems.[17]

Is sex bias present? _____

What form of sex bias is present? _____

Suggested revision: _____

_____

_____

_____

Case 6

The organized movement to win rights for women arose earlier in the United States than in any other nation, not because American women enjoyed so few privileges, but because they had so many that they demanded more.[18]

Is sex bias present? _____

What form of sex bias is present? _____

Suggested revision: _____

_____

_____

_____

_____

Case 7

Women in our society are already demanding new roles. By 2000, they may have complete equality with men. They will probably do as much work outside the home as men do. They will receive the same salaries. By 2000, women may also have equal social and political rights. There may be more women in government positions. Perhaps by then there will be a woman president. Many experts think that by 2000 the old saying, "A woman's place is in the home," will no longer apply.[19]

Is sex bias present? _____

What form of sex bias is present? _____

Suggested revision: _____

_____

_____

_____

_____

_____

_____

_____

_____

_____

Case 8

Besides men who can organize well and think clearly what other essentials are needed to build an industry? [20]

    Is sex bias present? _____

    What form of sex bias is present? _____

    Suggested revision: _____

_____

_____

_____

Case 9

Women were given the vote as a reward for their work in World War I.

    Is sex bias present? _____

    What form of sex bias is present? _____

Suggested revision: _____

_____

_____

_____

Case 10

The scientific advances of man in the twentieth century have been amazing.

Is sex bias present? _____

What form of sex bias is present? _____

Suggested revision: _____

_____

_____

_____

Case 11

These two problems appear on the same page of a mathematics book:

1. Nancy needs to make two batches of cookies for the Bake Sale. Help her double her recipe.
2. John wants to build a fence of 2-in. stakes to extend 20 feet. How many stakes should he buy?
    Is sex bias present? _____

What form of sex bias is present? _____

Suggested revision: _____

_____

_____

_____

_____

Case 12

The firefighters and police officers held a press conference to explain their grievances. The union president acted as spokesperson as she read the grievances to the reporters.[21]

    Is sex bias present? _____

    What form of sex bias is present? _____

    Suggested revision: _____

_____

_____

_____

Case 13

The last chapter of a social studies textbook is devoted to American life during the 1970s. It includes the following topics: The Economy, New Space Explorations, Contributions of Contemporary Women, Domestic Politics, Foreign Policy Decisions, Scientific Achievements, and the Energy Crisis.[22]

    Is sex bias present? _____

    What form of sex bias is present? _____

    Suggested revision: _____

_____

_____

_____

_____

_____

_____

APPLYING YOUR ANALYSIS SKILLS

The previous exercise has given you a chance to test your analysis skills on excerpts selected from texts. Now it's time to try your skill with some actual classroom textbooks. Select an elementary or secondary school text in a subject area of your choice. Examine this textbook for the six forms of sex bias and answer the questions below.

Name of Material Reviewed: _____

　　　Author(s): _____

　　　Copyright date: _____

1.　Is there sex bias in the textbook that you reviewed? If so, what form? Give examples of each form of bias found in the book.

Omission _____

_____

_____

_____

_____

Stereotyping _____

_____

_____

_____

_____

Selectivity/Imbalance _____

_____

_____

_____

_____

Unreality _____

_____

_____

_____

_____

Fragmentation/Isolation _____

_____

_____

_____

_____

Linguistic Bias _____

_____

_____

_____

_____

2.   How are minorities portrayed in this textbook? _____

_____

_____

_____

3.   How are minority females portrayed in the text? _____

_____

_____

_____

_____

4. What major changes would you make to eliminate sex bias in your text? (If you feel the text you analyzed is already nonsexist and needs no change, explain why.)

_____

_____

_____

_____

_____

_____

Did you find it difficult to analyze the textbook you selected? At this point you may be thinking that immersion in the day-to-day realities of teaching does not allow time for this kind of textbook analysis. It's true that textbook analysis is not a quick and easy task; however, as you continue to practice your skills you'll find the process becomes far less cumbersome and time consuming. Also, schools and organizations have developed a variety of aids that can help you evaluate your classroom instructional materials for sex and race bias. A selected list of these aids follows.

Aids for Analyzing Bias in Books

Biased Textbooks: Action Steps You Can Take. The Resource Center on Sex Equity, Council for Chief State School Officers, 400 North Capitol St., Suite 379, Washington, DC 20000.

Dick and Jane as Victims: Sex Stereotyping in Children's Readers. Women on Words and Images, P.O. Box 2163, Princeton, NJ 08540.

Equal Treatment of Sexes in Social Studies Textbooks: Guidelines for Authors and Editors. Westside Women's Committee, Box 24020, Village Station, Los Angeles, CA 90022.

How Fair Are Your Children's Textbooks? National Education Association, Publications Order Department, Academic Building, Saw Mill Rd., West Haven, CT 06516.

Sex Equality in Educational Materials. (AASA Executive Handbook Series # 4) American Association of School Administrators, 1801 N. Moore St., Arlington, VA 22209.

Stereotypes, Distortions and Omissions in U.S. History Textbooks. Racism and Sexism Resource Center for Educators, 1841 Broadway, New York, NY 10023.

Ten Quick Ways to Analyze Children's Books for Racism and Sexism. Council on Interracial Books for Children, 1841 Broadway, New York, NY 10023.

Beyond Pictures and Pronouns: Sexism in Teacher Education Textbooks. Education Development Center, 55 Chapel St., Newton, MA 02160.

THE IMPACT OF BIAS IN BOOKS

You may be saying, "Well, perhaps sex bias does exist in classroom materials. But can this really affect my students in any way?" Can bias in books promote sexist or racist attitudes and behaviors? Or is this bias only an annoying remnant of bygone days without any real significance for today's students and teachers?

According to a number of studies, bias in books cannot be dismissed as merely insignificant or annoying.[23] Students at various grade levels report that they have changed their attitudes and behaviors as a result of their reading. Changes occur in self-image, philosophy of life, interpersonal sensitivity, and opinions toward different cultural groups and social problems.[24] Therefore, if books distort or stereotype a certain group, this misrepresentation can affect student attitudes and perceptions. Here's how the process works. If you are a member of minority group or a female, or both, you may find yourself turning page after page before you find a character who represents you. Unfortunately, when minority and female characters do appear, they frequently have only minimal, stereotypic roles. As a female or minority reader, you are probably receiving a clear message that you are not as worthy and as important as others, and your self-image might be negatively affected.

But this need not be the case. Researchers have also found that books can have a positive influence on children. Several studies indicate that multicultural and nonsexist reading materials have a positive effect on children's attitudes toward minority group members and girls and boys who demonstrate nonstereotyped behavior.[25] For example, one study showed that black and white children demonstrated much more favorable attitudes toward blacks following exposure to multicultural readers.[26] Another study indicated that both boys and girls in grades one through five developed less stereotyped attitudes about jobs and activities after reading about people who successfully fought sex discrimination in nontraditional jobs.[27]

NOT BY THE BOOK ALONE

Obviously, books alone do not create attitudes. Children arrive at the schoolhouse door with a host of values and opinions that they have adopted or adapted from parents, friends, television, and other sources. In fact, studies reveal that both children and adults tend to interpret what they read so that it will conform to their previously internalized attitudes and behaviors.[28] For example, a child who holds stereotypic attitudes about the roles of men and women will tend to recall characters in books who demonstrate sex-stereotypic traits.[29]

This does not mean that nonsexist books are ineffective; rather it suggests that books alone may not make the difference. Books are only one component, although an important one, of an overall instructional program that you will have to implement in order to promote sex equity in your classroom. For example, one six-week project focused on children in kindergarten, and in fifth and ninth grade. Teachers used nonsexist books and other materials to encourage these students to develop nonsexist attitudes and behaviors. Evaluation of this nonsexist curriculum project revealed that many of the girls showed an improvement in their self-esteem and acceptance of the wide range of options available to them as adults. However, one of the most significant findings of this study was that teacher enthusiasm was a key factor in affecting attitudinal change of both boys and girls at all levels. Enthusiastic teachers used the materials more, and their students' attitudes were more likely to shift to egalitarian views.[30] These findings suggest that nonsexist books alone may not be enough to influence a change in attitudes. Teachers who positively and enthusiastically use nonsexist materials play a very important role in reducing or eliminating children's sex-role stereotypes.

YOU'VE COME A SHORT WAY, PUBLISHER! WHAT PUBLISHERS HAVE AND HAVE NOT DONE ABOUT SEX BIAS

Now that you understand how sex bias in educational materials can have a very real and injurious effect on students, your response is probably going to be, What is being done about this problem and how can I, as a teacher, change the situation? Obviously, one of the ways of dealing with sex bias in textbooks is to try and influence publishers to make changes. This is not as easy as it sounds.

The 1972 publication *Dick and Jane as Victims* called national attention to sex bias in children's readers. A number of women's groups and other organizations were making similar discoveries across the nation as they investigated the textbooks used in their local schools. With the pressure and publicity of such studies, most major publishing companies developed and disseminated guidelines for the preparation of nonsexist materials. Scott, Foresman was the first company to publish guidelines to improve the image of women in textbooks.[31] Some of the key points of these guidelines are:

1. The actions and achievements of women should be recognized.
2. Women and girls should be given the same respect as men and boys.
3. Abilities, traits, interests, and activities should not be assigned on the basis of male or female stereotypes,
4. Sexist language should be avoided.

The guidelines developed by Holt, Rinehart and Winston outlined three areas that should be addressed in a more equitable treatment of sex roles.[32]

1. *Role Models.* The traditional roles of women in society as homemakers and in the areas of childrearing, education, nursing, and the arts are both valuable and vital to the life of society. No effort should be made to downgrade or disparage these roles. Rather, an effort must be made to expand the roles of both sexes, to include men in nurturing and homemaking activities and to include women in areas such as business and science. An unbalanced assignment of such roles does a disservice to both sexes. Children should see people of both sexes in a variety of those models and thus develop their own individual talents and preferences to their best advantage.
2. *Subject Matter.* Educational materials should acknowledge the roles and contributions of both women and men. Materials that do not meet these criteria or which are biased in language or attitude should be avoided wherever possible.
3. *Language.* Careful and sensitive use of language is important in achieving a positive tone and in creating balance.

Publishers' Guidelines for the Preparation of Nonsexist Materials

Avoiding Stereotypes. Houghton Mifflin Co., College Division, 1 Beacon Street, Boston, MA 02107.

Guidelines for Creating Positive Sexual and Racial Images in Educational Materials. Macmillan Publishing Co., 866 Third Ave., New York, NY 10022.

Guidelines for the Development of Elementary and Secondary Instructional Materials. Holt, Rinehart and Winston, 383 Madison Ave., New York, NY 10017.

Guidelines for Eliminating Stereotypes from Instructional Material Grades K-12. Harper & Row, School Department, 10 East 53rd Street, New York, NY 10022.

Guidelines for Equal Treatment of the Sexes in McGraw-Hill Book Company Publications. McGraw-Hill, 1221 Avenue of the Americas, New York, NY 10020.

Guidelines for Improving the Image of Women in Textbooks. Scott, Foresman & Co., 1900 East Lake Avenue, Glenview, IL 60025.

Statement on Bias-Free Materials. Association of American Publishers, School Division, One Park Avenue, New York, NY 10016.

Suggestions for Developing Materials That Are Free of Racial, Sexual, Cultural and Social Bias. Science Research Associates, 259 East Erie Street, Chicago, IL 60611.

What Publishers Have Not Done

Unfortunately, the new editions of textbooks have not fulfilled the promise of the publisher's guidelines. Researchers have found that the language itself is not so blatantly masculine, but the number of male-centered stories has *increased* rather than decreased! Female major characters in stories and in illustrations are still grossly underrepresented. Ethnic minority males made the largest gain as characters in stories and in illustrations, but minority females remain almost nonexistent. And the newer texts still provide little about the historical reality of women's experiences and achievements.

In the everyday practice of teaching, we often are so busy we don't have time to review textbooks carefully. In quick "thumb-through" evaluations, we might be impressed by the changes we see. However, a more thorough examination would reveal that these changes are superficial rather than substantive. Following are some of the techniques publishers are using to make cosmetic rather than significant textbook change: [33]

1. *Inserts or Add-Ons:* New materials are added to a text, usually in the center or at the end of the book. These materials often appear as add-ons because they are inconsistent with the original book format.

2. *Cosmetic or Color Changes:* The same characters of previous editions are colored to appear black or tan. Sometimes the features are changed to match the corresponding ethnic groups, but sometimes the features remain Anglo.

3. *Name and Pronoun Changes:* An Anglo-type name is changed to an ethnic name without changing the cultural context of the story (e.g., Robert to Roberto). The same technique is used to change the sex of the character (e.g., Paul to Pauline). Researchers found that the stories in which such changes were made were character-

ized as the "weaker stories"—ones in which the main characters were less admirable or heroic.

4. *Story Clustering:* Stories about females or minorities are added or substituted in only one or two books of a series at only one grade level rather than in all of the books in the series at various grade levels.

5. *Neuter Character Syndrome:* An increase in the proportion of stories about neuter animals and objects causes the deletion of both male and female characters. What is needed is an increase of female characters, not more neuter stories.

Researchers who have analyzed the newer texts conclude that:

> . . . textbook companies which have published guidelines for reducing sexism and racism are to be congratulated for publishing excellent guidelines, yet criticized for failure to follow them. They have examined the issues and outlined some pioneering and innovative ideas for change for themselves and the entire textbook industry. What they have failed to demonstrate are "good faith" attempts to implement their own guidelines.[34]

The Excuse for Nonchange

Understandably, textbook publishers expect to make a profit from their sale of textbooks. This, however, has become the excuse for not making textbooks as equitable or representative as they should be. When confronted about the snaillike pace of change, the common response has been that such revisions are financially prohibitive.

As long as school districts continue to buy sexist textbooks, publishers will produce them. The profit motive encourages these companies to appeal to the largest possible market. Consequently, they will make some change to indicate sensitivity to racism and sexism. At the same time, they worry about the possibility of fewer sales in very conservative areas of the country where there is antagonism to such change.

Local groups or individuals can encourage textbook reform. They can exert influence and pressure so that schools will not purchase racist and sexist books. Only when educators, parents, and textbook publishers work cooperatively to eliminate sexism and racism will we begin to see instructional materials that are truly representative of the rich diversity that comprises this nation.

WHAT YOU CAN DO IN YOUR CLASSROOM

If the textbooks that you are given to use with students are biased, it is important to confront this bias rather than ignore it. A natural and legitimate way to begin this process is simply to "level" with your students. It's entirely appropriate to acknowledge that texts are not always perfect. You can engage your students in discussion about textbook omission and stereotyping. You may find that many students are initially reluctant to challenge any information that is housed between textbook covers; however, if you handle these discussions sensitively and constructively, you may find that you're developing their critical and analytic reading skills as well.

Being honest and direct with your students about bias in instructional material provides a way to begin, but it is critical that you go beyond simply calling attention to omission, stereotyping, and other forms of bias. It is not enough to recognize, for example, that there are few women in the classroom history text. Some students may remain skeptical, claiming that this is probably because women have done little that is worth recording. Other students in your class may believe that history texts are biased, but they may be unaware of the nature and extent of this bias. In order to develop students' awareness, it will be up to you to supply the information that is omitted from or distorted in your classroom text. This will inform the cynical students as well as the committed ones.

"That's quite a tall order," you are more than likely thinking. You may yourself be unaware of the contributions and history of women simply because you haven't been exposed to that information in your own school experience. Trying to fill these gaps may seem like an overwhelming assignment. Where do you begin?

Fortunately, there are a number of individuals and organizations concerned and angry about bias in texts; they have begun the production of supplementary information that should be in your texts. The final chapter of this book lists and discusses many of these organizations and materials. Another chapter of this book describes nonsexist lesson plans and approaches.

These supplementary materials can provide you with a bonanza of exciting and informative classroom lessons. Here are some suggestions on how you might use these materials in your classroom:

1. *Resource materials can be used as supplements to your textbook.*
   Although textbooks attempt to meet the needs of a wide variety of groups, they often fall short, and the treatment of women is a prime example of this failure. You may wish to prepare a discussion, lecture, fact sheet, case study, or other classroom activity based on the supplementary materials. In some cases, you can distribute the materials directly to the students as a reading assignment. In other situations, you will want to serve as a mediator of the materials and present them through classroom discussions and activities. Either approach provides students with ideas and information that go beyond the limits of textbooks currently available.

2. *Students can use supplementary materials to conduct their own research and to prepare original reports and papers.*

   The day to day realities of the classroom are hectic and pressured, and you cannot and should not be expected to spend hour after hour continually researching and preparing supplementary materials. However, through research, writing, and presentation assignments, you can share this learning responsibility with your students. If you do an effective job of calling attention to text bias and of stimulating students' curiosity about the women and other minorities who are missing from textbook pages, you can motivate students to undertake independent work, work that can be shared with the entire class to raise everyone's consciousness on these issues.

3. *Organizations identified in the resource chapter frequently provide speakers, films, and other educational aids that can be used in the classroom.*

   Although the initial response of many teachers concerned about the limitations of their texts is to seek out other print materials as supplementary resources, there is no reason to limit supplementary materials in this way. Many of the organizations identified in this book's final chapter will provide guest speakers for your class. Others have developed slide-tape presentations, posters, and films that are both motivating and informative. In our current media-oriented world, using this wealth of audiovisual materials and guest speakers can provide a real asset to your classroom activities and enhance the awareness of your students concerning sex equity.

In this chapter, we have tried to give you information and exercises that will help you develop skills to counteract bias in classroom instructional materials. But the real test of the effectiveness of this unit can only be determined in the months and years to come. As a teacher, the instructional decision maker in your classroom, you will be the one to determine how you will use classroom materials. You can accept biased books as "instructional givens," or you can work with your students to analyze, confront, and change this bias. The opportunity and the challenge are yours.

ANSWER KEY: Susan B. Who?

1.	e	6.	a	11.	g
2.	b	7.	m	12.	d
3.	h	8.	f	13.	l
4.	n	9.	k	14.	c
5.	i	10.	o	15.	j

ANSWER KEY: Test Your Recognition of Sex Bias in Texts

Following are potential responses to the exercises on pp. 74-79 of this chapter. Although your responses may show some variance from these answers, the discussion below focuses on the major biases in each case.

Case 1

The contemporary farmer is radically different from the frontiersman of the past. He is knowledgeable in a complex, scientific endeavor, and his livelihood is dependent upon his efficiency.

> *Is sex bias present?* Yes
> *What form of sex bias is present?* Linguistic Bias, Invisibility, and
>   Stereotyping
> *Revision and discussion:* Male and female farmers should both be referred to. The use of the pronoun *he* to refer to all farmers should be revised. The use of *frontiersman* is an example of sexist language and serves to deny the contributions and experiences of pioneering women. This noun should be replaced with *pioneers, frontier settlers,* or *pioneering men and women.*

Case 2

Soon after John arrived home from school, he received a call from his father who said he would be leaving the office later than usual. It was up to John to start dinner.

> *Is sex bias present?* No
> *What form of sex bias is present?* Not applicable
> *Revision and discussion:* The father and son in this excerpt demonstrate nonstereotyped roles. Because the father plans to work later than usual, it will be John's responsibility to start dinner.

Case 3

Sam led, and Helen went after him. Helen held his hand in a hard grip. She was timid in the darkness . . . Helen fell and Sam helped her get up.

> *Is sex bias present?* Yes
> *What form of sex bias is present?* Stereotyping
> *Revision and discussion:* The portrayal of a timid girl and a courageous boy is stereotypic. Revisions might include depicting both children as competent and capable or even describing a brave girl and a timid boy.

Case 4

In a mathematic workbook there are 31 word problems showing males and females involved in the following activities:

Boys	*Girls*
1. buying a model car & plane	1. deciding whether to plant grass around a doghouse
2. painting (2 times)	2. figuring out the living space
3. walking (4 times)	3. working for her father
4. making a map	4. drinking
5. doing an experiment	5. working
6. making a paper chain	6. making a paper chain
7. losing weight	7. gaining weight
8. riding a bicycle	8. growing taller
9. running a race	9. missing questions
10. swimming	10. driving boys home
11. using calories (2 times)	
12. driving a delivery truck	
13. buying land (2 times)	

Is sex bias present? Yes
What form of sex bias is present? Stereotyping and Invisibility
Revision and discussion: Over twice as many males as females appear in these 31 word problems—a characteristic of invisibility. Males are more active and participate in "more important" activities than females. Revisions should include females participating in an equitable number of active and important roles.

Case 5

Father came home early and noticed Tommy had been crying. He put off starting dinner and took Tommy for a "walk talk." Starting junior high school certainly had its problems.

Is sex bias present? No
What form of sex bias is present? Not applicable
Revision and discussion: This passage includes a father who takes responsibility for preparing dinner, and a teenage boy who is able to demonstrate emotions. Both break with the traditional male sex-role stereotype.

Case 6

The organized movement to win rights for women arose earlier in the United States than in any other nation, not because American women enjoyed so few privileges, but because they had so many that they demanded more.

Is bias present? Yes
What form of sex bias is present? Imbalance/Selectivity and Unreality
Revision and discussion: By equating right with privileges, this passage distorts the purpose of the women's movement for equal rights. It presumes that rights for women are privileges to be dispensed. This passage also presents an unrealistic view of the status of women in American society by implying that the women's movement for rights is an unwarranted struggle by an already overprivileged, but malcontent, group in society. No attempt is made to present information children need to recognize or understand problems that plague our society.

Case 7

Women in our society are already demanding new roles. By 2000, they may have complete equality with men. They will probably do as much work outside the home as men do. They will receive the same salaries. By 2000, women may also have equal social and political rights. There may be more women in government positions. Perhaps by then there will be a woman president. Many experts think that by 2000 the old saying, "A woman's place is in the home," will no longer apply.

Is sex bias present? Yes
What form of sex bias is present? Unreality
Revision and discussion: The passage is written with generalizations and it omits divergent views, emotional struggles, and the barriers to full equality, which are so much a part of the women's movement. This simplistic account of the struggle for equality is misleading. The passage could be made more realistic by including the barriers to equality, the sacrifices of feminists involved in the struggle, and the opponents to the feminist movement, including the opposition to the passage of the Equal Rights Amendment.

Case 8

Besides men who can organize well and think clearly what other essentials are needed to build an industry?

Is sex bias present? Yes
What form of sex bias is present? Linguistic Bias
Revision and discussion: The use of the supposedly generic *men* denies participation of women. This passage might be rewritten as "Besides people who can organize well and think clearly what other essentials are needed to build an industry?"

Case 9

Women were given the vote as a reward for their work in World War I.

> *Is sex bias present?* Yes
> *What form of sex bias is present?* Imbalance/Selectivity and Linguistic
> Bias
> *Revision and discussion:* This neglects the 70 years of struggle by
> women for the right to vote. The physical abuse and sacrifices
> suffered by leaders and participants in the struggle are negated
> by this oversimplification. The sentence might be rewritten as
> "Over 70 years after the Seneca Falls Convention, women won
> the right to vote."

Case 10

The scientific advances of man in the twentieth century have been amazing.

> *Is sex bias present?* Yes
> *What form of sex bias is present?* Linguistic Bias
> *Revision and discussion:* The use of the supposedly generic *man*
> denies the participation of women. The sentence might be rewritten as "Scientific advances in the twentieth century have been
> amazing."

Case 11

These two problems appear on the same page of a mathematics book:

> 1. Nancy needs to make two batches of cookies for the Bake Sale.
>   Help her double her recipe.
> 2. John wants to build a fence of 2-in. stakes to extend 20 feet.
>   How many stakes should he buy?

> *Is sex bias present?* Yes
> *What form of sex bias is present?* Stereotyping
> *Revision and discussion:* Both Nancy and John are shown in stereotypic roles. The problems might be revised by portraying Nancy
> and John working together at the bake sale or building the fence.

Case 12

The firefighters and police officers held a press conference to explain
their grievances. The union president acted as spokesperson as she read
the grievances to the reporters.

Is sex bias present? No
What form of sex bias is present? Not applicable
Revision and discussion: Nonsexist language is used, and women are shown in nonstereotyped roles.

Case 13

The last chapter of a social studies text is devoted to American life during the 1970s. It includes the following topics: The Economy, New Space Explorations, Contributions of Contemporary Women, Domestic Politics, Foreign Policy Decisions, Scientific Achievements, and the Energy Crisis.

Is sex bias present? Yes
What form of sex bias is present? Fragmentation/Isolation
Revision and discussion: The topic, "Contributions of Contemporary Women," should not be a separate section. Rather, this issue should be integrated throughout the text narrative.

ENDNOTES

[1] National Education Association, *Instructional Materials. Selection and Purchase* (Washington, D.C.: National Education Association, 1976).

[2] "Toward Improving National Efforts Related to Instructional Materials Selection," Report to NIE. (Washington, D.C.: National Institute of Education, June, 1977).

[3] *Report on a National Study of the Nature and the Quality of Instructional Materials Most Used by Teachers and Learners* (New York: EPIE Institute, 1977).

[4] Susan S. Klein, "Toward Consensus on Minimum Criteria for Educational Products," Paper presented at AERA Annual Meeting, April, 1976, in San Francisco.

[5] Myra Sadker and David Sadker, "The Teacher Educator's Role" in Shirley McCune and Martha Matthews (eds.) *Implementing Title IX and Attaining Sex Equity: A Workshop Package for Postsecondary Educators* (Washington, D.C.: U.S. Government Printing Office, 1978), TEW-3.

[6] Janice Law Trecker, "Women in U.S. History High-School Textbooks," in Janice Pottker and Andrew Fishel (eds.), *Sex Bias in the Schools: The Research Evidence,* (Cranbury, N.J.: Associated University Presses, 1977).

[7] Ibid.

[8] Women on Words and Images, *Dick and Jane as Victims: Sex Stereotyping in Children's Readers* (Princeton, N.J.: Women on Words and Images, 1975).

[9] Lenore J. Weitzman and Diane Rizzo, *Biased Textbooks: A Research Perspective* (Washington, D.C.: The Resource Center on Sex Roles in Education, 1974).

[10] Women on Words and Images, *Dick and Jane as Victims.*

[11] Weitzman and Rizzo, *Biased Textbooks.*

[12] Women on Words and Images, *Dick and Jane as Victims.*

[13] Quoted in Trecker, "Women in U.S. History High-School Textbooks."

[14] Shirley McCune and Martha Matthews (eds.), *Implementing Title IX and Attaining Sex Equity: A Workshop Package for Postsecondary Educators* (Washington, D.C.: U.S. Government Printing Office, 1978), TEW-3.

[15] Sadker and Sadker, "The Teacher Educator's Role."

[16] Glenn McCracken and Charles Walcott (eds.) *Lippincott Basic Reading Program,* Book E (New York: Lippincott, 1970).

[17] Sadker and Sadker, "The Teacher Educator's Role."

[18] Krug Quillen, *Living in Our America,* 4th ed., (Glenville, Ill.: Scott, Foresman, 1964).

[19] Lawrence Senesh, *Our Working World, The American Way of Life* (Chicago: SRA, 1973).

[20] Quillen, *Living in Our America.*

[21] Sadker and Sadker, "The Teacher Educator's Role."

[22] Ibid.

[23] Sara Goodman Zimet, *Print and Prejudice* (London: Hodder and Stoughton in association with the United Kingdom Reading Association, 1976).

[24] Shirley Fehl, "The Influence of Reading on Concepts, Attitudes, & Behavior," *Journal of Reading* (February 1969).

[25] Patricia Campbell and Jeana Wirtenburg, "How Books Influence Children: What the Research Shows," *Interracial Books for Children Bulletin* 11 (1980).

[26] J. Litcher and D. Johnson, "Changes in Attitudes Toward Negroes of White Elementary School Students after Use of Multiethnic Readers," *Journal of Educational Psychology* 60 (April 1969).

[27] K. Scott, "Elementary Pupils' Perceptions of Reading and Social Studies Materials: Does the Sex of the Main Character Make a Difference?" *Dissertation Abstracts* UMI 780973 (Ann Arbor, 1977).

[28] Anne Selley McKillop, *The Relationship Between the Reader's Attitudes and Certain Types of Reading Responses* (New York: Teachers College, Columbia University, 1972).

[29] Sally Gentry Koblinsky, Donna F. Cruse, and Alan I. Sugawara, "Sex Role Stereotypes and Children's Memory for Story Content," *Child Development* 49 (1978).

[30] Marcia Guttentag and Helen Bray, *Undoing Sex Stereotypes: Research and Resources for Educators* (New York: McGraw-Hill, 1976).

[31] *Guidelines for Improving the Image of Women in Textbooks* (Glenview, Ill.: Scott, Foresman, 1972).

[32] *Guidelines for the Development of Elementary and Secondary Instructional Materials* (New York: Holt, Rinehart and Winston, 1975).

[33] Gwyneth Britton and Margaret Lumpkin, *A Consumer's Guide to Sex, Race and Career Bias in Public School Textbooks* (Corvallis, Oreg.: Britton & Assoc., 1977).

[34] Ibid.

4

Between Teacher and Student:
*Overcoming Sex Bias in Classroom Interaction ***

Objectives

- To describe teacher expectations for and interactions with male and female students
- To analyze classrooms for sex-biased teaching patterns
- To develop nonsexist teaching behavior

> Our teacher, Mr. Greco, was a painter with a poetic soul. Mystical and idosyncratic in his art, he was real and direct in life. We thrived on this vital contrast. Most teachers warned us to face reality; Mr. Greco endowed us with a sense of mystery. Tragedy and joy were personal acquaintances of his. A refugee, he had known sorrow. Suffering brought him wisdom which he imparted with grace and nobility.[1]

> "Stupid idiot!"
> "Silly fool!"
> "Dumb blockhead!"

> Like a rattlesnake, he always had fresh venom. He used to tell us that in his mind he had a picture of a perfect pupil. Compared to this brainchild, we were a dismal disappointment. We were ignorant illiterates wasting professional time and public money. His relentless diatribes undercut our self-respect and ignited our hatred. When he finally fell ill, the whole class celebrated in thanksgiving.[2]

These descriptions show how vividly teachers, for better or worse, are remembered.

Did you ever meet a teacher who changed dry facts into drama and poetry? Can you remember a teacher who belittled you so that you felt incompetent—even worthless? What seem to be the qualities of those teachers who make a positive difference in the lives of their students?

---

* This chapter is adapted from Myra Sadker and David Sadker, *Between Teacher and Student: Overcoming Sex Bias in Classroom Interaction* (U.S. Dept. of Education, Women's Educational Equity Act Program, 1980).

When students are asked to describe successful teachers, one quality that comes up again and again is "fairness," the ability to establish a democratic classroom where all students are treated equitably. Although fair and equitable treatment of students is important, it is sometimes difficult to achieve this goal. One of the most pervasive barriers is sex bias.

Obviously, teachers would not consciously and intentionally stereotype students. Most teachers work very hard and are extremely conscientious; they try to treat both girls and boys fairly and equitably; they want all children to develop their full potential. However, educators, like members of other professions, have been raised in a society where sexism is prevalent. From parents and counselors, books and television, and a whole myriad of societal institutions, teachers have been taught that one set of jobs and behaviors is appropriate for girls and another different set is appropriate for boys. However, when teachers are able to recognize the subtle and unintentional sex bias in their behavior, they can make positive changes in their classrooms—and in the lives of their students.

TEACHER EXPECTATIONS: MIND OVER MATTER

It has been said that our thoughts, more specifically our expectations, can have marked effects on the behavior of others. In classroom terms, expectations mean the inferences that teachers make about the present and future behavior of their students. In fact, many studies show that when teachers hold certain expectations about their pupils, students actually mold their own behavior to conform to the expectations of their teachers. In schools, the impact of teacher expectations on children has been termed the "self-fulfilling prophecy." Since expectations can be so important, let's take a closer look at this phenomenon. Consider the following story:

> The children in an elementary school in a lower-class neighborhood were administered a special test designed to identify students who were "intellectual bloomers" and who would most likely show remarkable academic gains during the coming school year. About 20 percent of the students were identified by the test as "intellectual bloomers," and their teachers were informed of the test results. The validity of the test was demonstrated eight months later when these intellectual bloomers were given an I.Q. test and scored higher than they had on previous I.Q. examinations. Apparently the new test could be hailed as an important breakthrough, for it could effectively identify which students would demonstrate unusual I.Q. gains. Or could it?

And now, the rest of the story . . .

The test given was not a predictor of intellectual bloomers at all. It was a standard intelligence test, and students were not identified in any way through their test scores. In fact, the 20 percent were not really intellectual bloomers. Their names were selected at random. Yet, their I.Q. scores did increase while the scores of the rest of the students remained stable.

According to Rosenthal and Jacobson, who conducted this study, the key here was teacher expectations. Since teachers thought that these children would be intellectual bloomers, they behaved in various subtle ways to promote and encourage this development; in short, teacher expectations shaped and altered student academic performance. Further, by the end of the study, teachers described these randomly selected students as happier, more curious, more interesting, and more likely to succeed in later life than other children. This study was reported in a book entitled *Pygmalion in the Classroom,* and it is a well-known example of the "self-fulfilling prophecy." [3]

When this study first came out, it generated a good deal of interest not only among teachers and parents but among educational researchers as well. Study after study was conducted to determine if teacher expectations could really affect student behavior and achievement. Some studies have confirmed that teacher expectations can affect student behavior. Some have not. Even though conflicting evidence lies in the wake of the original *Pygmalion in the Classroom* study, many researchers conclude that teacher expectations can influence student behavior. Here's a little more background on how this process works:

1. Early in the school year, teachers form expectations about what students can achieve and how they will behave. Some of these expectations may be inaccurate; they may be resistant to change.
2. Based on these expectations, teachers treat students differently. When these expectations are inaccurate and rigid, treatment of students will be inappropriate.
3. Sometimes, students will actually change their own behavior so that it conforms to teacher expectations.

Two researchers, Brophy and Good, summarize this process:

> If continued indefinitely, such treatment constitutes a pressure on the student to begin to conform to the teacher's expectations by behaving in the ways that the teacher expects the student to behave. This in turn reinforces the teacher's expectations all the more, and a self-regenerating vicious circle is established. If the situation persists, a true expectation effect is likely to occur. [4]

LIVING UP—AND DOWN—TO SEX-STEREOTYPED EXPECTATIONS

As teachers enter the classroom, they carry with them more than their dittoes and chalk; they also bring socially influenced beliefs of what are appropriate behaviors, values, and careers for girls and for boys. Many teachers, like other members of society, have been socialized to believe that girls should be passive, demure, sweet, and dependent; they think that boys should be assertive, athletic, and competitive. For example, a group of junior high school teachers was asked to describe good female and male students. Here are their responses.[5]

Adjectives Describing Good Female Students		*Adjectives Describing Good Male Students*	
appreciative	sensitive	active	energetic
calm	dependable	adventurous	enterprising
conscientious	efficient	aggressive	frank
considerate	obliging	assertive	independent
cooperative	mature	curious	inventive
mannerly	thorough		
poised			

What happens to students who don't fit the stereotypes? The athletic girl who is super in math, assertive in her interpersonal style, and hopeful of becoming a corporate president may receive a variety of negative messages. The boy who likes poetry and ballet, or who expresses the hope of becoming a secretary or nurse or kindergarten teacher will also be treated to negative signals. Such messages confine students, limit their options, and restrict their aspirations and potential.

One researcher conducted in-depth interviews in which she asked women to remember their school days and what it was like to grow up female. Their recollections show that they were very aware of sex-stereotyped teacher expectations.[6]

> We always expect the boys to be doing funny things, like putting pencils in the heater, or putting the teacher's chair outside or yelling in the class—all those kinds of things. . . . And I always felt that when I did the same things that I thought were funny and were neat to be in on, that I got scolded in a way that they never did. . . .

When men think back over their experience in school, they also talk about the pressures and the pain of conforming to sex-role stereotypes—especially in athletics.[7]

> The two best players (never me) were captains, and they chose—one by one—players for their teams. The choosing went on and on, the better players getting picked first and me and my type last.

During the game, I always played outfield. Right field. Far right field. And there I would stand in the hot sun wishing I was anywhere else in the world.

Sex-stereotyped expectations can also have a harmful impact on boys in academic areas. For example, research shows that when teachers expect boys to do as well as girls in beginning reading, male students live up to these expectations. However, when teachers do not expect boys to perform as well as girls in beginning reading, they actually fail to match the performance of their female classmates.[8]

For girls an expectation problem is more likely to occur in math and science. Math has been stereotyped as a male domain and girls get the message.[9] While girls' performance in math is equal to that of boys at age 9, their performance continues to drop as they "progress" through school.[10] These young women learn to perceive math as inconsequential for future careers, and they are far less likely to take advanced math courses than are boys. By young adulthood, the gap between male and female achievement in math can only be described as staggering. Further, math acts as a "critical filter" that denies women access to the whole range of scientific and technical occupations.

Most teachers care deeply about the students in their classrooms. When asked if they treat boys and girls differently, they are usually startled. "Of course not," they reply. "I treat all my students, girls and boys, in the same manner." However, when teachers are encouraged to analyze their attitudes and behaviors, they discover the subtle and pervasive nature of sex bias in the classroom; they become concerned, and they make changes. In fact, teachers, because of the special relationship they have with their students, can help counteract the limiting cycle of sex bias.

In the next section, we'll focus on how expectations can lead to differential treatment of girls and boys in classrooms. Then we'll present a series of exercises and observation instruments to help you analyze patterns of interaction in your classroom.

TEACHERS TALK (BUT NOT IN THE SAME WAY TO EVERYONE)

The noted educator, Haim Ginott, used to tell the story about the little girl who came home from her first day of school . . . "How did you like it?" her anxious mother queried. "Oh, school was just fine," the young scholar replied, "except for this one lady who kept interrupting."

On one level this anecdote captures the funny notions young children have about what school is supposed to be like. On another level this story shows how insightful young children can be about the operation of classroom rituals and norms. This girl accurately picked up one of the patterns that is likely to characterize not only the first day of school, but every day thereafter. Teachers do a lot of interrupting.

In fact, they do a lot of talking in general. For example, Ned Flanders, one of the earliest and best known researchers in classroom interaction analysis, determined that approximately two-thirds of classroom talk is teacher talk.[11] Another researcher, Phil Jackson, noted that teachers typically engage in over 1,000 verbal exchanges in their classrooms every day.[12] And another researcher tells us that teachers typically ask between three and six questions per minute,[13] and after asking a question, they are likely to wait only one second for a student to answer.[14] If this instantaneous response is not forthcoming, they will call on someone else, answer the question themselves, or ask a new question. If the impression you are getting from studies like these is that teachers do a lot of fast talking, you are exactly right.

Given the hectic pace of classroom life, it is no wonder that teachers have little time to think about the subtleties and specifics of verbal interaction. They are amazed to discover the "bombing rate" at which they ask questions. They are also surprised to learn that they do not interact with female students in the same way they do with males. The only sex difference in verbal interaction that teachers typically are aware of is in classroom discipline. "Yes, I suppose I reprimand boys more and punish them more," many teachers will agree. "But the boys seem to be the ones who are misbehaving."

Educators who are concerned about equality of opportunity in schools have been examining life in classrooms. Who do teachers talk to? Praise? Reprimand? Question? Do certain students fail to receive their fair share of the teacher's verbal attention, not only in terms of quantity but in quality as well? Are minority students and female students the "invisible" members of our classrooms, those who are ignored when questions are asked and who are passed over when teacher praise, encouragement, and reward are passed out? And researchers are trying to determine if the way teachers interact with students makes a difference. Does the quantity and quality of teacher interaction appear to have any impact on student self-concept, behavior, and achievement? These are some of the questions we will look at very closely in this section on classroom interaction.

Following are some classroom scenarios. As you read each one, try to determine if there are differences in the way the teachers treat male and female students. Each scenario is followed by a review of the research on which it is based. If the vignettes appear to be somewhat exaggerated, it is because they are illustrations designed to reflect information drawn from several research studies.

TEACHERS TALK WITH BOYS AND GIRLS: A PLAY-BY-PLAY RESEARCH REVIEW

The Play

It is a hot Friday afternoon in June a few days before the release of summer vacation. Jim Bernstein's loosened tie hangs askew around his neck, his wilted jacket has been tossed across a pile of ungraded papers, and his shirt is pasted to his back. It has been one of those difficult days with the sixth graders, and his patience is thin.

"O.K. class. Cut the noise. You boys in the back row. I think I've made it clear that the assignment is in-class reading, not in-class talking. This is your last chance." (Despite this warning, the back-row clamor continues unabated.)

"That does it! Jim, Pete, Mark! Put your names on the board! Stop stalling—you know where. Right there on the after-school list. It's a half an hour detention tonight . . . maybe longer if you don't watch out. Now, unless the rest of you want to join this unholy trio, you'll get back to your reading assignment." (The class grows momentarily still except for the shuffling of books and the turning of pages. But the lull is short-lived, and Mr. Bernstein turns disciplinarian again.)

"Alan and Susan. This is not a place for your own private gab fest. You know the penalty. Alan, your name goes on the after-school list. Put it up there right now. And Susan," Mr. Bernstein's voice softens, "I'm surprised to have to talk to you like this. You know better. One more chance, and then your name goes up on the list and you'll join the boys after school."

Before you read ahead, take a few moments to summarize the interaction patterns in Mr. Bernstein's classroom.

The Research

Did you notice that Mr. Bernstein spent most of his time reprimanding the boys in his classroom? How typical is this interaction pattern? Do boys in classrooms usually get reprimanded more often than girls?

Researchers have looked at how teachers dispense disapproval: in study after study, they find that boys get most of it. Moreover, most of the disapproval male students receive is directed at classroom behavior. One study indicates that boys receive eight to ten times as many prohibitory control messages as their female classmates [15]—comments such as "Stop talking, Bob." "Put that comic book away, Bill." "Back to your seat, Andrew."

At this point you may be wondering why boys are disciplined more frequently. A logical and simple answer is that boys tend to misbehave more, and classroom observation studies support this conclusion. However, this is only a partial explanation.

One study of 15 preschool classes showed that when teachers were faced with disruptive behavior, from both boys and girls, they were over three times as likely to reprimand the boys as the girls. Further, they more frequently punished the boys through a loud public reprimand. In contrast, when they did reprimand girls, they were likely to do it quickly and quietly.[16] So even when *both* girls and boys are misbehaving, boys receive more frequent and more harsh discipline.

This difference in intensity as well as quantity of disapproval emerges as a finding in several studies. Besides getting more than their share of disapproval messages, boys are scolded more loudly and more harshly than girls, even when the offenses are similar or identical. In the preceding vignette, did you notice that Susan received a softer rebuke than her classmate Alan? Also, she was not given the same punishment as Alan, even though she was involved in identical classroom misbehavior.

It is important to realize that all boys do not receive these disapproval messages. It is the low-achieving boys who attract most of this negative attention. For example, one study showed that, while low-achieving boys raised their hand to respond less than half as often as their classmates, they were criticized more than twice as frequently.[17]

The research indicates that Mr. Bernstein is quite representative in the way he reprimands boys and girls. There was no information in this vignette on the socioeconomic or racial background of his students. If there were, and if Mr. Bernstein remained representative, you might have found him disciplining minority students and children from lower socioeconomic groups more frequently.[18] This is another pattern that emerges from the educational research on classroom interaction.

The Play

It looked as though a cyclone had swept through Ms. Washington's classroom. In fact, it was a cyclone of a human sort—final rehearsal of the eighth-grade play. The students were getting ready to put on *Light in the Forest,* the story of an Indian boy caught between two cultures. Despite the chaos of last-minute rehearsal, Gloria Washington was clearly a teacher in charge of the situation. She moved smoothly from one knot of students to another, offering advice on costumes, scenery, sound effects, and script.

"John, that teepee of yours seems to be a little shaky. I doubt it will make it through the first act, let alone the whole play. Why don't you fasten the poles together more tightly at the top? Go get the box of rope from the resource room. That should make it strong enough."

"Maria, how are those headbands coming along? They seem to

be shedding feathers. Here, give them to me and I'll show you how to fasten the feathers more firmly. Just let me add a little glue, and you'll find your problem is solved."

"Laura and Ann, you look like you're having trouble measuring the canvas to fit over that drum. Give me the tape measure for a second. There, I've marked it off. I think that will fit."

"Brian and Tony. That background mural really looks great. Just add a little more orange to the sunset, and you're finished."

"Mike, let me hear the background music you've got on the tape recorder. That sounds good. It does a nice job setting the mood for the play."

"What's the matter, Joseph? Part of the script giving you trouble? The dialogue in Scene II just doesn't sound right, does it? Here's what I suggest. Reread the first chapter in *Light in the Forest* and that will give you a better idea of how True Son's mind works and how he would be likely to talk and behave."

"Dennis, let's take a look at the opening narration you're working on. Hmmm, this does a pretty good job, but as you revise it, I want you to think about these questions: How much background information will the audience need to understand the first scene? What words could you use that will get the audience's attention and give them a feeling for the problem that True Son faces?"

Because this scene is fairly complex, you'll notice that we focused on teacher comments, and we did not include student responses. Before you read ahead, think about the comments Ms. Washington made. Were there any sex differences in the way she talked and worked with her students?

The Research

In this scene, the teacher does not spend her time reprimanding; nevertheless, did you notice that the boys still received more of her attention? In fact, teachers not only disapprove of boys more, but they also interact with them more in general. While the research is not entirely consistent on the nature of this interaction, certain patterns emerge.

- Teachers appear to interact more with boys in four major categories: disapproval, praise and approval, instruction, and listening to the child.[19]
- They initiate more work contacts, more academic contacts, and more positive contacts with boys.[20] Teachers are also more likely to engage in extended conversations with male students.[21]

- Teachers ask boys more direct questions, more open-ended questions,[22] more complex and abstract questions.[23]
- When working with gifted students, teachers favor boys, and are more restrictive with girls.[24]
- Teachers are more likely to give male students extended directions, detailed instruction on how to do things "for oneself." In contrast, they are less likely to explain things to girls. They tend to "do it for them" instead. Here's a specific example of how this happens in the classroom.

> In one classroom, the children were making party baskets. When the time came to staple the paper handles . . . (the teacher) showed the boys how to use the stapler by holding the handle in place while the child stapled it. On the girls' turns, however, if the child didn't spontaneously staple the handle herself, the teacher took the basket (and) stapled it.[25]

These studies show that boys are the salient members of classrooms and receive more of teachers' positive and active attention. In contrast, girls are more frequently passed over and ignored. Were you able to analyze the classroom scene above to determine some of these patterns? Did you notice that the boys received more academic contacts, more questions and more approval? Also, did you notice that when male students were having difficulty, Ms. Washington gave them directions on how to solve the problem for themselves? But when girls needed help, Ms. Washington took over and did *for* them instead of instructing them on how to "do for themselves."

It is important to qualify the research we've presented. Not all boys are receiving this positive and active attention. Low-achieving boys receive more teacher criticism; in contrast, high-achieving boys receive more teacher approval and active instruction. The difference is so clear that some researchers have concluded: "In many ways, in so far as teacher-student interaction data are concerned, it makes sense to speak of low-achieving boys and high-achieving boys as separate groups rather than to speak of boys as a single group." [26]

So, we have more information on the classroom interaction picture. Boys, especially high-achieving boys, receive approval, questions, detailed instructions and, in general, more active teaching attention. Girls of all ability levels do not interact as frequently with teachers. Nor do students who are members of minority groups. For example, one study showed that teachers gave less attention to black students; they requested fewer statements from blacks, encouraged them to expand on ideas less frequently, praised them less, and criticized them more.[27] Other studies show similar patterns of invisibility for Mexican-American and Native American children.[28]

The Play

It is a few minutes before third period, and the students in Ms. Watson's seventh-grade English class are anxious.

"Do you think she's got the tests graded?"

"That test was so long. I don't know if she's had the time."

"You know Watson. She always gets tests back the next day. She's famous for it."

"I'm scared. She said this test would be half our grade. Do you think she means it?"

Eyes turn to the front of the room as Ms. Watson enters and places her brief case on the desk. She pulls out a pile of papers decorated with red pencil, and the class grows quiet.

"As you know, students, yesterday you took a very important English exam. It covered a lot of information—everything that we've been discussing for the last four weeks in our unit on poetry. We'll use this class period for individual conferences on the test. I'm going to call each of you up to my desk so that we can discuss this test in some detail. I want to make sure that you understand why you got the grade you did and what area you need to work on."

"While I'm having these individual conferences, I'd like the rest of you to be working on your assignment in the language skills book. Tom Johnson, come up to my desk, please.

"Here's your exam, Tom. Take a few minutes to look it over, and then we'll discuss it."

(The students glance from their assignment to see Tom's reaction. They watch as he skims through the test and then smiles.)

"What's your reaction to the grade, Tom?"

"I'm really happy. I thought I'd done O.K., but I wasn't sure."

"You did a very fine job on this exam. An A— is something to be proud of. You identified all the spot passages accurately and you gave correct definitions for the figures of speech. I particularly like the original poem you wrote in the extra-credit section of the exam, and I wrote you a long comment about it that you can read more carefully at your seat.

"On the negative side, I must say something about the appearance of this exam. Maybe you were nervous while you were taking the test, but that still doesn't excuse this kind of careless writing. The prescriptions my doctor writes out are easier to read than this. And you know the rules about margins, headings, and the proper form for all work that gets handed in. Work on getting things in proper shape and in the next test maybe you can turn an A— into a straight A. Next, Beth Galente."

(Beth reluctantly accepts the paper Ms. Watson hands her.)

"Take a few minutes to read the test over, Beth, and then we'll talk about it."

"A C+! I thought I had done better than that."

"Well, you confused the definitions of metaphor and simile, and you left out personification. Also, you seem to have irony mixed up with alliteration."

"I didn't realize I missed so many of the questions."

"Why don't you look your paper over more carefully at your desk to make sure you understand the errors. Next, Frank Campone."

(Frank slumps down in the chair next to Ms. Watson's desk and looks despondent as he goes over the test.)

"Do you have any questions about the exam, Frank?"

"I don't know if I have questions, but my parents sure will. They're gonna kill me. They expect me to get A's and B's."

"Well, they're right, Frank, you should be getting A's and B's. But you can't just walk in and take the exam without studying. Also, you've got to pay more attention during class. Passing notes to your buddies and doing social studies homework behind your poetry books isn't going to get you those A's and B's that both you and your parents want. Neither will turning in hastily scrawled work—obviously done at the last minute—that I can hardly read. Now, I know you can do better than this—but you have to give it more effort."

(As Frank returns to his seat, Ms. Watson calls Marilyn Miller to her desk.)

"Here Marilyn, look over your paper and then we'll discuss your grade." (Marilyn spends a few minutes intently going over the questions.)

"What's your reaction?"

"Well, a B+ is a pretty good grade, but I wish I could have gotten an A on this test . . . I knew I couldn't remember a few of those spot passages, so I just guessed. I guess I guessed wrong."

"I know you would have liked a higher grade. You're very well behaved in class—you seem to be paying attention, your papers are always handed in on time, and your work is neat and careful. However, you did miss some of the questions. You should check over the spot passage section. You identified several of these incorrectly. Also go over your explanation of the Robert Frost poem. I don't think you've picked up how complex this poem is."

What teacher–student interaction patterns characterize this classroom? Do you notice any differences in the way Ms. Watson evaluates the work of her male and female students? Summarize these patterns in your mind before you read ahead.

The Research

As we have discussed, there are a number of studies showing that, in general, boys are disciplined more frequently and more harshly in schools, and that they receive more extended conversation and direct instructions, and more praise. In contrast, girls get less attention and are more likely to be the "invisible" members of our classrooms.

At this point, there has been less research that explores subtleties in the different ways that teachers talk to boys and girls about their academic work. While the educational literature is not conclusive in this area, the studies that have been done must be looked at carefully because they have important implications for teachers. Recent studies by Carol Dweck and her colleagues provide a more fine-grained analysis of the kinds of criticism that girls and boys receive in classrooms. These studies make a persuasive case that there are striking sex differences in the amount and kind of praise and criticism students receive concerning their academic work.

Researchers observed fourth- and fifth-grade classrooms over a period of five weeks. The observers coded and analyzed the evaluative feedback teachers gave to girls and boys. These researchers found that approximately 90 percent of the praise boys received for their academic work was directly concerned with intellectual quality (i.e., John, you did a good job of analyzing the causes of the Civil War). In contrast, for girls only 80 percent of praise for academic work was directly concerned with intellectual quality. The other 20 percent of the praise girls received for their work did not focus on intellectual quality. Instead this praise was directed at papers being neat, pretty, and following the rules of form (i.e., That's a nice paper, Suzy. Your margins and headings are exactly right.).[29]

In the classroom scene above, did you notice the different ways Ms. Watson handled the male student and the female student who did well on the exam? Tom was praised for the intellectual quality of his answers. Marilyn was praised for promptly handing in neat papers.

Studies also indicate that in terms of criticism for academic work the sex differences are even more striking. Approximately half the criticism boys receive on their academic work is for intellectual inadequacy. The other half of the criticism boys get is for failure to obey the rules of form and to turn in papers that are neat and attractive. In contrast, almost 90 percent of the criticism girls receive for academic work is specifically directed at intellectual inadequacy. Girls get little criticism on neatness and rules of form.[30]

Did you notice the different kinds of criticism for academic work that Ms. Watson gave to boys and girls? Both A− student Tom and C− student Frank were criticized for handing in sloppy work that violated rules about margins, headings, and the like. The two girls did not receive this kind of disapproval. Instead both C+ student Beth and B+ student Marilyn received criticism that focused directly on the intellectual inadequacy of their exam responses.

Researchers who analyze differences in the ways teachers criticize the academic work of girls and boys have discovered another very important pattern. When teachers criticize boys, they tend to attribute their academic inadequacies to lack of effort.[31] (You defined these terms incorrectly, Bill. I know you can do better if you try harder.) However, when teachers criticize girls, they usually do not attribute intellectual inadequacy to lack of effort. (You defined these terms incorrectly, Alice.) In the preceding classroom scene, did you notice that Ms. Watson attributed Frank's C— grade to lack of effort and encouraged him to try harder? In contrast, no such attribution to effort was made for C+ student Beth. Following is a table that summarizes the research on how teachers evaluate the academic work of boys and girls.

	Boys	*Girls*
Praise for Academic Work	Approximately 90% of praise is for intellectual quality	Approximately 80% of praise is for intellectual quality
	Approximately 10% of praise is for following the rules of form	Approximately 20% of praise is for following the rules of form
Criticism for Academic Work	Approximately 50% of criticism is for intellectual inadequacy	Approximately 90% of criticism is for intellectual inadequacy
	Approximately 50% of criticism is for failure to obey the rules of form and other non-intellectual factors	Approximately 10% of criticism is for failure to obey the rules of form
	There is frequent attribution to effort (you can do better if you try harder)	There is infrequent attribution to effort

IMPACT AND IMPLICATIONS

This play-by-play research has presented information on differences in the ways teachers interact with girls and boys in their classrooms. It's important to mention that there doesn't seem to be much difference whether it is a man or woman who stands behind the teacher's desk. The interaction patterns we have discussed remain pretty much the same.[32]

If you've been thinking something like a researcher yourself, you're probably already considering the next question. Does it matter if teachers interact differently with girls and boys? Do these differences in any way affect student learning and behavior?

This seems to be a pretty straightforward question. Paradoxically, the answer has to be somewhat roundabout and complex. It's difficult to make direct cause-and-effect links between teacher behavior and pupil attitudes and achievement. Therefore, we can't make definitive statements about how teacher interaction affects student behavior. However, we can look very carefully at what educational researchers and theorists tell us and draw some implications for teaching.

One researcher, Pauline Sears, studied classroom interaction patterns over 15 years ago, long before the concept of sex equity emerged on our educational consciousness. Here is what she concluded:

> One consequence might be a cumulative increase in independent, autonomous behavior by boys as they are disapproved, praised, listened to, and taught more actively by the teacher. Another might be a lowering of self-esteem generally for girls as they receive less attention and are criticized for their lack of knowledge and skill.[33]

Her words set the scene for contemporary educational research and practice. In fact, the studies of Carol Dweck and her colleagues indicate that this indeed is the result.

Dweck has found that there are sex differences in a pattern of behavior called "learned helplessness." Learned helplessness exists when failure is perceived as insurmountable. Children who exhibit learned helplessness attribute failure to factors that they cannot control, for example, lack of ability. After receiving negative evaluation, children characterized by learned helplessness are likely to show further deterioration in performance. In contrast, children who emphasize factors that can be modified or changed, such as effort, tend to see failure as surmountable. After negative evaluation, these children will often show improved performance.

Girls are more likely than boys to exhibit learned helplessness. They are more likely to blame poor performance on lack of ability rather than on lack of effort. They are also "more prone than boys to show decreased persistence or impaired performance following failure, the threat of failure or increased evaluative pressure."[34]

Why are girls so ready to give up after receiving failure feedback? Why do boys exhibit greater confidence in their ability and show greater persistence in failure situations?

At least part of the answer can be found in the way teachers talk with students regarding their academic work. As we've discussed, teachers give boys more general and intellectually irrelevant disapproval. They criticize them for misbehavior, for not following directions, for violating the rules of form. They give less criticism to boys for the intellectual quality of their academic work. When they do criticize boys for intellectual inadequacy, they frequently attribute failure to not trying hard enough. As a result of such frequent and diffuse negative feedback, boys are more likely to attribute failure, not to themselves, but to a generally negative attitude on the part of the teacher or to the fact that they haven't expended sufficient effort.

For girls, the pattern is different. Girls do not receive frequent, general, and intellectually irrelevant disapproval. They are not often criticized for misbehavior or for failing to comply with the rules of form. Almost all the criticism they get is related directly and specifically to intellectual inadequacy. Moreover, this feedback is not usually tempered by comments such as, "You could have done better. You just didn't try hard enough." As a result, girls are left with few options for placing blame. They can't attribute failure to a teacher who is "against" them or to lack of effort. The cause of failure must then lie in their own lack of ability. In short, Dweck hypothesized that teachers' evaluative feedback regarding the intellectual quality of academic work may actually cause sex differences in learned helplessness.

In order to test this hypothesis, Dweck and her colleagues conducted an interesting experiment with 60 fifth-grade children. Ten boys and ten girls were randomly assigned to each of three experimental conditions. In one experimental condition, ten boys and ten girls were taken individually to a testing room where they were presented with word puzzles. The children were given two kinds of failure feedback on their performance. One kind of feedback was specifically addressed to the correctness of the solution. ("You didn't do very well that time— you didn't get the word right.") The other kind of failure feedback was explicitly addressed to a nonintellectual aspect of performance. ("You didn't do very well that time—it wasn't neat enough.") This was called the "teacher-boy condition" because it is similar to the kind of negative evaluation that boys are more likely to receive in classrooms. Each of the other two experimental conditions consisted of ten boys and ten girls. In these conditions the children also worked individually in a testing room on word puzzles. However, the failure feedback these children received was addressed specifically to the correctness of the solution. These children did *not* receive failure feedback addressed to a nonintellectual aspect of their performance, such as neatness. These were called the "teacher-girl conditions" because they approximated the kind of negative evaluation girls are more likely to receive in classrooms.

At the end of the word puzzle trials, the children in all three conditions were given written questions that assessed whether they attributed failure to the instructors' unfairness, to their own lack of effort, or to their own lack of ability. Most of the children in the "teacher-boy condition" did not view failure on the word puzzles as reflecting a lack of ability. Both boys *and* girls in this condition indicated that *insufficient effort* was the cause of failure. In sharp contrast, both girls *and* boys in the two "teacher-girl conditions" overwhelmingly interpreted the failure feedback as indicating a *lack of ability*. This research led the experimenters to conclude that "the pattern of evaluative feedback given to boys and girls in the classroom can result directly in girls' greater tendency to view failure feedback as indicative of their level of ability." [35] And so, the way teachers interact with boys and girls can have important consequences—an impact that causes sex difference in learned helplessness as girls see failure as insurmountable since it appears to be caused by their own lack of ability.

Another potential impact results from the greater amount of active instruction that boys receive, not only praise and disapproval, but also questioning, opportunities for recitation, extended conversations and directions. It appears that this active instruction may not only increase "independent autonomous behavior" in boys, as Pauline Sears noted, or confidence in ability and persistence in the face of failure, as Carol Dweck noted. It may also influence sex differences in achievement.

Recent research on teacher effectiveness tells us that a pattern of teaching behavior called "direct instruction" appears to be very important in increasing student achievement. Direct instruction involves active teaching; it includes the setting of goals, assessing student progress, making active and clear presentations of the concepts under study; giving clear instruction both for class and individual work.[36] The interaction research we have discussed indicates that teachers appear to be instructing boys more actively and directly than girls. And, as we discussed in Chapters 1 and 2, there are clear sex differences in patterns of achievement.

What happens to girls after the middle elementary years that puts an end to their promising academic start? Obviously, many factors must be considered. And one of these factors may be the more active and direct teaching that male students receive in our nation's classrooms.

Teachers can make a difference in the lives of their students. If you are to have a positive impact on the achievement of all your students, it is essential that you not only become aware of biases in teacher-student interaction patterns, but that you consciously, intentionally, and affirmatively develop interaction skills that are fair, equitable, and designed to actively compensate for student differences in behavior and achievement. The next sections of this chapter will help you begin this process.

PICK A PATTERN: AN ASSESSMENT OF YOUR INTERACTION AWARENESS SKILLS

We have reviewed the research on sex differences in classroom interactions; also we've drawn some classroom vignettes to show you how this research gets translated into classroom action. Now it's your turn. Following is a summary of the classroom interaction patterns that have been discussed in this unit. There are also several scenarios of classroom life. After reading each scenario, determine which pattern fits the scene. In the space indicated, offer example(s) of the specific teacher behaviors that result in this pattern. In the last space provided, suggest how the teacher can change his or her behavior and eliminate this pattern of sex bias. In some cases, none of the patterns fit the scene. Simply note "No Pattern Applies" and explain why. When you've finished, check your responses with the answer key at the end of the chapter. Here is a brief review of the patterns:

Pattern A: Disciplinary Pattern

- Teachers reprimand, disapprove of, and criticize boys more often than girls. This criticism is frequently directed at inappropriate classroom behavior. Low-achieving boys, in particular, are likely to get this negative attention. Girls at all achievement levels are not reprimanded as frequently or as harshly for classroom misbehavior.

Pattern B: Active Teaching Pattern

- Teachers not only disapprove of boys more, they also approve of them more and give them more positive, active teaching attention. Teachers tend to praise boys more, ask them more questions, initiate more work-related contacts with them, and give them more extended directions. Girls of all ability levels do not receive this active attention and instruction. They are more likely to be the quiet and invisible members of classrooms. They are less likely to get extended directions and more likely to get fewer opportunities to participate in classroom discussions.

Pattern C: Evaluation Pattern

- Teachers give more verbal praise to boys for the intellectual quality of their work. They are more likely to praise girls' academic work for its neatness and compliance with rules of form.
- When teachers criticize girls' academic work, comments focus directly on intellectual inadequacy. When teachers criticize boys' academic work, almost half their comments focus on neatness and failure to follow the rules of form. Moreover, teachers are likely to attribute boys' poor academic performance to lack of effort. This attribution to effort does not occur as frequently for girls.

Situation 1

SCENE: Mr. Francisco is working on multiplication and division in his third-grade classroom. Selected students have written multiplication and division examples on the board, and the teacher is going over the work with the class. The students have been having a good deal of trouble with the "math facts" and the teacher is getting frustrated.

TEACHER: O.K. class, let's take a look at these examples. Who wrote the first group of examples on the board? Oh, Eric, several of these examples are incorrect. You've just got to do some studying. If you work harder at memorizing your tables, you'll be able to do these. That's all there is to it.

Let's look at the next set of examples. Jennifer, you wrote these? Jenny, there are several mistakes here. I can't understand why you're having trouble learning these. It's not so difficult.

All right class. It looks like we're not ready for these exercises. It's back to the flash cards for more drill.

Pick the pattern: _____

_____

Examples of the pattern: _____

_____

_____

_____

_____

Suggestions for eliminating the pattern: _____

_____

_____

Situation 2

SCENE: Sixth-grade accelerated English class.
TEACHER: Class, the poem I have put up on the board is called "Stopping by Woods on a Snowy Evening." It's one of the poems that you had for your assignment last night. Can you remember who wrote the poem? Marsha?

MARSHA: Robert Frost.

TEACHER: Yes, he's a poet from New England who writes a lot about nature. What is the setting for this particular poem, Alice?

ALICE: There's someone in a sleigh, and he's watching the woods get covered with snow. I think he says that there aren't any farm houses nearby, so it must be far away from people.

TEACHER: That's right. Describe in more detail what this scene is like. How does the man feel about it? Put it in your own words, Arthur?

ARTHUR: It's night. The man is all alone. There's no people and no noise—except for the sounds of the horse. The woods are turning all white in the dark and it's beautiful. The man feels very peaceful. It's almost like he wants to walk right into the woods and stay there. But at the end of the poem he says he can't because he's promised things to people and he has responsibilities.

TEACHER: Arthur, you've captured the mood exactly. Arthur says that the man feels so drawn to the scene before him that he almost wants to walk into the woods and stay there. Why do you think he feels this way? Jim?

JIM: It seems like there are two reasons. He says that the woods are "lovely, dark, and deep." They're so beautiful and peaceful, they're pulling him to become part of them. It also sounds like he's got some hassles on his mind because he's got these promises he's made to people. Maybe he'd just like to stay in the woods and forget about these problems.

TEACHER: That's an excellent analysis, Jim. In the last line of the poem the man says that he has miles to go before he sleeps. I want you to think carefully about this line. Is there another meaning sleep could have besides just resting for the night? Tony?

TONY: It's probably way-out, but when the man talks about "miles to go before I sleep," he could mean before he dies? It's like he's saying that he has a lot to do during his life before he can rest at peace in the woods forever.

TEACHER: Tony, that's not way-out, at all. You've done a wonderful job interpreting this poem. It's one of those poems that can be read on more than one level. And, on a deeper level, it may be a poem about death and how this man feels about it.

Pick the pattern: _____

_____

Examples of the pattern: _____

_____

_____

_____

_____

Suggestions for eliminating the pattern: _____

_____

_____

Situation 3

SCENE: A second-grade class has been given an assignment to cut out current events items from the newspaper. The children have brought in several articles on the "Energy Crisis," and they are discussing this problem.

TEACHER: Well, class, I think we've defined what this energy problem is about. What signs have you seen in your own life that there is not enough fuel? Has anything happened directly to you or your family because of this? Selma?

SELMA: There are gas lines all over the place. I saw them yesterday when I drove downtown with my parents. Some of the lines went all the way around the block.

TEACHER: Yes, Selma. I've seen them too. Has anybody had to wait in these lines? Jack?

JACK: The other day I was in the car with my mother. Our gas tank was almost empty so we went to the gas station. There was a long, long line that went around the block. We waited in it for almost an hour. It was really boring, and my mother was mad.

TEACHER: I know. I've waited in those lines too. What else has happened? George?

GEORGE: Last week our family was going on a vacation, and we were going to the ocean in Maine. But my parents were so worried about the gas shortage that we stayed home instead and went to the swimming pool.

TEACHER: I'll bet that was disappointing. Any other problems? Alice?

ALICE: Well, you know how we were talking about the president's speech and how we have to keep our thermostats at a certain level. Well, in my mother's office, the thermostats all have to be set at 78 degrees. She says it gets very hot in there.

TEACHER: I know that it's not pleasant to work when you feel too hot. Your mother must find that difficult. We've talked about some of the problems the energy crisis has caused. What can we do to help? Martha?

MARTHA: We can make sure the thermostats in our own homes are set at 78 degrees this summer.

WILLIAM: We can encourage our parents to car pool to work.

SARAH: We can turn off lights and not play the record player too much. And turn off the air conditioner.

TEACHER: Those are good ideas. I'm going to start writing them on the board so that we can develop an energy action plan for our class.

Pick the pattern: _____

_____

Examples of the pattern: _____

_____

_____

_____

_____

Suggestions for eliminating the pattern: _____

_____

_____

Situation 4

TEACHER: Today, we're going to start our new social studies unit on children in other countries. I've got our new texts and I'm going to ask the first person in each row to come up and get them and distribute them to his or her row.

(The front seat people immediately start for the books and, in the rush, a stack of texts hits the floor.)

TEACHER: Hey, Phil, Kenny, Richard. The rest of you back to your seats. I didn't tell you to come up yet. One at a time. Alison, you come first. Then Kenny. Then Rita. And we'll go on down the rows. I expect the rest of you to be quiet while these books are given out. It'll just take a few minutes to distribute them. Jerry, I said quiet. That was not an invitation to talk. And that goes for your cohort in crime, Tim. You boys have been causing trouble all day, and I've about had all I'm going to take. If I have to speak to you again, it's the principal's office.

(The teacher turns her back to check the dwindling supply of texts on her desk. She turns back to the class just in time to intercept a paper airplane flying across the room.)

TEACHER: Sheila, did you throw that? Bring it up here, young lady. You know better than to act like this. You should be ashamed of yourself.

Pick the pattern: _____

_____

Examples of the pattern: _____

_____

_____

_____

_____

Suggestions for eliminating the pattern: _____

_____

_____

Situation 5

SCENE: It is one of the early lessons in an eighth-grade science lab. The teacher has just explained the use of the microscope to the class, and now she is working with individual students to make sure that light sources, slide platforms, and lenses are all functioning properly. As she passes Bob's desk, she notices that his mirror is pointed away from the light source. She explains the problem, and watches as Bob adjusts the mirror. As she walks by Alice's table, she notices that the wrong lens magnification is being used. She points out the problem, and as Alice watches, she quickly adjusts the microscope for the appropriate lens and moves on to the next table.

Pick the pattern: _____

_____

Examples of the pattern: _____

_____

_____

_____

_____

Suggestions for eliminating the pattern: _____

_____

_____

Situation 6

SCENE: The teacher is working with two fifth-grade students in the writing center.

TEACHER: Gwen and Dick, let's take a look at the stories you've been working on. I understand your stories are called "Jaws Revisited" and you're doing a sequel about the shark. Gwen, this is coming along nicely but I can't find your topic sentence for the first paragraph. Why don't you start the paragraph with an overview sentence about the shark, and then your scary description will hold together better. Dick, you're also off to a good start, but you've got the opposite problem. You've got a topic sentence, but you don't support it. Think what details you could put in to describe that New England fishing town.

Pick the pattern: _____

_____

Examples of the pattern: _____

_____

_____

_____

_____

Suggestions for eliminating the pattern: _____

_____

_____

PUTTING YOUR KNOWLEDGE TO WORK

At this point, you are familiar with how teacher expectations and interactions can create and reinforce patterns of sex bias in the classroom. The next move is yours. It is up to you to move sex equity from the written word to the reality of the classroom. The last part of this chapter provides observation tools to help you accomplish this.

The rapid pace of classroom life makes careful observation a real challenge; however, by keeping some general principles in mind and using the observation instruments provided, you can acquire a number of helpful insights into your teaching behavior. The first step is to collect objective information about your teaching. You can do this on your own in a number of ways. You can set up a video or audio recorder in your classroom to record your teaching. Or, you can cooperate with another teacher and take turns visiting and observing in each other's classroom. The point to remember here is that the demands on you as a teacher are far too great for you to try to maintain an ongoing and objective analysis of your own behavior. The first step, therefore, is to identify a source to help you collect information on your teaching.

The following suggested observation techniques run the gamut from the simple to the complex. You may want to start out slowly with some of these initial techniques, and, as you become more comfortable with the observation process, move on to the more complex approaches. Obviously, the more information you acquire, the better you will be able to pinpoint and alter potentially biased teaching patterns.

To get the best results, it is advisable to use each technique for about 30 minutes, and, if possible, for several times. This will provide you with the most representative sample of your teaching behaviors.

Observation Technique 1

In order to determine if you are giving approximately equal attention to both boys and girls, ask an observer to count the number of times you interact with each. Or, if you have an audio or videotape set up, you may be able to assess your own interaction style. For this initial technique, all your comments are counted, including questions, answers, rewards, directions, and so forth that are given to either a boy or a girl. Only when you speak to the entire class or to a mixed group of girls and boys are the comments not counted.

Since any given class might consist of more students of one sex than the other, you can get an accurate proportion by dividing each total by the number of boys and girls in the room.

	Teacher Interactions	Total
Boys	1111 1111 1111 1111 1111 1111 1111 1111 1111 111	= 48
Girls	1111 1111 1111 1111 11	= 22
Boys	48 (total number of teacher interactions) = 3.7 average interactions 13 (total number of boys in the class) with each boy	
Girls	22 (total number of teacher interactions) = 1.8 average interactions 12 (total number of girls in the class) with each girl	

Finding: The teacher gives boys more than twice as many interactions as girls.

Obviously, this is a very global indicator of who is receiving teacher attention. If you want more specific information, you may want to divide the tallies into academic and nonacademic attention, and see how attention to boys and girls is distributed in these two areas. Academic attention would involve questions, rewards, and other comments directed at the student's work. Nonacademic comments would include disciplining students, class routine and decorum, and other remarks not concerned with a student's academic work.

When you use this observation system to observe other teachers, or when this approach is used to analyze your own teaching, you will be able to compare these results with research findings that indicate that most of the teacher's attention, academic and nonacademic, is given to boys. Do your teaching behaviors reflect this pattern, or do you distribute attention in a fair manner to both female and male students?

Observation Technique 2: Praise and Criticism

To obtain more specific information, you can use the same procedure as described in the first technique, but this time distinguish between teacher interactions that praise students and those that criticize students. So when the teacher says, "Good answer, Betty," tally one mark for girls in the reward category. A comment such as, "Pay attention, Joan," would be recorded by a tally for girls in the criticism category. The remark, "Don, see me after class about your poor behavior," would receive a tally in the boys' criticism column. A comment such as, "Good work, Jim," would be noted in the boys' reward column. As in the first procedure, you then divide each tally by the total number of boys and the total number of girls in order to get the average. This procedure will allow you to compare how frequently you reward boys versus girls, and how frequently you reprimand one sex compared to the other.

	Teacher Rewards	Total
Boys	1̶1̶1̶1̶ 1̶1̶1̶1̶ 1̶1̶1̶1̶ 1̶1̶1̶1̶ 1̶1̶1̶1̶ 1	= 26
Girls	1̶1̶1̶1̶ 1̶1̶1̶1̶ 11	= 12
Boys	$\dfrac{26 \text{ (total number of teacher rewards to boys)}}{13 \text{ (total number of boys in class)}} = \dfrac{2}{1} = 2$ rewards per boy	
Girls	$\dfrac{12 \text{ (total number of teacher rewards to girls)}}{12 \text{ (total number of girls in class)}} = \dfrac{12}{12} = 1$ reward per girl	

Finding: The teacher rewards the average male student twice as often as the average female student.

	Teacher Reprimands	Total
Boys	1̶1̶1̶1̶ 11	= 7
Girls	1	= 1
Boys	$\dfrac{7 \text{ (total number of teacher reprimands of boys)}}{12 \text{ (total number of boys in class)}} = 0.6$ per boy	
Girls	$\dfrac{1 \text{ (total number of teacher reprimands of girls)}}{12 \text{ (total number of girls in class)}} = 0.08$ per girl	

Finding: The average boy has a 60 percent chance of being reprimanded. The average girl stands only an 8 percent chance of being reprimanded. Boys are being reprimanded more than six times as often as girls.

As with the first procedure, you may want to get more specific information on praise and criticism. To do this, divide the tallies between praise and criticism that are related to academic attention of the teacher.

Your use of questions represents another area which can reflect either sex bias or sex equity. How do you distribute your questions among boys and girls?

Observation Technique 3: Teacher Questions

Using the same procedure described in Observation Techniques 1 and 2, tally the distribution of questions given to girls and boys. Divide these tallies by the number of girls present and the number of boys present to determine the average number of questions a typical boy and a typical girl would receive. Compare these averages to see if you are practicing equity or promoting bias.

Observation Technique 4: Assessment of Sex Equity in Teacher Interactions

This observation technique is far more comprehensive than the first three techniques that have been described. In fact, this procedure subsumes those three techniques and goes beyond them to analyze a wide variety of teacher behaviors. If you have had previous experience in recording and analyzing teacher behaviors, you may want to bypass the first three techniques and begin with this one.

Although this technique uses the same basic procedure as the previous ones, i.e., tallying teacher behaviors, this observation technique investigates a wide spectrum of teacher behaviors, and you will be kept busy counting them all. However, you will be rewarded for this effort by obtaining a fairly comprehensive picture of your teaching in relation to sex equity.

Let's begin by looking over the observation sheet and reviewing the definitions of each of the categories.

Observation Categories

I. *PRAISE*
   A. *Academic*—Teacher rewards and reinforcement given directly for the intellectual quality of work: "Good answer." "You've written a very interesting report." "Your evaluation of the problem is excellent."
   B. *Nonacademic*—All teacher rewards and reinforcement that are not directed to the intellectual quality of academic work: "You're being nice and quiet today." "That's an attractive dress." "That's a very neatly written paper."

II. *CRITICISM—ACADEMIC*
   A. *Intellectual quality*—Critical teacher remarks directed at the lack of intellectual quality of work: "Perhaps math isn't a good field for you." "Is this experiment too difficult for you?" "You don't seem able to grasp this material."

B.   *Effort*—Teacher comments attributing academic failure to lack of effort: "You're not trying hard enough." "I know you can do the work if you put your mind to it and study harder."

III.   CRITICISM—NONACADEMIC
A.   *Mild*—Negative teacher comments that reprimand violations of conduct, rules, forms, behavior, and other nonacademic areas: "Tom, stay in line." "Sally, quiet down." "Jim, your paper is too messy."
B.   *Harsh*—These negative comments are "scene-makers" and attract attention. They are louder, often longer, and always stronger than the mild criticism: "Tom, get back in line. I've had more than enough from you today. Stay in line or suffer the consequences. Move." "Harriet, the rules are quite straightforward, and you are talking and disturbing others. For violating the rules, you are to stay after class today for one hour in the detention hall."

IV.   QUESTIONS
A.   *Low level*—Teacher questions that require memory on the part of the student: "When did Columbus arrive in the Americas?" "Who was the fifth president?" "What is the name of this color?"
B.   *High level*—Teacher questions that require higher intellectual processes and ask the student to use information, not just memorize it: "In your opinion, why did Columbus come to America?" "Analyze the causes of the Viet Nam War." "Determine the range of possible answers in this quadratic equation." "How would you evaluate this painting?" "Can you apply the rules of supply and demand to the following example?" "How would you write your own personal statement on human rights?"

V.   ACADEMIC INTERVENTION
A.   *Facilitate*—This category is concerned with teacher behaviors that facilitate learning by providing students with suggestions, hints, and cues to encourage and enable them to complete the task for themselves. The teacher helps, but the student does: "Think of yesterday's formula, and try to do that problem again." "Are your facts correct? Double check them." "Your explanation isn't complete. Review the purpose of the law, and then try it again." "Watch me do this experiment, then you try it again by yourself."
B.   *Short-circuit*—If the above comments are designed to encourage the student to reach a successful conclusion, comments in this category prevent or short-circuit such success because the teacher intrudes and takes over the process. The teacher

does the task for the student. When the teacher provides the answer instead of the direction, this category is tallied: "Let me do that for you." "That's wrong. The answer is 14." "You're way off base. Watch me do it."

An analysis of your findings can be made by averaging the tallies and comparing the average results for girls with the average for boys. As you assess your results, see if you are practicing equitable teaching behavior. Consider the following guidelines and potential problems as you evaluate your teaching.

Praise—Are boys and girls receiving approximately the same amount of praise? Are boys and girls receiving praise for academic and nonacademic efforts in about the same proportion? Or, are boys more likely to receive praise for the intellectual quality of their work?

Criticism (Academic)—Are equal amounts of academic criticism given to girls and boys? Or, are boys admonished for not trying hard enough while girls are criticized for lack of ability and competence?

OBSERVATION SHEET FOR TECHNIQUE 4
ASSESSMENT OF SEX EQUITY IN TEACHER INTERACTIONS

Directions: For each category indicated, tally the teacher comments directed at boys and girls. Refer to the definition of each category if necessary.

		Boys	Total	Girls	Total
		Teacher Comments Directed At:			
I. Praise	A. Academic				
	B. Nonacademic				
II. Criticism—Academic	A. Intellectual quality				
	B. Effort				
III. Criticism—Nonacademic	A. Mild				
	B. Harsh				
IV. Questions	A. Low level				
	B. High level				
V. Academic Intervention	A. Facilitate				
	B. Short-circuit				

Criticism (Nonacademic)—Are boys and girls receiving the same amounts of criticism at the same level? Or, are boys receiving more frequent and harsh criticism for classroom misbehavior?

Questions—Are the number and types of questions asked divided equally? Or, are boys asked more questions, particularly higher level questions?

Academic Intervention—Is the learning of girls as well as boys facilitated or encouraged? Or, are boys shown how to solve problems and accomplish tasks, while girls get these activities done for them?

Observation Technique 5: Descriptive Data

The previous four techniques rely on counting certain types of teacher behaviors. However, you may want to uncover additional information about your teaching, information that will offer you specific examples of your classroom interaction style. Such data are best obtained by recording objective descriptions, verbatim if possible, of the classroom activity being analyzed.

For example, let's select the first category on the previous observation sheet, Praise. To develop a more in-depth understanding of the use of praise in the classroom an observer would record precisely all statements of praise and reward. If you are using an audio or video recorder, you would play it back after class and write down these comments yourself. This procedure will give you more precise information about the kind of praise you are using for boys and girls.

Here's an example:

Praise given boys:	*Praise given girls:*
Excellent answer, Miguel.	Good, Shari.
Right, Bill.	That's a beautiful cover for your
Good thinking, Joe.	project, Myra.
Fine response, Tony.	O.K., good answer, Consuelo.
O.K., Rey.	That's a neatly written paper,
That's a great idea, David.	Chantal.
I really like that solution, Tom.	Jane, that's the right idea.
That's right on target, Tulsi.	
Excellent, Joe.	

From this kind of descriptive information, you can discover several aspects of teacher behavior. You can see that the teacher is giving more praise to boys than to girls, and more of this praise is directed at academic achievement. You can also see that the teacher is praising girls for neatness and attractiveness of work as well as for intellectual accomplishments.

As you can see from this brief example, obtaining descriptive data provides you with more information than simply tallying the behaviors. You can apply this process to the other categories as well, recording your questions, criticism, and the like. Although this technique is somewhat more demanding than the previous ones, it has potential for providing you with some very specific and very valuable information.

Another technique for obtaining more precise information is to tally not the number of teacher comments in a particular category, but the amount of time a teacher gives to that category. For example, a teacher may ask only one question, but that question could require 3 seconds of classroom time, or it might require 30 seconds of classroom time. A more precise observation procedure would take into consideration these differences in time. After all, the more time that a teacher spends in a category, the more important that category becomes in its impact on students.

Those of you familiar with the well-known Flanders Interaction Analysis system will already know about the procedures for measuring how much time a teacher spends in each category. Some observers rely on stop watches, while others can mentally count with remarkable accuracy the time spent by the teacher in each category. If you have had experience using the Flanders or a similar procedure, we invite you to apply that knowledge to one or more of the observation techniques described in this unit. This will obviously give you a more precise indication of patterns of sex bias or equity in the classroom.

If, on the other hand, you have not had the opportunity to clock teacher behaviors previously, we suggest that you keep this factor in mind. It will be extremely difficult to develop this skill at this point, for it takes hours of practice to time teacher behaviors in a reliable and accurate fashion. However, you should be aware that the time spent by a teacher in each category is one important consideration in analyzing classroom behavior, and you may want to devote the energy necessary to acquire this skill at a later time. Whichever techniques you choose, obtaining information on your classroom teaching behaviors represents an important step on the road to providing equity in the classroom and improving your teaching effectiveness.

TEACHING THEM ALL

I have taught in high school for ten years. During that time, I have given assignments, among others, to a murderer, an evangelist, a pugilist, a thief, and an imbecile.

The murderer was a quiet little boy who sat on the front seat and regarded me with pale blue eyes; the evangelist, easily the most popular boy in the school, had the lead in the junior play; the pugilist lounged by the window and let loose at intervals a raucous laugh that startled even the geraniums; the thief was a gay-hearted Lothario with a song on his lips; and the imbecile, a soft-eyed little animal seeking the shadows.

The murderer awaits death in the state penitentiary; the evangelist has lain a year now in the village churchyard; the pugilist lost an eye in a brawl in Hong Kong; the thief, by standing on tiptoe, can see the windows of my room from the county jail; and the once gentle-eyed little moron beats his head against a padded wall in the state asylum.

All of these pupils once sat in my room, sat and looked at me gravely across worn brown desks. I must have been a great help to those pupils— I taught them the rhyming scheme of the Elizabethan sonnet and how to diagram a complex sentence.[37]

In "I Taught Them All," Naomi White talks with despair about her years as a teacher. All teachers have moments of futility but, at its heart, teaching is not an insignificant, paper-shuffling job. It has meaning, worth, and value. It gives you the opportunity to touch a young and impressionable life and make it better.

We were the luckiest class in the school. We had a homeroom teacher who knew the core truth of education. Self-hate destroys, self-esteem saves. This principle guided all her efforts on our behalf. She always minimized our deficiencies, neutralized our rage, and enhanced our natural gifts. She never, so to speak, forced a dancer to sing or a singer to dance. She allowed each of us to light his own lamp. We loved her. . . .[38]

Mr. Jacobs won our hearts, because he treated us as though we were already what we could only hope to become. Through his eyes we saw ourselves as capable and decent and destined for greatness . . . Mr. Jacobs introduced us to ourselves. We learned who we were and what we wanted to be. No longer strangers to ourselves, we felt at home in the world.[39]

You can become the kind of teacher that students will remember. Information, exercises, and observation techniques in this chapter are designed to help you become a more equitable and sensitive teacher, one who can reach all students, both girls and boys. But in the end, it is your own ability, initiative, and commitment that will translate these ideas into classroom practice. By affirmative and intentional nonsexist teaching, you can treat both girls and boys fairly. By eliminating stereotypes and bias from your classroom, you can introduce all your students to who they are—and to what they are capable of becoming.

ANSWER KEY: Pick a Pattern: An Assessment of Your Interaction Awareness Skills

The following section provides suggested responses to the exercise. Although your responses may vary slightly from these answers, we have tried to provide explanations that focus on the major issues involved in each classroom scenario.

Situation 1

Pattern C: Evaluation Pattern
Examples: When Mr. Francisco criticizes Eric's math examples, he attributes errors to lack of effort or studying.
Eliminating the pattern: Research by Dweck and others suggests the importance of attributing failure to lack of effort rather than to lack of ability. Mr. Francisco should also encourage Jenny to study harder and to memorize her math facts.

Situation 2

Pattern B: Active Teaching Pattern
Examples: The teacher interacts more frequently and extensively with male students in this classroom. Boys are asked more high-order questions, and are given more opportunity for extended recitation and response. They also receive more praise for their classroom participation.
Eliminating the pattern: The teacher should make an active effort to encourage the participation of both female and male students. This could be accomplished by asking female students more high-order questions and by praising them for their answers.

Situation 3

No pattern applies. The teacher actively instructs both male and female students.

Situation 4

Pattern A: Disciplinary Pattern
Examples: The teacher disciplines male students more frequently and harshly. When Sheila misbehaves, she receives a less intense rebuke than her male classmate.
Eliminating the pattern: This situation could be used as a springboard not only for equitable interaction, but also for strategies for effective management of classroom behavior. This teacher's reactions to inappropriate behavior may actually serve to reinforce rather than eliminate it. Also, it should be emphasized that both female and male students should be held to the same standards of classroom conduct.

Situation 5

Pattern B: Active Teaching Pattern
Examples: This science teacher gives Bob instructions on how to solve the problem with his microscope. In contrast, when Alice has a problem, the teacher takes over and solves it for her, instead of giving her directions on how to solve the problem for herself.
Eliminating the pattern: "Doing for" female students can lead to dependency and lack of initiative. Whenever possible, both female and male students should be given explicit instructions so that they can work independently and solve problems for themselves.

Situation 6

No pattern applies. Both Gwen and Dick are given praise as well as extended directions on how to work on their own to revise their compositions. Further, when criticism is given, both students are encouraged to expend more work and effort.

ENDNOTES

[1] Haim Ginott, *Teacher and Child* (New York: Macmillan, 1972).

[2] Ginott, *Teacher and Child.*

[3] Robert Rosenthal and Lenore Jacobson, *Pygmalion in the Classroom: Teacher Expectation and Pupils' Intellectual Development* (New York: Holt, Rinehart and Winston, 1968).

[4] Jere Brophy and Thomas Good, *Teacher-Student Relationships: Causes and Consequences* (New York: Holt, Rinehart and Winston, 1974).

[5] B. J. Kemer, "A Study of the Relationship Between the Sex of the Student and the Assignment of Marks by Secondary School Teachers" (Ph.D. dissertation, Michigan State University, 1965).

[6] Sari Knopf, "Lessons of Consequence" (paper delivered at the American Educational Research Association, San Francisco, April 1979).

[7] "Out in Right Field," in Joseph Pleck and Jack Sawyer (eds.), *Men and Masculinity* (Englewood Cliffs, N.J.: Prentice-Hall, 1974).

[8] J. Palardy, "What Teachers Believe—What Children Achieve," *Elementary School Journal* 69 (1969).

[9] Julia Sherman and Elizabeth Fennema, "The Study of Mathematics by High School Girls and Boys: Related Variables," *American Educational Research Journal* 14 (1977).

[10] "Puzzles and Paradoxes: Males Dominate in Educational Success," *The Educational Digest* 31 (1976).

[11] Ned Flanders, *Analyzing Teacher Behavior* (Reading, Mass.: Addison-Wesley, 1970).

[12] Phil Jackson, *Life in Classrooms* (New York: Holt, Rinehart and Winston, 1968).

13 W. D. Floyd, "An Analysis of the Oral Questioning Activity in Selected Colorado Primary Classrooms" (Ph.D. dissertation, Colorado State College, 1960).

14 Mary Budd Rowe, "Wait-Time and Rewards as Instructional Variables: Their Influence on Language, Logic and Fate Control" (paper presented at the National Association for Research in Science Teaching, Chicago, April 1972).

15 Phil Jackson and Henrietta Lahaderne, "Inequalities of Teacher-Pupil Contacts," *Psychology in Schools* 4 (1967).

16 L. Serbin, K. O'Leary, R. Kent, and I. Tonick, "A Comparison of Teacher Response to the Preacademic and Problem Behavior of Boys and Girls," *Child Development* 44 (1973).

17 Brophy and Good, *Teacher-Student Relationships.*

18 Ibid.

19 Robert Spaulding, "Achievement, Creativity, and Self-Concept Correlates of Teacher-Pupil Transactions in Elementary School" (Washington, D.C.: Department of Health, Education and Welfare, 1963).

20 V. Jones, "The Influence of Teacher-Student Introversion, Achievement and Similarity on Teacher-Student Dyadic Classroom Interactions" (Ph.D. dissertation, University of Texas at Austin, 1971).

21 Lisa Serbin and Daniel O'Leary, "How Nursery Schools Teach Girls to Shut Up," *Psychology Today* (December 1975).

22 V. Jones, "The Influence of Teacher-Student Introversion, Achievement and Similarity on Teacher-Student Dyadic Classroom Interactions."

23 J. Sikes, "Differential Behavior of Male and Female Teachers with Male and Female Students," (Ph.D. dissertation, University of Texas at Austin, 1971).

24 W. Cosper, "An Analysis of Sex Differences in Teacher-Student Interaction as Manifest in Verbal and Nonverbal Behavior Cues" (Ed.D. dissertation, University of Tennessee, 1970).

25 Lisa Serbin and Daniel O'Leary, "How Nursery Schools Teach Girls to Shut Up."

26 Brophy and Good, *Teacher-Student Relationships.*

27 P. Rubovits and M. Maehr, "Pygmalion Black and White," *Journal of Personality and Social Psychology* 25 (1973).

28 Brophy and Good, *Teacher-Student Relationships.*

29 Carol Dweck, William Davidson, Sharon Nelson, and Bradley Enna, "Sex Differences in Learned Helplessness: II. The Contingencies of Evaluative Feedback in the Classroom and III. An Experimental Analysis," *Developmental Psychology* 14 (1978).

30 Dweck et al., "Sex Differences in Learned Helplessness." *See also* Spaulding, "Achievement, Creativity, and Self-Concept Correlates of Teacher-Pupil Transactions in Elementary School."

31 Ibid.

32 Brophy and Good, *Teacher-Student Relationships.*

33 Pauline Sears and David Feldman, "Teacher Interactions with Boys and Girls," *National Elementary Principal* 46 (November 1966).

[34] Dweck et al., "Sex Differences in Learned Helplessness."

[35] Ibid.

[36] Thomas Good, "Teacher Effectiveness in the Elementary School," *Journal of Teacher Education* 33 (1979).

[37] Naomi White, "I Taught Them All," *The Clearing House* (November 1937).

[38] Ginott, *Teacher and Child.*

[39] Ibid.

5
Nonsexist Teaching

Objectives

- To become aware of guidelines for nonsexist teaching
- To consider a variety of lesson plans, learning center activities, enrichment projects and, value clarification activities in developing a nonsexist classroom
- To develop your own ideas and approaches to nonsexist teaching

> I just can't understand what's going wrong. I've worked hard to set up a nonsexist classroom. I have a library shelf of nonsexist children's books. I check myself all the time to make sure that I don't discriminate in the way that I talk to boys and girls in my classroom. And still I don't feel that I'm getting anywhere. The kids still seem to behave in stereotyped ways. Just the other day I had to break up an argument where a group of boys was insisting that a woman couldn't be president. After all I've done, this really is frustrating.

Many teachers and parents often comment that they are teaching and raising their children in a nonsexist fashion; they go out of their way to bring nonsexist books and toys into their classrooms and their homes; they try to expose children to nonstereotyped role models in the community; they assure their children that they are free to choose how they want to behave and what they want to become.

But if you listen carefully, you will also hear these committed teachers and parents express confusion and bewilderment. Despite these efforts, their daughters and their sons often seem to be stuck inside stereotypes. One feminist educator tells of coming home from a conference on nonsexist teaching to find her 9-year-old daughter insisting that she couldn't become a doctor because only boys were doctors. A mother tells about how she drives to the other end of her city to take her daughter to a female pediatrician—and that child unwaveringly claims that girls are nurses and boys are doctors. And a physician tells how she was utterly dumbfounded when her 6-year-old son patiently explained to her how women couldn't be doctors. A junior high school teacher describes how she made elaborate preparations to expose her class to nonsexist career models in the medical profession. She took her seventh-graders on a field trip to a local hospital. A male nurse talked to the children about what his job was like. A female doctor talked to the children about her job and she conducted a tour around the hospital. When the students returned to their classroom, the teacher was surprised when some of the children still insisted that men were supposed to be doctors and women were supposed to be nurses. "How can you say that?" the teacher asked. "Today you saw a male nurse, and the woman who took you around the hospital was a doctor." The children were undaunted by reality. "Oh, those people lied," was the quick response.

These may be extreme examples—but they are also illustrations of how difficult nonsexist teaching and child rearing is. Children are exposed to a continual bombardment of sexist messages in almost every aspect of their lives. They go to the toy store and see science kits with pictures of boys looking through microscopes and conducting experiments. They see rows of well-endowed female dolls with pretty dresses and wavy hair. They turn on their television sets on Saturday morning and watch the super heroes—all male except for Wonderwoman—perform amazing feats. They watch detectives and police officers and doctors—almost always male—rescue victims in trouble—almost always female. Every day, several times a day, they are bombarded with short and cleverly devised commercials where women fight ring-around-the-collar and greasy-waxy-build-up so their homes will be spotless when their husbands return from work. In fact, television's ring-around-the-collar may be the universal electronic curriculum, the ring that binds and unites all children in a common sexist environment. Exposing children to an occasional nonsexist book or taking them to visit a female doctor is not enough. More powerful medicine is needed to counteract the sexist messages that society delivers.

There are several lessons to be learned from those teachers who have pioneered experiments in creating nonsexist classrooms. Their early attempts provide important direction on how to create nonsexist classrooms so that we can go about changing the facts and figures on the report card in the first chapter of this book.

GUIDELINES FOR NONSEXIST TEACHING

1. *Nonsexist teaching should be continuous and integral to daily instruction.*

Most research shows that the attitudes and behaviors of children, particularly girls, can become less stereotyped after they read nonsexist materials. The problem is that these changes often don't last from year to year—or even month to month or week to week. This means that to truly open up options for children, teachers need to incorporate nonsexist materials, books, activities, and lessons on a continual basis in the day to day teaching of children. Think about the form of bias called fragmentation that we talked about in the chapter, "Beyond the Dick and Jane Syndrome." When a text presents a separate chapter or boxed-off section on issues related to sex equity, children learn that this information is isolated from and not integral to the main body of information the text presents. Similarly, if there is a separate lesson or even a separate unit on changing roles for women and men, the message is that the topic is an interesting diversion but not really an important issue for children to learn. In a later part of this chapter, there are a variety of teaching techniques and learning center and lesson plan ideas that will help you incorporate nonsexist teaching into your classroom on a daily and integrated basis.

2. *Nonsexist teaching must direct attention to the stereotypes and problems that affect boys as well as girls.*

Those who have worked with nonsexist curriculum in elementary and secondary schools frequently comment that boys seem to be more resistant than girls to these materials. For example, in one research project a nonsexist curriculum intervention was taught at the kindergarten, fifth-, and ninth-grade levels. Female students in these different grades showed less stereotyped attitudes toward occupational and socioemotional roles after instruction in the nonsexist curriculum. However, male students were more resistant to changing stereotyped attitudes and, at the ninth-grade level, they actually exhibited stronger sex-role stereotyping after the nonsexist curricular intervention.[1]

A high school teacher who taught a unit on outstanding women in U.S. history notes that the boys in her class were actually hostile to the unit. Several claimed that they were being brainwashed with reverse sexism and that they were being left out. These early teaching attempts show us very clearly that when we talk about nonsexist teaching we need to pay attention to the harmful impact of stereotyping on male as well as female students. In the next chapter there is a discussion of male sex-role stereotyping as well as a variety of classroom exercises that focus on this issue.

3. *Nonsexist teaching must also be concerned with discrimination on the basis of race/ethnicity/religion/class/age/and handicap.*

Discrimination on the basis of sex is a growth from the same kind of prejudice that harms people who are members of various minority groups. Nonsexist teaching must be broad in its application and should work toward confronting prejudice and discrimination in its widest sense.

For example, when you develop nonsexist lesson plans and learning centers, it is important to include the experiences and achievements of women and men from various racial and ethnic groups. The struggles and accomplishments of individuals who are handicapped should be demonstrated and discussed. At its essence, nonsexist teaching should highlight and celebrate the rich diversity that comprises contemporary society.

4. *Nonsexist teaching should be a partnership between the teacher and parents and community members.*

Changing the stereotypes that close off children's aspirations and options is no easy job. It needs help and cooperation from others who care about the well-being and positive potential of children. You may need to form a partnership with parents and work closely with them. In communities where parents are resistant and even hostile, you may have to explain to them what nonsexist teaching is about and why it is an important educational issue. Show them the facts and figures in the report card in this book. Explain how nonsexist teaching may actually work toward improving boys' achievement scores in reading and girls' achievement scores in math. In communities where parents are already concerned about the impact of sexism on their children, enlist this important resource in an active teaching partnership. Explain to the parents what you're doing in your classroom so that they can reinforce these lessons at home. Some of these parents may themselves be involved in nonstereotyped careers and life styles. They as well as other community members may want to come into your classrooms to talk about their occupations and their experiences. These parents and community members may also be an influential group ensuring that the school district complies with both the letter and the spirit of Title IX.

5. *Nonsexist teaching is a total process. It should involve all aspects of the classroom environment.*

Nonsexist teaching involves the total classroom including:

- the physical arrangement and organization of your room
- verbal and nonverbal classroom language and interaction
- selection and use of print and audiovisual curricular materials
- development of classroom lessons, units, and learning centers

Every aspect of the classroom environment can teach about roles and options for females and males, and students are sensitive to inconsistencies. For example, if you include women who have made outstanding achievements in your social studies lessons but fail to represent women in bulletin board displays, students will be aware of the incongruity. If you talk about the importance of women and men working together but allow sex segregation in classroom groups, lines, and other activities, students will be confused by this contradiction. All aspects of the classroom should consistently reinforce the message that equal educational opportunity is a reality for both female and male students.

6. *Nonsexist teaching is good teaching.*

Enthusiasm, humor, creativity, patience, careful planning, flexibility, respect for diverse student opinions—these are some of the qualities that characterize good teaching—and they are essential for effective nonsexist teaching. There are many obstacles to nonsexist teaching, including parent and student misunderstanding and resistance. But research on nonsexist instructional interventions show that highly skilled and enthusiastic teachers can overcome these obstacles and help both boys and girls become less stereotyped in their attitudes and behaviors.[2]

7. *Nonsexist teaching must include both the affective and cognitive domains.*

Students usually have strong feelings about appropriate behavior and roles for women and men. Consequently, nonsexist instruction must help students reflect about and examine not only their ideas but also their attitudes and feelings. For example, one student read a U.S. Department of Labor summary of facts and statistics concerning the increasing participation of women in the salaried work force. His attitude that "woman's place is in the home" was so strong that he refused to believe the statistics; the facts denied reality as he wished it to be. After participating in value clarification activities on changing roles for men and women, the student was able to consider cognitive information on working women in a more intellectually open manner. In the final section of this chapter, there are a variety of value clarification activities that you can use to help students consider, discuss, and analyze their attitudes on sex-role issues. When these affective activities are used in conjunction with cognitive approaches, they can lead to a comprehensive and powerful approach to nonsexist teaching.

8. *Nonsexist teaching is active and affirmative.*

Because children are bombarded with sexist messages and signals, nonsexist teaching must be an *active* and *intentional* process of incorporating into daily instruction those books, audiovisual materials, discussions, research projects, field trips, enrichment activities, learning centers, and lesson plans and units that teach girls and boys about changing roles and widening options. In short, it's not enough to have a classroom library that includes nonsexist books. It's not enough to bring in nontraditional role models on career awareness day and to refer to "firefighters" instead of "firemen." These are all good and positive steps but they are not enough to make the report card in Chapter 1 obsolete. In order to change that report card for your students, in order to help them question and condemn prejudice on the basis of sex you will need to include examples, references, lesson plans, and learning center ideas every day in your discussions and assignments.

At this point you may be thinking that this is a naive, idealistic recommendation—and that with all the other problems there is not time for such an active and all-encompassing approach. After all, there are more pressing problems to worry about such as achievement scores and back to basics. But if you're tempted to dismiss this recommendation, remember that there is nothing more basic than equal opportunity for all your students.

NONSEXIST TEACHING: A WHOLE CLASSROOM CATALOG

In the remaining sections of this chapter, you will find a catalog of activities and lessons that you can adopt or adapt for use in your classroom. Some of the activities are more appropriate for elementary children; others can be used more effectively in secondary classrooms. Many can be modified for use with a variety of age levels. Some, such as the value clarification activities, are primarily affective; others focus on the cognitive domain.

These activities and lesson plan ideas are organized in four main sections: (1) generic lesson plans, (2) math and science lesson plans, (3) ideas and projects for language arts and social studies, and (4) values clarification activities.

There is such a wealth of activities and approaches for nonsexist teaching that no single chapter could include all the possibilities. These are only samples—a beginning—to jog your mind and encourage you to formulate your own nonsexist teaching style.

GENERIC LESSON PLANS

These lesson plans deal with a variety of sex-equity issues. They can be used in many different content areas from social studies to math, from language arts to career awareness. While each lesson plan notes recommended age levels, with a bit of creative revision, you can adapt these for younger or older students. You may notice that these lesson plans vary slightly in format. This simply reflects the different styles that educators use when they write lesson plans.

Catalog Contents

- Families
- Choosing Gifts
- The Fable of He and She
- Take a Look at the Story Problems in Your Math Book
- Going to the Source
- You Can Fight City Hall
- A Woman's Place Is . . .
- A Case Study of Paul
- What's in a Job? A Skills Analysis
- Language Matters
- A Fine Kettle of Fish

Lesson Plan 1

FAMILIES

Target Group

Grades K–3

Objective

To examine and understand the roles of family members of different ages and sexes

Related Curriculum Areas

Language Arts, Social Studies

Related Occupational Areas

All

Classroom Time Required

30–60 minutes

Materials/Resources Needed

- Copies of the My Family handout
- A Families Poster. The instructor may make this, and students can help by cutting out pictures from old magazines. There should be several different types of families represented: a traditional family, a single-parent family, an extended family including grandparents or aunts or uncles. The families' members should be different ages and sexes: babies, children, senior citizens. Minority families and families with disabled members should be represented.
- Related stories for possible follow-up activities:

  Families—A coloring book for families to share. c/o McNamara, 6 Madison Avenue, Ossining, NY 10562
  Eichler, Margrit. *Martin's Father.* Chapel Hill, N.C.: Lollipop Power, 1971.
  Simon, Norma. *All Kinds of Families.* Chicago: Albert Whitman, 1976.
  Families Grow in Different Ways. Waterloo, Ontario: Before We Are Six Press, 1976.

The Activity/Procedures

1. Ask students what things people need to know how to do in order to take care of a home and family. Write their responses on the chalkboard.
2. Write the following six job categories in another list on the board:

   a. Child care
   b. Cooking
   c. House cleaning
   d. Earning money
   e. House repair and maintenance
   f. Paying bills

   Explain that these are probably some of the more important categories of things people have to do. Next have students try to decide who in each family on the Families Poster does each of the six jobs. Consider each family separately and discuss each person in the family. When students identify a person with a task, ask if any other family member could do the job.

3. Following this discussion, distribute the student activity sheets. Read the directions to the students and have them complete the sheets.

Follow-up Discussion

4. Ask students to tell who in their family does each of the six jobs. There will probably be some different family members in each category.
5. Have students put the initials of other members of their families who *could* do the job next to their drawing in each space.
6. Make the following points in this discussion:

   ● Adults of both sexes can do all the jobs.
   ● Children of both sexes can do most of the jobs.
   ● Only babies and very old people cannot do most of the jobs.

7. Ask students to think of ways different family members can share some of the jobs. For example:

   ● Two adults can earn money for the family.
   ● Adults and children can share house cleaning, cooking, and maintenance.

Source

Reprinted from *Choices: Learning about Changing Sex Roles*. Copyright © 1977 by Sherri Wagner, Minneapolis, MN.

The *Choices* materials include posters, a teacher's guide, and 20 additional activities for elementary and secondary students.

FAMILIES

My Family

Directions: List the people in your family below:

_____   _____

_____   _____

_____   _____

_____   _____

Draw a picture of the person or persons in your own family who does each job in the spaces below.

Housework	Cooking	Earning money
Fixing the house, the car	**Paying bills**	**Child care**

Lesson Plan 2

CHOOSING GIFTS

Target Group

Grades K–4

Objective

To examine how interests and preferences are thought to be associated with different sexes.

Related Curriculum Areas

Language Arts, Social Studies, Mathematics

Related Occupational Areas

All

Classroom Time Required

15 to 60 minutes

Materials/Resources Needed

- Copies of the Gift List handout
- Play money
- Store catalogs from which pictures of objects can be cut out
- Construction paper and paste

The Activity/Procedures

1. Use Ward's or Sears' or any other large catalog to cut out a variety of objects which might be gift items. (Avoid clothes.) Mount each item on construction paper and print a one-word label and the price in even dollars underneath each picture. Display the pictures on a table or bulletin board. If students prepare these pictures for the class, they may wish to display them in a store arrangement.

2. Distribute $100 in play money to each student. Distribution can take place through student bankers.

3. Distribute gift lists and tell each student to choose gifts for each member of his or her family and to pay the storekeeping students the amount of each chosen gift. Note that gift lists allow personalization due to differences in families. For writing practice, have each student write the name of chosen gifts on his or her list.

    Alternate plan for younger students: The economic lesson is optional; therefore, the money exchange may be eliminated. Beginning readers would benefit in copying gift words onto their lists, but students could cut pictures from catalogs to paste on their sheets beside family names. If this plan is followed, more than one catalog will be needed.

4. When gift lists are completed, conduct a class discussion around the following questions:

    a. Why did you choose certain gifts for certain people? Did you choose gifts because you thought:

    - The person would really use the gift?
    - It was a gift *you* wanted the person to have?

CHOOSING GIFTS

Play Money

$1.00	$1.00
$1.00	$5.00
$10.00	$5.00
$10.00	$20.00

CHOOSING GIFTS

Gift List

Let's pretend. Suppose someone gave you a lot of money and you could buy gifts for your family. Choose something for each person.

NAME _____	*NAME* _____
_____	_____
_____	_____
GIFT _____	*GIFT* _____
_____	_____
_____	_____
_____	_____
NAME _____	*NAME* _____
_____	_____
_____	_____
GIFT _____	*GIFT* _____
_____	_____
_____	_____
_____	_____

- It was something the person *should* want?
- It was something *you yourself* liked?

b. Did you select something that:

- The person needs?
- The person wants?
- You want?

c. Would you reverse the gifts you gave:

- Mother—Father?
- Sister—Brother?

Why or why not?

d. What gifts would you like to receive? What gifts would you give a girlfriend? A boyfriend?

e. Do girls ever play with boys' toys? Do girls ever want to play with boys' toys? Do boys ever play with girls' toys? What are girls' toys . . . boys' toys? Do boys play with dolls? (How about Action Jackson and GI Joe?) Who decides what's right?

f. Do the gifts we give to people always need to cost a lot of money? What gifts can you think of that don't cost anything?

Source

From *Today's Changing Roles: An Approach to Non-Sexist Teaching* prepared by Educational Challenges, Inc. Copyright 1974 by the National Foundation for the Improvement of Education.

Lesson Plan 3

THE FABLE OF HE AND SHE

Target Group

Grades 2–4

Objectives

- To become aware of how sex-role stereotyping occurs
- To become aware of how sex-role stereotyping handicaps people in life situations
- To discover how females and males can share skills and work together

Related Curriculum Areas

Language Arts, Social Studies, Creative Dramatics

Related Occupational Areas

All

Classroom Time Required

30 to 60 minutes each for the original and follow-up activities.

Materials/Resources Needed

Copy of "The Fable of He and She." Optional: The "Fable of He and She," an animated 11-minute film available from Learning Corporation of America.

The Activity/Procedures

1. Read "The Fable of He and She" to the students. (Summary: On an island live two kinds of creatures, the "hardybars," who hunt and build, and the "mushamels," who cook and take care of the children. When the island is split in two by a storm, everyone has to learn to do everything. When the hardybars and mushamels are reunited, they share their newly acquired skills in a spirit of cooperation.)
2. After you have read the story, make two charts on the board. Label one "Before the Storm" and label the other, "After the Storm." Have students list jobs done by the mushamels and the hardybars before and after the storm.
3. Discuss with the students:

    a. How do the mushamels and the hardybars feel about sharing their skills after the storm?
    b. How do their attitudes change?

Follow-up Activities

Creative Dramatics

1. Divide the class into four groups of about six students each
2. Ask each group to practice and act out the following scenes:

    a. Before the Storm—showing divided roles of mushamels and hardybars
    b. First Celebration—showing respective contests for mushamels (cooking, beauty) and hardybars (building and hunting) and crowning of king and queen
    c. After the Storm—showing each group learning new skills

    d. Second Celebration—sharing of skills, crowning of She-mel and He-
       bar

Art

Make puppets or clay or playdough figures for acting out the story. Follow procedure for "Creative Dramatics" above.

Source

From *The House that Jill and Jack Built*. Copyright © 1976 by the Berkeley United School District.

THE FABLE OF HE AND SHE
Film adaption by Lyn Reese

    A long time ago, on an island called Baramel there lived wonderful birds
and beasts. Among them were the savage chuck-a-chuck, the fierce mushmoo,
and the wild melachuck. On the island there were two kinds of people, hardybars
and mushamels. There were old and young hardybars and mushamels and they
lived together in families. The hardybars did all the building and hunting.
    "Mushamels are too timid to face the fierce melachucks," they said.
    "Right," said the mushamels.
    "They are too soft to escape the fangs of the awful chuck-a-chuck. We
are strong, we will hunt," declared the hardybars. "Mushamels don't know how
to build houses. So we will build all the houses that need to be built."
    "Oh, yes," said the mushamels.
    Only one hardybar, called He-bar, wanted to do things differently.
    "Can't we do some cooking? Can't we make houses pretty? Put some
paint on them?"
    "He-bar, hardybars do *not* paint. That is *not* a hardybar thing to do," cried
all the others. So he didn't.
    The mushamels were best at cooking and watching babies.
    "Mushamels make things sweet and nice. That's what *all* mushamels like
to do best," they said.
    Only one mushamel, She-mel disagreed.
    "Oh, not me, I'd rather be fighting chuck-a-chucks instead of standing
over a stove in a hot kitchen all day."
    The other mushamels groaned, "She's so peculiar. So odd." So She-mel
didn't do what she wanted.
    Each year in Baramel there was a great holiday called Om-pah Day. The
hardybars went to one end of the island to celebrate, the mushamels to the other.
Each held all sorts of contests. The hardybars had contests in sawing wood, pole
climbing, and mushmoo catching. The fastest and bravest hardybar was named

hardybar of the year. The mushamels held contests too. Their contests were in gardening, cooking, dancing, and beauty. The winner, with cheers and tears, became mushamel of the year.

Suddenly, in the midst of the festivities, disaster struck! The skies darkened, the wind blew, lightning struck. Then, with a shudder and a shake—earthquake! And the island split in two!

When the storm was over, much to their surprise, the hardybars found themselves separated from the mushamels by a huge body of water. And there was no way to reach each other across that cold and swift ocean.

"What are we going to do? We need houses," the mushamels loudly cried.

"I can't hunt chuck-a-chuck, " said one.

"I can't build shelters," said another.

"We'll freeze," they all said.

Then She-mel took charge.

"Hold it everyone and stop crying! I, for one, do not plan to freeze—or starve. Come on."

Finding clay, She-mel constructed a sturdy hut. In front she planted some flowers.

"Oh, yea for She-mel," everybody cheered.

"And now, we're going hunting."

"Now She-mel, you're going too far," said an older mushamel. "Only hardybars can face the fierce mushmoo."

"Don't worry, I have a plan."

She-mel had everyone sneak up to the nearest mushmoo and surround it.

"Now, everybody sing as loud and high as you can," she commanded.

All did as they were told and the noise was so piercing that the mushmoo roared and stamped and fell over dead.

"Hey, we did it!" cheered the mushamels.

Meanwhile, the hardybars had problems of their own.

"If those children don't stop crying I'll lose my mind," moaned one. "Be quiet, be quiet! Oh, I hate little children."

That made He-bar speak up. "Wait, that doesn't work very well. I have an idea."

And he made some clever swings which held the children firmly and kept them happy. The children were happy, the adults were delighted.

"Hooray for He-bar," everybody cheered.

"Okay, hardybars, dinnertime," one hungry person called.

"Oh, dear, hardybars can't cook," was the reply.

"I believe I could whip up a little something," said He-bar. "Get me some pom-pom berries, a kettle, and dig a hole":

He-bar's first meal was chuck-a-chuck and pom-pom berry stew in peanut butter sauce. But little by little all the hardybars learned and their cooking improved.

Time passed. Hardybars and mushamels lived separately on each side of the great gap. Then one day—REVERSEQUAKE! A great force pushed the island together again. With much kissing, the two groups were united.

"Now that we're together again, everything will return to normal," said one hardybar.

"Oh no, things are going to be different. We've learned to do some new things. Watch!"

And the mushamels showed them how they built their houses.

"Wow. Interesting construction technique," commented the hardybars. "Let's show the mushamels what we can do!"

Soon the hardybars announced, "Fried chuck-a-chuck pie with pom-pom pudding topped with creamy mushmoo whip."

"Mmm," sighed the mushamels.

From then on things were different in the land of Baramel. Both hardybars and mushamels built homes, hunted, cooked, planted gardens, and tended children. And they both shared with each other new ways to do their work.

That year, on Om-pah Day, everyone was grateful to He-bar and She-mel for helping them change their ways.

"The prize of hardybar of the year goes to He-bar and the prize of mushamel of the year goes to She-mel."

"Yea, yea." Everybody was happy with the choices.

The people wanted the names of He-bar and She-mel to be remembered. So from then on they called all hardybars "he" and all mushamels "she." And so they still are called in Baramel—and in a few other places.

Source

From *The Fable of He and She:* sale, $185.00; rental $20.00 (3 days), color, 11 minutes, Learning Corporation of America, 1350 Avenue of the Americas, New York, NY 10019.

Lesson Plan 4

TAKE A LOOK AT THE STORY PROBLEMS IN YOUR MATH BOOK

Target Group

Grades 3–7

Objectives

- To use data collecting skills
- To use writing skills
- To decrease sex stereotyping

Related Curriculum Areas

Math, Language Arts

Related Occupational Areas

All

Classroom Time Required

30–45 minutes for four consecutive days

Materials/Resources Needed

- Copies of the "Survey of Story Problems in Math Books" handout
- Students' standard math textbooks

The Activity/Procedures

Day One

1. Divide the class into six groups. Assign each group a certain number of pages in the math text. Each group will further divide their pages among themselves. Each student, using the data collection form will record each story problem, within the assigned pages, which depicts only males, only females, or both males and females, and list the activity of each story problem.

    Example: Bill has 42 cents and wants to buy a comic book for 50 cents. How much more money does Bill have to earn?

    This story problem would be counted as one that depicts only males, because only Bill was mentioned, and buying comic books would be listed as the activity of the story problem.

    Example: Nancy paid 27 cents for lunch on Monday, 19 cents on Tuesday, and 24 cents on Wednesday. How much money did Nancy spend on lunches?

    This problem would be counted as one that depicts only females, because only Nancy was mentioned, and buying lunches would be listed as the activity of the story problem.

Day Two

2. Have each of the six groups select a recorder. Hand a blank survey form to each recorder. The students in each group will report the information on their survey forms to the recorder. This will result in one completed

survey form for each group which contains data for the group's assigned pages.

a.   Have the students in each group look at the numerical counts for each of the three groups on their survey form:

How many problems were counted in the "only male" group?
How many problems were counted in the "only female" group?
How many problems were counted in the "both male and female" group?

Do each of these groups have about the same number of story problems? Is there a greater number of problems in one of the groups? If, for example, the "only male" group has a greater number of story problems, then some of those story problems should be changed to depict "only females" or "both females and males." Point out that both males and females take mathematics and must make use of mathematic skills in their daily lives. Therefore a balance should be reflected in the text book.

b.   Have students in each group look at the types of activities for each of the three groups:

What kinds of activities were in the "only male" group?
What kinds of activities were in the "only female" group?
What kinds of activities were in the "both female and male" group?

Do these activities differ? Can females do the activities listed for the "only male" group? Can males do the activities for the "only female" group? Point out that both males and females can do most activities. Therefore, a balance should be reflected in the text.

3.   After looking at the data, the student groups should decide how many story problems need to be rewritten to make the number and types of story problems more balanced.

Day Three

4.   Discuss with the class the necessity of changing some of the activities of the story problems in order to create a balance between the kinds of activities in which males and females are involved.

5.   Give an example of how a story problem could be changed; e.g., change the male name to a female name, or change buying lunches to buying tools.

6.   Have each group meet and rewrite story problems to create a balance in number and kind of activities in which females and males are involved.

Day Four

7.   Have each group read two story problems they rewrote on Day Three. Reading the original version and the changed version would be helpful.

8.   Have the students turn in all the newly written problems and use these when students are working in that section of the book.

Source

The Yellow, Blue, and Red Book
Project Equality
John D. Ross and LaRae Glennon, Directors
Highline Public Schools
Seattle, Washington

Lesson Plan 5
GOING TO THE SOURCE

Target Group

Grades 5–12

Objectives

- To analyze different sources in our society that may promote and reinforce sex-role stereotyping
- To compare and contrast ways that these sources portray sex-role stereotyping
- To identify situations in which these sources influence personal decision making

Related Curriculum Areas

Language Arts, Social Studies

Related Occupational Areas

All

Classroom Time Required

3–5 class periods

Materials/Resources Needed

Copies of the following handouts:

Going to the Source: Television Commercials
Going to the Source: Television Programs
Going to the Source: Magazines (worksheet and summary sheet)
Going to the Source: Personal Interviews

The Activity/Procedures

1. Explain to students that sex-role stereotyping is taught in many ways and comes from many sources. Tell students that they will get a chance to go directly to some of these sources to see how these stereotypes are taught.

2. List "television," "magazines," and "personal interviews" on the board. Tell students to choose from these three the source of sex-role stereotyping they would like to analyze. Make certain that each of the three areas has both female and male students represented.

3. Have the students form three groups according to the stereotyping source they have selected.

4. Distribute the appropriate worksheets to each group. Give students some time to read the directions and plan their strategy for analyzing their sex-role stereotyping source. The planning groups should consider such factors as:

    Television: Who will analyze which channels? Which nights and times will be viewed? Make certain that the Public Broadcasting Network is also analyzed. Which student or students will be responsible for summarizing the group's findings? Will each student record both commercials and programs?

    Magazines: Who will analyze which magazines? Which student or students will be responsible for summarizing the group's findings?

5. Inform students that in three days each group will report on its findings. Tell the groups that they will have time to meet during the next few days, report on their progress, iron out any potential difficulties, and make plans for the summary presentation.

6. After each group has a chance to give a summary of its findings, conduct a class discussion:

    a. How are the male sex-role stereotypes in television, magazines, and personal interviews similar? How are they different?
    b. What words and phrases would you use to describe the male role stereotype you found?
    c. Were there any exceptions to the stereotype? Where were they found?
    d. How were the female sex-role stereotypes in television, magazines, and personal interviews similar? How were they different?
    e. What words and phrases would you use to describe the female sex-role stereotype?
    f. Were there any exceptions to this stereotype? Where were they found?

g. How accurately do these stereotypes reflect what you are like? How accurately do they portray males and females that you know?

h. Which do you think is the most powerful in channeling people to conform to sex-role stereotypes? (1) television, (2) magazines, (3) people you interact with on a daily basis? Why?

i. Think back to a time when one of these three sources encouraged you to make a nonstereotyped decision. Share the situation as honestly and as accurately as you can.

j. What can you do to change sex-role stereotyping in these three sources?

k. What other sources can you identify that promote sex-role stereotyping?

Source

Being a Man: A Unit of Instructional Activities on Male Role Stereotyping
Resource Center on Sex Roles in Education
National Foundation for the Improvement of Education
U.S. Department of Health, Education, and Welfare
Office of Education

GOING TO THE SOURCE: TELEVISION COMMERCIALS

Directions

Your television viewing for the next day will be not only relaxing, but also part of your homework. Watch as many television commercials as possible and fill out a chart like the one below for each commercial you analyze. If possible, try to analyze some commercials that sponsor shows for young children.

Commercial for _____

Program   _____

Main Characters	Males	Females
Physical appearance		
Personality characteristics		
Activities in which the character is involved		
If there is a problem what is it? Who has the problem?		
Who resolves the problem? How?		

Key Questions: How does this commercial promote or inhibit sex-role stereotyping for men? For women?

Suggested Activity for Reporting: Recorded Medley

If you have a tape recorder available, you might record some of the T.V. commercials that you think are most powerful in reinforcing or inhibiting sex-role stereotypes. Your group may wish to play some of these when it summarizes its findings for the class. A good idea might be to prepare a recorded medley of stereotyped and nonstereotyped T.V. commercials.

GOING TO THE SOURCE: TELEVISION PROGRAMS

Directions

View as many T.V. shows as possible and complete the following chart for each one. Be sure to analyze some shows that are viewed by young children.

Program _____

	Male	**Female**
Names of leading characters		
Personality characteristics		
Most frequent activities		
If there is a problem, what is it? Who has the problem?		
Who resolves the problem? How?		

Key Questions: How does this program promote or inhibit sex-role stereotyping for men? For women?

Suggested Activity for Reporting: Role Plays

If you wish, you may want to role play for the class one or two scenes from these shows that you and your group feel are the most powerful in reinforcing or inhibiting sex-role stereotypes. Be sure to explain to the class why you have selected these scenes and what you feel they demonstrate.

GOING TO THE SOURCE: MAGAZINES—WORKSHEET

Directions

For each advertisement in the magazine, answer the following questions.

Advertisements You Think Are Directed to Men

	Male	Female
Number of characters in advertisement		
Activities of characters		
Dress and physical appearance of characters		
Products advertised		
Advertisement's message, e.g., if you buy . . .		

Advertisements You Think Are Directed to Women

	Male	Female
Number of characters in advertisement		
Activities of characters		
Dress and physical appearance of characters		
Products advertised		
Advertisement's message, e.g., if you buy . . .		

GOING TO THE SOURCE: MAGAZINES—SUMMARY SHEET

Name of magazine _____

Intended audience _____

Total number of advertisements _____

    Number directed to men: _____

    Number directed to women: _____

List the activities illustrated in the advertisement.

Advertisements Directed to Men	Advertisements Directed to Women

Count the number of characters and the types of dress (e.g., casual, businesslike, formal, sportswear).

Advertisements Directed to Men	Advertisements Directed to Women

List the products advertised.

Advertisements Directed to Men	Advertisements Directed to Women

List the advertising messages.

Advertisements Directed to Men	Advertisements Directed to Women

GOING TO THE SOURCE: PERSONAL INTERVIEWS

Directions

Choose several different people to interview. Try to interview both males and females, and people you don't know well in addition to friends and relatives. Explain that the interview will be anonymous and that it is for a class project. Then, complete the following interview form. Read each question, but do not rephrase any. Each person will answer the exact question as well as he or she can.

1.   Sex: _____

2.   Age range:

     Under 10 _____

          10–18 _____

          19–30 _____

          31–50 _____

     Over 50 _____

3.   What is a "real man"? _____

     _____

4.   What is a "real woman"? _____

     _____

5.   What are some good jobs for women in our society?

     _____

     _____

6.   What are some good jobs for men in our society?

     _____

     _____

7.   In marriage should the man or the woman have the leadership role?

_____

_____

8.   Would you vote for a woman to be president of the United States?

_____

_____

Lesson Plan 6

YOU CAN FIGHT CITY HALL

Target Group

Adaptable to grades 1–12

Objectives

- To present findings and opinions concerning bias in books, television, or other media
- To write a letter, in appropriate form, summarizing findings and opinions concerning bias in books, television, or other media

Related Curriculum Areas

Language Arts, Social Studies

The Procedure

After students have completed the worksheets from "Going to the Source," they may feel concerned or even angry about sex bias in television, commercials, books, and other sources. One constructive way to help students channel this concern is to teach them how to write to people who publish the books and produce the T.V. shows. You will need to compile a list of publishers' names and addresses. There are a variety of books that index publishers' addresses, and these are available from a public or university library.

Review the correct form of writing a business letter with students and have this outline available for reference. Discuss with students the best way to present the data they have collected so that their letters present logical and convincing arguments for eliminating bias from television and other media. Review letters with students before mailing. Share any replies that are received, and post these on the bulletin board.

Evaluation

When you review the students' letters with them, you will be able to determine if they have used correct letter form and if they have developed their summaries in a logical and convincing fashion.

Other Ways to Fight City Hall

- Students may also wish to present their "Going to the Source" data and their opinions on sex bias by writing Letters to the Editor in local or national magazines. If their letters get printed, be sure to share them with the class and post them on the bulletin board.
- Students may want to write less formal letters about sex bias in books and television—letters that they don't plan to send. These letters, like the ones by elementary school children reproduced below, will give the students the opportunity to be angry, funny, or even a little silly. Put letters like these on the bulletin board—but not in the mail.
- Students can draw posters to express their points of view. Fourth-grade children developed the posters below. Posters can be exhibited on bulletin boards. They can also be sent to various associations and organizations concerned with sex equity (see the resource list of organizations in the final chapter of this book).
- When people care about a cause, they develop slogans that are worn on buttons, bumper stickers or T-shirts—for example, "Uppity Women Unite" or "Men of Quality Are Not Afraid of Women for Equality." Students can develop their own slogans. If you wish, you can sponsor a contest for the best student slogan on roles and rights for women and men.

YOU CAN FIGHT CITY HALL: SAMPLE LETTERS FROM STUDENTS

Washington D.C. Television
Tower Number 5
06905

Dear T.V. People,

    I've watched your shows and they make me disgusted. I hate even to see the commercials. All the women do the housework while the men advertise tools and things that are used outside of the house.

    The shows that have girls on them usually show them going to ballerina class. The boys go to football practice and things like that.

    I would really want to see more equality on your shows!

                     Your Mad T.V. Watcher,

                     Robin

Women's Liberation League
555 Minnesota Avenue
Washington, D.C.
20015

Dear Women,

     I don't like discrimination against women anymore than you. I don't like the way they don't put very many pictures in the text books.

     The children might get men, men, men into their heads.

     I was just wondering whether you could fight about this text book discrimination.

                Sincerely,

                Alison

Men Science Book Publishers
330198 Chovenistic Drive
Upstate Alaska

Dear Sirs,

        I feel that it is my duty to speak out on the subject of women's
rights in textbooks. I've recently looked through a science book of
yours, just looking for pictures of men and women. Now, I'm really
gonna speak my mind. I found 88 men and 50 women. Do you know what
an ugly feeling is? Well, that's what I get when I read your books.
I just would like to throw up. It is preposterous the way you cut
the opposite sex down. And what's more, I think that its truly dis-
gusting having 38 more men than women in a 3rd grade science book.
How do you know, there maybe another Susan B. Anthony in that class, and
when she's grown up, guess who'll be in trouble!

                            Ungratefully,

                            Joanna

P.S. I didn't learn a thing from your ever detested book!

New York Book Corporation
6328 Fifth Avenue
New York, New York 60058

Dear Sirs,

    I looked at one of your science books that you put out, just to see how many men and how many women there were in the book, and I found about four times as many men in the book as women.

    It really was not very fair putting almost all men in it. I mean they didn't do it all!

    A lot of women found out different experiments also.

                    Your Angry Reader

                    Amy

why should texts exclude the other SEX?

Women want their Freedom.......

N O W!

Not in ten years!

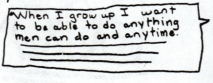

When I grow up I want to be able to do anything men can do and anytime.

Lesson Plan 7

A WOMAN'S PLACE IS . . .

Target Group

Grades 4–12

Objectives

- To write an essay with a consistent point of view
- To analyze how roles for women are changing
- To become aware of facts about women in the salaried labor force

Related Curriculum Areas

Language Arts, Social Studies

Background and Procedure

As part of the 1974 National Assessment of Education Progress (NAEP) survey in writing, 4,600 17-year olds were given the following writing assignment: "Some people believe that a woman's place is in the home. Others do not. Take one side of this issue. Write an essay in which you state your position and defend it."

About half the students said that "a woman's place is where she wants it to be"—in the home, in the salaried labor force, or combining both roles. About 20 percent said women should be allowed to work in the salaried labor force under certain conditions. Almost 30 percent said that women belong in the home. Twenty-one percent of the females and 37 percent of the males felt that women belonged in the home.[3] How do you think your students would respond to this question?

Instruct students to develop an essay on the NAEP topic. Tell students they will not be graded on their opinion but rather on how well they support their position.

Before you collect the essays, hand out "Nothing but the Facts: Quiz on Women in the Salaried Labor Force." Students can work individually or in small groups to answer the quiz. Then discuss student responses as a total class. On the chalkboard tally how the students answered the six questions. Then provide students with the correct responses listed below:

1. c   4. a
2. b   5. b
3. d

Discuss the correct responses with students. Then ask them to read their essays over one more time and write an answer to the following question. "After taking the Quiz on Women in the Salaried Labor Force I would/would not change my essay because _____." Stress that students do not have to change their essays unless they want to.

Evaluation

Checking the students' essays will provide information on their writing skills, while listening to student comments in the discussions will be indicative of ability to analyze changing roles and awareness about women in the salaried labor force. It will also be interesting to see how many students decide to make changes in their essays.

Other Ways to Think About "A Woman's Place"

If there is controversy in your class about where a woman's place is, hold a debate on the issue. Emphasize that students who participate need to do research to support their points of view.

- Ask students to bring in records and tapes of popular songs that define traits and roles of women and men. Have the students discuss and/or write essays characterizing the most prevalent images of men and women that emerge from these songs. Students may wish to try their hand at writing songs that portray nonstereotyped images of males and females.
- Ask students to list the life survival skills that both women and men need to be competent individuals both inside and outside the home. If your school still has separate home economics and shop courses, the students may wish to design an integrated Survival Skills course and present it to the appropriate school curriculum committee for potential adoption.

A WOMAN'S PLACE IS . . .

Nothing but the Facts: Quiz on Women in the Salaried Labor Force [4]

1. What percentage of women in the United States are in the salaried labor force?

   a. 20 percent
   b. 35 percent
   c. 55 percent
   d. 75 percent

2. Why do most women work:

   a. to get out of the house
   b. they need the money

c.   to buy extras
d.   to develop careers

3.   The average married woman is likely to work outside the home for

a.   3 years
b.   5 years
c.   15 years
d.   25 years

4.   The average unmarried woman is likely to work outside the home for

a.   45 years
b.   30 years
c.   60 years
d.   25 years

5.   What percentage of girls in high school today can expect to be part of the salaried labor force?

a.   70 percent
b.   90 percent
c.   60 percent
d.   50 percent

Lesson Plan 8

A CASE STUDY OF PAUL

Target Group

Grades 9–12

Objective

To identify values, traits, skills, and experiences of a fictitious individual and use them in arriving at a career decision for the individual

Related Curriculum Areas

Language Arts, Social Studies

Related Occupational Areas

All

Classroom Time Required

1–3 hours

Materials/Resources Needed

Copies of the five handouts:
1.   Gathering Information About Paul
2.   Paul's Background
3.   Paul Speaks About Himself
4.   Statements Made by Paul's Friends and Family
5.   Paul's Alternatives

The Activity/Procedures

1.   Have students read handouts 2, 3, and 4 individually, or have them read aloud to the entire class. Discuss each aspect of Paul's resume, his comments, and those of family and friends.
2.   Using the information presented in handouts 2, 3, and 4, have students complete handout 1.
3.   Then have each student complete handout 5. Have students present the alternative they chose to the class and give the reasons for their choices.

Source

© 1974 J. C. Penney Company, Inc., Consumer Affairs Department Career Development: Education for Living. Used by permission

A CASE STUDY OF PAUL

Gathering Information About Paul

Directions

Use this worksheet to record what you will learn about a young man named Paul, so that you can help him make a career decision.

Information will be given to you about what is important to him—his values, skills, talents, personality traits, experiences at work, in the home, in the school, and in his community. Begin with "Paul's Background Resume" (worksheet #2) then go on to "Paul Speaks About Himself" (worksheet #3) and finally note any other facts and impressions you pick up about him through "Statements Made by Paul's Friends and Family" (worksheet #4).

What Paul seems to value and hold important about work	Personality traits and interests
Skills and talents	Work experience in the home, school and community, as well as jobs

Other points of information that you feel are important to record about Paul

A CASE STUDY OF PAUL

Paul's Background

RESUME

Education
  High School: Graduated one year ago in a general educa-
                                  tion program
  Academic Record: Good in English, science, and math; fair
                                  marks in social studies and languages;
                                  elected courses included: shop (woodwork-
                                  ing), family life, sociology, mechanical
                                  drawing, health and driver's education—did
                                  well in all of these
  Extracurricular Activities: Ridgefield High Students for a Cleaner Envi-
                                  ronment
                                  Ridgefield Township Swim Team
                                  Intramural Basketball Club
                                  Camping

Post-secondary Education:	Attending Community College in evenings; courses in: elementary psychology, photography, biology
Work Experience:	Magic Garden Flower Shop; part-time during senior year in high school. Responsibilities: delivered flowers, assisted in floral arrangement during holiday season
	Ridgefield Recreation Center; summer following senior year in high school. Responsibilities: lifeguard at pool, assistant coach junior swim team
	Ruggles Garden Supply; full-time following summer position, employed 6 months. Responsibilities: delivery of supplies, some planting and landscaping
	Red Robin Nursery School; presently employed 4 months. Responsibilities: bus driver (drives children to and from school), handyman (small repairs of equipment and toys, cares for grounds around the school)
Volunteer Activities:	Assistant Coach Ridgefield Township Junior Swim Team, during summer and presently

A CASE STUDY OF PAUL

Paul Speaks About Himself

"So I'm 19, and I haven't got a job that my folks think is really right for me—but I don't think I'm so different from other kids my age.

My father, although he doesn't really pressure me, offered to pay for college or technical school after high school, but only on the condition that I enroll in a full-time program. My mother kind of takes my side and tells Dad "I'm finding myself," which is really how I feel.

When I graduated from high school I found myself with no clear-cut direction to take. I still needed time to explore several areas to decide what would be best for me. I've taken three courses at the local community college in three different areas—so you can't say I'm not trying. I did pretty good too.

I like my present job. Driving those little kids to nursery school has turned out to be fun. It amazes me how you look at kids differently when they're not your own brothers or sisters. But I must admit I wouldn't want to drive a bus forever.

There's a job opening up at the nursery school that I have a chance of getting. It would involve working with the children as a Child Care Assistant. Of course I'd have on-the-job training and would be required to take some child development courses at night. Mr. Patton, the director of the nursery school, assures me it's a field both guys and girls are going into, but I'm hesitant.

I have to give this some thought if I'm going to commit myself to one area—maybe I should think about the other things that interest me like environmental science—the whole plant and ecology scene interests me—must be some good jobs in that field.

One of the teachers at work thinks I'd be good working with the children, but it's something I've never really tried before—I wonder what other people would think?"

A CASE STUDY OF PAUL

Statements Made by Paul's Friends and Family

Mom:	"Saturday fishing trips and hikes were a regular thing for Paul. He and his younger brother, Johnny, were up and gone at the crack of dawn."
Sister:	"Paul's got a really good sense of humor. He's an artistic person too, although he doesn't always show that side of his personality. He used to make great-looking terrariums when he worked for the florist shop—gave me one for my birthday."
Father:	"He had decent marks in school—I wonder what happened to his ambition?—I'm sure he'd make a great architect—look how well he did in mechanical drawing."
Mr. Ruggles:	"I often wonder why Paul stopped working for me in my garden supply store. He was a good worker, even started taking on more responsibility and helped me in planning some landscaping projects. Guess he got tired of working only with me—he seems to enjoy being with people more than I do."
A friend from high school:	"I could never stand the activity of a nursery school the way Paul does. My own brothers and sisters cause enough confusion; but then again Paul's always been more organized than I am. In high school he was one of the guys who planned the intramural basketball program."

Mr. Patton, Director of Red Robin Nursery School:	"I think Paul's a responsible individual, that's why I hired him for the bus-driving job. He also takes care of the property, and repairs items such as toys and broken equipment. I'm thinking about offering him a position working with the children in the nursery school. I just wish he wouldn't wear blue jeans to work—but that's his easy going style."
Paul's brother Johnny:	"Paul's nice to me but sometimes he's pretty mean—like the time I went into his room, and accidentally broke the lamp he had made in shop class. I thought it was funny looking anyway—but I guess he was sort of proud of it."
A friend:	"Paul's a generous person. He doesn't seem to worry about expenses, but if he plans to do all the things he's thinking of in the future . . . he better start saving now."
Supervisor of Lifeguards, Ridgefield Park Pool:	"I met Paul when he worked as a lifeguard and he has helped coach the junior swim team. He works well with the kids, but sometimes forgets the important details that are required on the job."
A classmate, Ridgefield Community College:	"Paul is a sensitive person. I noticed that when viewing some of the pictures he took for his portfolio in our photography class. He has a feeling for people and a good sense of design."

A CASE STUDY OF PAUL

Paul's Alternatives

Paul has been offered the job of Child Care Assistant by Mr. Patton, the Director of the Red Robin Nursery School. As he begins to think over the decision he must make, he feels he is faced with three alternatives. Based on the information you have gathered about Paul, which alternative do you think he should take?

What information do you have to support this?

What values and needs will be met through this choice?

Are there some needs he will not be able to satisfy by making this particular choice?

What are other ways he might meet these needs?

Lesson Plan 9

WHAT'S IN A JOB: A SKILLS ANALYSIS

Target Group

Grades 5–12

Objectives

- To determine the various skills that are needed in several occupations
- To assess which jobs are sex-role stereotyped and whether this stereotyping has any basis in competencies necessary for job performance
- To analyze why stereotyping in jobs exists

Related Curriculum Areas

Language Arts, Social Studies, Career Awareness

Procedure

Write the following list of jobs on the board

computer programmer	secretary
nursery school teacher	farmer
auto mechanic	nurse
dentist	T.V. station manager
high school principal	journalist
U.S. senator	

Ask the students to write down the specific skills an individual would need to perform these jobs effectively. For example, a high school principal would need the ability to:

- communicate effectively with students, faculty, parents, and other community members
- develop school objectives and curricula
- manage school budgets
- handle discipline problems
- supervise teachers to improve their teaching skills
- determine in-service training that would improve teachers' morale and effectiveness
- schedule classes and other school events
- write grants to obtain funding from state, federal, and other agencies
- ensure school compliance with state and federal regulations
- resolve interpersonal conflicts

The students can work individually or in small groups to determine the necessary skills for each job. Discuss the skills needed for the jobs with the whole class and ask the students whether these jobs could be handled most effectively by men, by women, or by both males and females. Discuss whether these jobs are held mainly by men or mainly by women. Ask the students:

Why are some jobs held mainly by men and others by women?

Is this imbalance based on skills needed to do the jobs, or are there other reasons? What are some of these reasons?

Is it important to get more men into traditional women's jobs and more women into jobs that traditionally have been held by males? Why or why not?

What could be done to get both males and females to go into a wider range of job options?

Evaluation

You can assess whether the objectives have been met by checking the students' skills analysis sheets and listening to student comments in small and large group discussions.

Other Ways to Learn What's in a Job

Set up a regular schedule in which men and women in nontraditional jobs come into your class to talk about their work. To add variety and humor, you may wish to structure some of these visits in a "What's My Line?" format. Students ask the visitor several questions about her or his line that can be answered by yes or no. Students have a specified number of questions and a designated time allotment to guess the visitor's occupation. Or hold a career day workshop where several people in nontraditional jobs discuss their work, including both frustrations and satisfactions. Encourage these visitors to talk about the training necessary for employment and job prospects for women and men.

Hand out "Best Bet: Jobs for Women in the Next Decade," and discuss with your students. Ask the students to research the topic: "Best Bet: Jobs for Men in the Next Decade" and develop a similar sheet for men. (Your school guidance counselor should be able to provide assistance.) Have students compare the sheets. Are the "Best Bet Jobs" similar or different? Why?

What's in a Job: A Variation for Younger Students

This lesson can be adapted for younger grades by handing out "Who Does the Jobs in My Community" and discussing whether both men and women should do these jobs. When discussing this question, help students determine the specific tasks and activities that comprise these jobs.

WHAT'S IN A JOB

Best Bet: Jobs for Women in the Next Decade

According to Kathryn Stechert in the January 1980 edition of *Woman's Day* the best jobs for women in the 1980s will be nontraditional jobs—the ones that men have held in the past. The jobs on this list promise good employment prospects and higher salaries than typically paid in the traditional women's fields.

Best Bet Jobs

Accountant/Auditor
Automobile mechanic
Bank officer or manager
Carpenter
Computer programmer
Computer systems analyst
Dentist
Drafter
Electrician
Emergency medical technician
   (ambulance attendant)
Industrial machinery repairer
   (maintenance mechanic)
Lawyer
Manufacturer's sales representative
Machinist
Pharmacist
Plumber and pipefitter
Police officer
Truck driver (local only)
Welder

WHAT'S IN A JOB

Best Bet Job Resource Guide

Here is a list of places to call or write for more information on these jobs, including approximate salaries, the kind of education or training needed, and an updated forecast on employment prospects.

Emergency Medical Services Division of the Health Dept. or the Governor's Office
for Highway Safety in your state

Society of Women Engineers
345 E. 47 St.
New York, NY 10017

International Union of Electrical, Radio and Machine Workers
1126 16 St., N.W.
Washington, DC 20036

American Bar Association
1155 E. 60 St.
Chicago, IL 60637

Sales and Marketing Executives International
Career Education Division
380 Lexington Ave., N.W.
Washington, DC 20036

International Association of Machinists and Aerospace Workers
1300 Connecticut Ave., N.W.
Washington, DC 20036

American Association of Colleges of Pharmacy
4630 Montgomery Ave.
Suite 201
Bethesda, MD 20014

National Association of Plumbing, Heating and Cooling Contractors
1016 20 St., N.W.
Washington, DC 20036

National Association of Women Police
1100 NE 125 St.
Miami, FL 33161

American Trucking Associations, Inc.
Public Relations Dept.
1616 P St., N.W.
Washington, DC 20036

The American Welding Society
2501 N.W. 7 St.
Miami, FL 33125

National Association of Accountants
919 Third Ave.
New York, NY 10022

Automotive Service Industry Association
444 Michigan Ave.
Chicago, IL 60611

National Association of Bank Women
111 E. Wacker Drive
Chicago, IL 60601

> Your state's dept. of labor can put you in touch with the nearest office of the U.S. Bureau of Apprenticeship and Training.

Association of Computer Programmers and Analysts
294 Main St.
East Greenwich, RI 02818

American Federation of Information Processing Societies
1815 N. Lynn St.
Suite 800
Arlington, VA 22209

American Dental Association Council on Dental Education
211 E. Chicago Ave.
Chicago, IL 60611

American Institute for Design and Drafting
3119 Price Road
Bartlesville, OK 74003

International Brotherhood of Electrical Workers
1125 15 St., N.W.
Washington, DC 20005

WHAT'S IN A JOB

Who Does the Jobs in My Community

Think about the people who do different jobs in your community. Then read this list of jobs and circle the answer that tells who does the job in your community.

My teacher is	a man	a woman
My doctor is	a man	a woman
In my library the person who checks out books is	a man	a woman
My dentist is	a man	a woman
The person who delivers mail to my house is	a man	a woman
The police in my community are	men	women
The nurses in my community are	men	women
The principal of my school is	a man	a woman

Here are some questions to think about and talk over. Can men do each of these jobs? Can women do each of these jobs? Why, or why not?

Lesson Plan 10

LANGUAGE MATTERS

Target Group

Grades 4–8

Objectives

- To become aware of ways that sex bias is reflected in language
- To consider the impact of language on thought and behavior
- To begin developing a nonsexist vocabulary

Curriculum Areas

Language Arts and Social Studies

Procedure

Give half the class copies of the "Early Caveman: Draw a Picture" sheet. Give the rest of the class copies of the "Early Cave People: Draw a Picture" sheet. Do not tell students about differences in their assignments. When the students have completed their drawings, collect them and count the number of males and females in the drawings generated by the two assignments. It is likely that students who have been told to draw pictures of early cavemen will take their instructions literally and draw mainly men. Students who have been instructed to draw pictures of early cave people will probably draw both men and women as well as scenes of family life. Discuss how the instructions led to differences in the drawings. Talk about words that are supposed to be universal and generic— *man, mankind, he.* Ask the students: Is it important to use words that clearly include both females and males? Why or why not? Do you think language can influence how people think or believe? Give examples to support your point of view.

Generate a list of words and phrases that reflect sex bias and write these on the chalk board. For example:

1. mankind
2. the best man for the job
3. Will each student hand in his test?
4. fireman
5. policeman
6. salesman
7. mailman

8. All men are created equal.
9. men and women; boys and girls; he or she
10. man and his nation

Help students figure out nonsexist alternatives to these terms. For example:

1. people; society; humanity
2. the best (person; individual; man or woman; woman or man) for the job
3. Will the students hand in their tests?
   Will each student hand in his or her test?
4. firefighter
5. police officer
6. sales representative
7. mail carrier
8. All people are created equal.
9. (vary the order) women and men; boys and girls; she or he
10. people and their nation; citizens and their nation

Ask students to collect examples of sexist words and phrases they see in their textbooks, magazines, and other reading materials. Have them develop nonsexist alternatives to these examples.

Evaluation

Hand out the "Fair Talk" sheet and have students work individually or in groups to provide nonsexist alternatives. By checking these sheets and listening to student comments during discussion, you can assess whether the students have met the objectives of the lesson.

LANGUAGE MATTERS

Early Caveman: Draw a Picture

Imagine what life was like for early caveman. Where did he live? What kind of food did he eat? Think about how he made his weapons and cooking utensils. Then draw a picture of early caveman.

LANGUAGE MATTERS

Early Cave People: Draw a Picture

Imagine what life was like for early cave people. Where did they live? What kind of food did they eat? Think about how they made their weapons and cooking utensils. Then draw a picture of early cave people.

LANGUAGE MATTERS

Fair Talk

Try your skill at making the language more fair and inclusive. Analyze the sentences below and then provide a nonsexist alternative for each example.

1. Each teacher in this nation makes an enormous contribution. She has the opportunity to change the lives of children.

    Alternative: _____

    _____

2. One small step for man; one giant step for mankind.

    Alternative: _____

    _____

3. man and wife

    Alternative: _____

    _____

4. The stewardess will assist each passenger as he leaves.

    Alternative: _____

    _____

5. The pioneers took their wives and children and moved westward.

    Alternative: _____

    _____

6. Dear Sir: (salutation to a letter)

    Alternative: _____

    _____

Lesson Plan 11

A FINE KETTLE OF FISH

Target Group

Adaptable to grades 2–8

Objectives

- To become aware of women and men who have made outstanding achievements in various fields of endeavor
- To organize either written or oral presentations concerning these outstanding people

Curriculum Areas

Language Arts and Social Studies

Procedures

Place a large bowl or kettle in your classroom and make a "fishing pole." Simply tie a string to a stick and attach a magnet to the end of the string. Cut fish shapes out of construction paper, write the name of a woman or man who, either in the past or present, has made an outstanding contribution as a politician, inventor, labor leader, artist, author, civil rights/women's rights worker and so on. Attach paper clips to the fish and place them in the bowl. It is important that an equal number of females and males be represented and that people from different racial, ethnic and religious groups be included. Since outstanding men fill the history books, you will probably have no trouble finding enough famous names for this activity. Since outstanding women have often been left out of the books, finding the names may be more difficult. Here is a list to start things off.

Jane Addams	Prudence Crandall	Margaret Mitchell
Marion Anderson	Isadora Duncan	Marion Mitchell
Susan B. Anthony	Emily Dickinson	Lucretia Mott
Clara Barton	Amelia Earhart	Rosa Parks
Mary McLeod Bethune	Margaret Fuller	Alice Paul
Judy Blume	Martha Graham	Leontyne Price
Anne Dudley Bradstreet	Sarah and Angela Grimke	Eleanor Roosevelt
Pearl Buck	Fannie Lou Hamer	Margaret Sanger
Mary Cassatt	Helen Hayes	Rose Schneiderman
Carrie Chapman Catt	Mother Jones	Ann Howard Shaw
Willa Cather	Helen Keller	Elizabeth Cady Stanton
Shirley Chisolm	Edna St. Vincent Millay	Harriet Beecher Stowe

Maria Tallchief	Harriet Tubman	Emma Willard
Sojourner Truth	Eudora Welty	Victoria Woodhill
Sacajawea	Phyllis Wheatley	

Procedure

Each student "fishes" from the fine kettle of fish. Once a fish is caught, the student is responsible for finding out about the life and achievements of the individual named on the fish. Students can write papers on those outstanding people, or they can present oral reports to the class. Since there may only be limited information on some of these women in standard reference sources, you may need to compile a library of nonsexist reference books that the children can use. See the last chapter for additional resources.

Evaluation

Student knowledge and organizational skills can be checked by reviewing the written or oral reports.

Other Ways to Learn About Male and Female Famous Folks

- Mystery Guest

    Cut out a slip of paper for every student in your class, and write the name of a famous person on each paper. Be sure that males and females are represented equally. Pin one name on each student's back, and make sure the other students do not tell the hidden name.

    The children sit in a circle and one child stands in the middle so everyone can see the famous name on her or his back. The person tries to guess the name by asking the other students questions like: "Am I living today?" "Was I a president?" "Did I work for women's rights?" All questions must be answered by yes or no. Once the child guesses the correct name, another student gets a turn to be the Mystery Guest.

- Famous Folk Cards

    Have students cut out thin pieces of cardboard about the size of baseball or football cards. Have students write minibiographies of their famous people on one side of their cards. On the other side, they can attach photographs of their famous people. (If these are not available, the students can draw their own pictures.) Students can collect different kinds of Famous Folk cards and swap them with their friends. Remember—it's important that Famous Folk cards include equitable representation by sex and that famous people from various minority groups be included.

LESSON PLANS: MATH AND SCIENCE

Math and science are content areas that need special attention if sex equity is to be achieved. According to the National Assessment of Educational Progress (NAEP), the largest testing of educational achievement that occurs in the United States, males demonstrate higher achievement in these areas particularly at the secondary level. Researchers tell us that math and science have been stereotyped as male domains. Boys are more likely than girls to value these subjects and see them as useful to future occupations. Girls are more likely to drop out of advanced math and science courses in high school and college. In fact, math has been termed the critical filter which keeps young women from entering careers in accounting, engineering, medicine, as well as a variety of other scientific and technical occupations.

How High the Sky? How Far the Moon? is a nonsexist program in math and science. It was developed by Sharon Menard under a grant from the Women's Educational Equity Act Program, U.S. Department of Education.[5] The next six lesson plan ideas were taken from this program. If you would like more information and activities for achieving sex equity in math and science, the entire program can be obtained from: Education Development Center, 55 Chapel Street, Newton, MA 02160.

Catalog Contents

- Reading and Writing Word Problems
- Science and Mathematics in the Kitchen
- Using Tools
- Family Finances
- Locating Jobs for Which Mathematics and Science Skills Are Needed
- Lost Women of Science

Lesson Plan 12

READING AND WRITING WORD PROBLEMS

Target Group

Primary, Intermediate

Objectives

- To develop mathematical vocabulary
- To provide auditory training for mathematical language
- To develop skill in mental translation of mathematical language into computational symbols.

Activity Description

Mathematical problems are read aloud and students verbally translate the problems into computational procedures.

Materials Required

Mathematics problems, tape recorder (optional)

Instructions

1. Teacher reads mathematics problem aloud. A tape recorder can also be used for this.
2. The students identify the mathematical operations which are necessary to solve the problem, e.g. addition.
3. The students write the procedure for working the problem.
4. After some training, the students can work in a buddy system, taking turns reading problems to each other.
5. After the students have practiced reading problems, have them write their own word problems. Then follow this by having them write the procedure for working the problem.
6. Working the problem may not be necessary every time.

Discussion

1. Why do you think the identified operation will work?
2. What other operations might be used to solve the problem?

Lesson Plan 13

SCIENCE AND MATHEMATICS IN THE KITCHEN

Target Group

Primary, Intermediate, Junior High

Objectives

- To learn science and mathematics applications
- To develop awareness of science and mathematics in other subjects
- To learn that science and mathematics are part of everyday life

Activity Description

Science and mathematics are used and explained as part of kitchen activities.

Materials Required

Recipes, food, kitchen equipment and supplies

Instructions

1. Select a recipe. For the primary level, the recipe can be written on large sheets of paper using pictures to illustrate cups, teaspoons, etc.
2. Use the measurements to explain fractions, e.g. half cup; one-fourth of a teaspoon.
3. Have students note and try to explain the physical and chemical change process as the recipe is carried out and the food is cooked.
4. Introduce science vocabulary, e.g. molecules, boiling point.
5. Other activities include using kitchen procedures to experiment with chemical reactions. Shalit has experiments that can be done with soap, salad oil, and tea. Any cookbook for children will also supply some appropriate recipes.

Discussion

1. Why does water boil?
2. What does your sense of taste tell you about substances, e.g. acids, salts?
3. What does color tell you in the cooking process?

References

Shalit, Nathan, *Cup and Saucer Chemistry.* New York: Grosset & Dunlap, 1974.
Viorst, Judith, *150 Science Experiments Step by Step.* New York: Bantam Books, 1973.

If you want to expand the concept of this activity, the following reference may be useful:

Simon, Seymour, *Science in a Vacant Lot.* New York: Viking Press, 1970.

Lesson Plan 14

USING TOOLS

Target Group

Primary, Intermediate, Junior High

Objectives

- To learn the use of hand tools
- To develop applied science skills
- To enhance mechanical aptitude

Activity Description

Hand tools are identified and demonstrated. Principles behind familiar engines and machines are explained.

Materials Required

A selection of hand tools, a bicycle, automobile engine

Instructions

1. Display a selection of hand tools, such as hammer, screwdriver, pliers, etc. Name each tool, explain how it works and the scientific principle behind its operation. Demonstrate its use. (You might have a speaker come to the class and do this or make it part of a field trip. Try to find a woman who can do this.)
2. Have the students practice with the tools themselves.
3. Follow up with a unit on bicycle repair or automobile repair, depending on the grade level. This can be done by speaker or field trip.
4. In connection with the tools and repair units, teach a unit from the reference listed below.

Discussion

1. Where are the hand tools located in your house?
2. Who uses them?
3. When are they used?
4. What are some of the things you can do with these tools? What could you repair?

Reference

Keen, Martin L., *How It Works*. New York: Grosset & Dunlap, 1974.

Simple explanations of the principles of common, familiar machines, such as the telephone, tape recorder, light bulbs, electric iron, vacuum cleaner, flashlight, internal combustion machine, and ballpoint pen

Related Activities

Plan a field trip to a hardware store. Or, bring a box of nuts and bolts, wires, etc., to school and let students handle them and try them. This is a good classifying activity for the primary level.

Lesson Plan 15

FAMILY FINANCES

Target Group

Junior High

Objectives

- To develop mathematical skills
- To learn a mathematical application
- To learn the relevance of mathematics to everyday living
- To become aware of the amount of money needed for everyday living

Activity Description

The students will create a family budget, learn basic record keeping, and learn checking account procedures.

Materials Required

Pencil, paper, blank checks, deposit forms (if not available, students can make their own)

Instructions

1. Set an upper limit on the amount of money each student is allowed to spend and has deposited in the bank.

Objectives

- To create awareness of women scientists and their work
- To develop research skills

Activity Description

The work and dates of the work of women scientists are listed.

Materials Required

"Women Scientists List" (on next page or create your own); encyclopedia, biographical dictionary, or other reference material

Instructions

1. Give students copies of the list of women scientists.
2. Have students research the scientific contributions of the women and the time of the work.
3. Have students complete the list.
4. Have students include their research bibliography with their list.
5. Collect lists and identify those women on the list for which no information was found. Add the information or direct the students to where they can find the information.
6. Have students take turns presenting their findings about each woman.

Discussion

1. Where was the information about the women located? Was it hard to find? If it was hard to find, why do you think this is so?
2. Were the contributions of women scientists surprising to you? If they were a surprise, why?

LOST WOMEN OF SCIENCE

Women Scientists List

How many women scientists can you name? How many mathematicians and engineers? Most people can think of at least one—Marie Curie, who won two Nobel Prizes, one in physics and one in chemistry. In addition, her daughter, Irene Joliet-Curie, won a Nobel Prize in chemistry, becoming the second female Nobelist. How many of the following women can you identify? Do you know about their work and when they did it?

Name	Her Work	Time Period
Annie Jump Cannon		
Rachel Carson		
Gerty Cori		
Mari Goeppert-Mayer		
Alice Hamilton		
Florence Sabin		
Helen Taussig		
Grace Hopper		
Hypatia		
Maria Mitchell		
Lise Meitner		
Chien-Shiung Wu		
Lillian Gilbreth		
Ellen Richards Swallow		
Ada Byron Lovelace		
Mary Somerville		
Jane Goodall		
Virginia Apgar		
Sonya Kovalevski		

RIGHTING THE STORY: PROJECTS FOR LANGUAGE ARTS AND SOCIAL STUDIES

This section includes a variety of project ideas specifically targeted for language arts and social studies. They can be used in learning centers or developed into full scale lesson plans. You can determine how to use them most effectively as you develop your own approach to nonsexist teaching.

Catalog Contents

- Fairy Tale Sequels
- Tall Tales
- Commercials
- Interviews
- Story Starters
- Story Stoppers
- Wheels of Fortune
- Author Analysis
- Times-They-Are-A-Changin' Situations
- Out-on-a-Limb Cards
- Focus on the Future
- Student-Made Materials

Fairy Tale Sequels

Many fairy tales have been called sexist because the prince saves a stereotyped princess who is sometimes so passive that she sleeps through half the story. Ask students to try writing nonsexist sequels to the following stories:

> Cinderella
> Snow White
> Sleeping Beauty
> Rapunzel

To help students develop their sequels, ask them to think about questions like the following:

> What will the lives of these fairy tale heroines be like after they get married? For example, what did Cinderella and Prince Charming talk about? Did they have a lot in common? What kind of event might happen to get these princesses to take a more active and assertive role?

Tall Tales

There have been many tall tales about characters in the early days of this country—men like Paul Bunyan, Mike Fink, and Pecos Bill. Ask students to write a tall tale about a female main character and read it to the class. To help students develop their tall tales, ask them questions like the following:

> Tall tales are based on exaggeration; they often stress characteristics such as size and strength. Are there other characteristics that you could emphasize in your tall tale? Many tall tales are set in the frontier and in undeveloped parts of the country. Would a female tall tale character face situations or problems different from those of a male character? Why or why not?

Commercials

Many commercials on television show men and women in stereotyped roles. Have students turn the tables on their TV set by writing nonsexist commercials about:

> coffee
> ring around the collar
> greasy wax build-up
> perfume
> any other product of your choice

The students may wish to put on skits dramatizing these commercials for their classmates.

Interviews

Some people criticize our history books for focusing too much on the lives of extraordinary people and events and not telling enough of what the lives of ordinary women and men were like. Ask students to interview their grandparents, great grandparents, or other older members of their community. Then suggest that students think about the following topics when developing their interview questions. How many children did they have? How did they cook and refrigerate food? What did they do with their leisure time? What kind of toys and games did they play with? What were schools like? Medical facilities? Stores? Ask students to record the answers to their interview questions and then organize the responses into an essay about the person interviewed.

Another project for students is interviewing men and women who work in nontraditional jobs (a male nurse, homemaker, secretary; a female firefighter, physician, police officer, etc.). Students can ask questions about the following: How do these people describe their jobs? How do they feel about them? Are there special satisfactions in working in a nontraditional job? Special frustrations?

Students may also wish to interview people who are homemakers, and ask them questions such as: How do they describe their jobs? How do they feel about them? What do they like best? Least? Do they think the new emphasis on women in the salaried labor force has had a negative impact on the role of the homemaker? Why or why not? Can men be as effective as women in the job of being a homemaker? Why or why not?

Story Starters

Write a nonsexist story that begins with one of the following sentences:

"A woman can also become president," Anne insisted.

Nadine put on the boxing gloves and stepped into the ring.

Chantal Deniro stepped forward to interrogate the witness for the defense.

"I have no idea what I want to do when I get out of high school," Bernard told his counselor.

"Watch out. The rapids are below," Jackson called to Sandi, but his voice was drowned out by the sound of the water.

Donna and Miguel were riding down a deserted street in their patrol car.

The haunted house loomed up in front of the two girls.

"Look at Tommy. He's playing with a doll."

"I'm going to strike, Batman!" Batgirl was clearly angry. "Robin makes twice as much as I do for doing the same work."

Sarah checked the bulletin board and saw that she had the highest grades in her medical school class.

"Tom, we found it," called Valerie. "The buried treasure is here."

"I'm sorry we can't send you to college," Angela's parents told her. "We only have enough money to send one of you—so your brother, Tony, will get to go."

Story Stoppers

Here are ending lines for student stories. The student's assignment is to write a nonsexist story that ends with one of these sentences:

The first woman president had been elected.

Cinderella had learned that it takes more than good looks to live happily ever after.

Let's stop wasting time and get ready for the operation," said Dr. Andrea Morgan.

"You see," Tommy's father said. "Sometimes it is O.K. to cry."

Juan and Jennifer had done it. The gold medal was theirs.

"There's no substitute for good team work," Mr. Jackson told Julian and Consuelo.

Robert smiled when he opened the package and saw the new doll.

The kindergarten class loved Mr. Johnson. He was their favorite teacher.

Donald checked the bulletin board and saw that he had the highest grades in his nursing class.

Wheels of Fortune

Make wheels of fortune, like the ones below. Students spin a fortune, or plot line, and their assignment is to write a nonsexist story based on their spin. (An easy way to make wheels of fortune is to ask students to bring in spinners from discarded games. Then you simply paste the plot lines on these spinners.)

WHEEL OF FORTUNE: OLDER GRADES

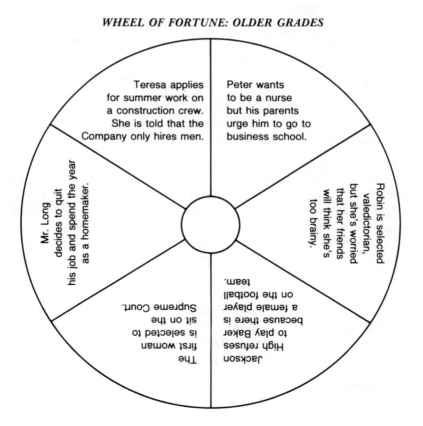

WHEEL OF FORTUNE: YOUNGER GRADES

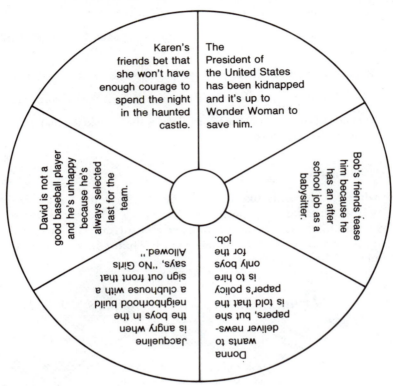

Karen's friends bet that she won't have enough courage to spend the night in the haunted castle.

The President of the United States has been kidnapped and it's up to Wonder Woman to save him.

David is not a good baseball player and he's unhappy because he's always selected last for the team.

Bob's friends tease him because he has an after school job as a babysitter.

Jacqueline is angry when the boys in the neighborhood build a clubhouse with a sign out front that says, "No Girls Allowed."

Donna wants to deliver news-papers, but she is told that the paper's policy is to hire only boys for the job.

Author Analysis

Suggest that students conduct an in-depth study of various authors to analyze their treatment of female characters. Ask students to read a variety of one author's works, compile lists of the female characters, and then, viewing the work in its entirety, write a summary or make a presentation of their conclusions to the class. One such author might be Charles Dickens. The students could read about and analyze the characters listed below and then draw conclusions regarding Dickens' views of women and how he portrays them.

Biddy   Lucie Manette
Mrs. Sarah Gamp   Miss Murdstone
Peggotty   Estella
Sissy Jupe   Miss Havisham
Little Nell   Madame De Farge
Miss Flite   Nancy
Rosa Bud

The students could discuss, debate and write about whether female authors differ from males in their portrayal of women. Similar assignments could be conducted on the portrayal of male characters.

Assign the students to investigate the "greatest love stories" of all time. The following examples could provide a point of departure.

Napoleon and Josephine	Superman and Lois Lane
Romeo and Juliet	David and Bathsheba
Anthony and Cleopatra	Scarlet O'Hara and
Duke of Windsor and Wallis Simpson	Rhett Butler
Blondie and Dagwood	Archie and Edith Bunker
Paris and Helen of Troy	Zebulon and Esther Walton
Orpheus and Eurydice	

Ask the students to write a paper on the following topic: How are females and males portrayed in these relationships? Would you consider these relationships role stereotyped? Why or why not? [6]

Times-They-Are-A-Changin' Situations for Discussion Writing, Role Playing and Improvisation

Whenever there is social change, as in the area of male and female roles, people are often confused about how they should behave in various situations. Below are situations that may lead to confusion, discomfort, and even some difficult problems. You can use these Changin'-Times Situations for classroom writing topics or role plays. They are also excellent for improvisation—role plays where students are not given a script but rather need to improvise the dialogue and what happens in the situation as they go along.

1. A twelfth-grade boy opens the door for a woman who is entering the school building. She tells him, politely but firmly, that she is quite capable of opening the door for herself.

Points to ponder and discuss:

Should the boy have opened the door?

Should the woman have rebuked the boy, or should she have walked in without saying anything?

Why do men open doors for women? Do they like to?

Do most women like men to open doors for them?

Should a woman ever open a door for a man?

Why do some women object to this social custom?

2. A sixth-grade teacher punishes a disruptive male student by making him sit with the girls.

Points to ponder and discuss:

Is this an effective punishment strategy?

How would the boy feel in this situation?

How would the girls feel?

What message is the teacher giving the class by disciplining the boy in this way?

3. An eleventh-grade girl asks one of her male classmates to go to the prom. He tells her that he's the boy and it's his role to do the asking.

Points to ponder and discuss:

Should the girl have invited the boy?

Should he have responded in this way?

Would most boys be pleased if a girl invited them out?

Why traditionally have boys been supposed to do the asking?

What are the advantages and disadvantages of doing the asking?

What are the advantages and disadvantages of waiting to be asked?

4. The personnel director tells a female applicant for a job in a large business firm, "I see by your records that you just got married. I'm afraid that we can't hire you. After we spend a lot of time and money training you, you may just get pregnant and leave. I expect you'll want to start a family pretty soon now."

Points to ponder and discuss:

How would you feel if you were the applicant?

Do you think the personnel director is right?

What assumptions is she making?

Are there any legal issues in this situation?

5. Jack invites Helen to go to the movies with him. When they arrive at the theater, he takes out his wallet to buy the tickets, but she insists on paying her own way.

Points to ponder and discuss:

Should Jack expect to pay for Helen?

Do you think Helen is right to object?

Do most boys want to pay for dates?

Do most girls want to pay their own way?

Why might a girl want to pay for herself? After all, isn't it easier to have someone pay for you?

Why has it been an accepted custom that men pay for women on dates?

6. Douglas invites Maria to go to the movies with him. When they arrive at the theater he buys his own ticket and waits for her to purchase

her own. She is amazed. She didn't even bring any money along because she expected him to pay for her.

Points to ponder and discuss:

Should Douglas expect Maria to pay for herself?

Do you think Maria should expect the boy to pay for her?

Are most boys happy with changing social customs so that they are not always expected to pay?

When boys pay, particularly if it has been an expensive evening, do they expect anything in return?

7. At a personnel director's meeting Shirley's supervisor makes the following comment: "Shirley is a very responsible and capable worker. Her background is excellent. She would be an ideal candidate for manager, but I don't know how the men would feel about working for a woman boss. I guess we'd better give the job to Dave." Shirley makes an appointment to see her supervisor. She is furious.

Points to ponder and discuss:

Is the personnel director right?

How would you feel if you were Shirley?

Do most men object working for a woman boss?

Should the male employees' feelings be a factor in the personnel director's decision, or should the fact that Shirley is the most qualified person for the job be the only consideration?

Are there any legal issues in this situation?

8. Tom and Marlene are planning on getting married. They both have excellent jobs. Tom says that when they eventually have children he would stay home and care for them when they are young. He loves to care for babies and he's a marvelous cook. He feels that Marlene's salary could easily support the family for a few years. Marlene is amazed. She had planned on quitting her job when they began a family.

Points to ponder and discuss:

Does Tom have the right to stay home and care for young children?

Is Marlene's reaction justified? Should she expect to be able to stay home and care for the children?

This is an unusual situation. More typically both parents want to continue their careers outside the home. How can this situation be resolved?

Out-on-a-Limb Cards

Concern for the rights and potential of both boys and girls has caused us to read critically and evaluate pronouncements about women that have been made. Share these out-on-a-limb cards with your students as part of a lesson or in a language arts or social studies learning center. The students can write down or discuss their reactions.

All the following statements are about women. You or your students may want to collect statements made about men and then develop out-on-a-limb cards from these.

Out-on-a-Limb Card

"Frailty, thy name is woman." (Shakespeare)

1. What does frailty mean? Put the quote in your own words.
2. Do you think women are more frail than men? Why or why not?
3. Is it possible for a person to be frail in some things and strong in others.
4. Is frailty ever a positive trait?
5. Have you ever known or read about a woman who was not frail? What was she like?
6. Have you ever known a man who was frail? What was he like?
7. How does this quote make you feel?

Out-on-a-Limb Card

"Men hate learned women." (Tennyson)

1. Who was Tennyson?
2. Do you think men dislike women who are smarter than they are?
3. Do girls ever "play dumb" when they're with their boyfriends? Do they ever purposely lose games or competitions?
4. (For girls) Have you ever pretended you didn't know or understand something when you were with a boy you liked? Why did you do this? How did this make you feel about the boy? About yourself?
5. (For boys) Would you want to go out with a girl who was smarter than you? Why or why not?
6. Did you know: Until recently, it was very difficult for a girl to become a learned woman. During the early 1800s women were not allowed into most colleges. Do some research on women and education. What you learn may startle you.

You can make your own out-on-a-limb cards from these:

Never any good came out of female domination. God created Adam Master and Lord of living creatures, but Eve spoiled all. (Martin Luther)

Woman reduces us all to the common denominator. (George Bernard Shaw)

A woman doth mischief brew in nineteen cases out of twenty. (W. S. Gilbert)

God made the woman for the use of man, and for the good and increase of the world. (Tennyson)

A wise woman is twice a fool. (Erasmus)

The education of women should always be relative to that of men. To please, to be useful to us, to make us love and esteem them, to educate us when young, to take care of us when grown up; to advise, to console us, to render our lives easy and agreeable. These are the duties of women at all times, and what they should be taught in their infancy. (Jean Jacques Rousseau)

I am one of those who believe—broadly speaking—that women are better than men. We have not wrecked railroads, nor corrupted legislatures, nor done many unholy things that men have done; but then we must remember that we have not had the chance. (Jane Adams)

A woman should not be president; it's not the way God intended it to be. Yes, a woman could become president, but she'd have to become more and more like a man to handle the job. One of our problems today is that women are becoming more like men and men are becoming more like women. That's against God's will. (Anita Bryant)

There is nothing in the world so unbecoming to a woman as a nonconformist conscience. (Oscar Wilde)

Girls need only sufficient geography to find their way around the house and enough chemistry to keep the pot boiling. (Anonymous)

Oh, had I received the education I desired, had I been bred to the profession of the Law, I might have been a useful member of society. (Abigail Adams)

Women, in general, want to be loved for what they are and men for what they accomplish. The first for their looks and charms, the latter for their actions. (Theodore Reik, psychoanalyst)

As long as a woman is prouder and happier to bring a boy rather than a girl into the world, it will be proof that woman's victory has not been won. (Françoise Paurturier)

Focus on the Future: A Brainstorming Activity

The world is going through a radical change. Alvin Toffler's book *Future Shock* captured the imagination of our society and the title literally became a household phrase. The Educational Policies Center at Syracuse notes that:[7]

- One out of three items now on the supermarket shelf did not exist ten years ago.
- Twelve years from now, 75 percent of all people employed by industry will be producing products that don't exist now.
- Half of what a young person learns today will no longer be valid by middle age.

You can use the technique of brainstorming to help students use their imagination and predict how changes may affect the roles traditionally assigned to men and women. Here are some fundamental rules for conducting brainstorming activities:

1. Encourage as many ideas as possible. Don't worry if solutions seem far out. What's important is to help students go beyond the trite and the obvious.
2. Encourage students to offer as many ideas as possible. The more ideas students generate, the better the chances of getting creative and insightful predictions.
3. Avoid making judgements. Evaluations tend to discourage students from offering suggestions; there is plenty of time after suggestions have been offered for a closer examination of the responses.
4. Encourage students to build on each other's ideas.

How would roles for men and women change if

1. Parents could select the sex of their children in advance?
2. Each female was allowed to have only one child during her lifetime?
3. Marriage contracts were for a limited period of time instead of for life?
4. New inventions almost completely replaced cooking, cleaning, and other household chores?
5. A national system of quality child care was available?
6. Children were required to attend school beginning at age 2?
7. Both males and females were required to serve in the army or some other form of national service?
8. A typical work schedule was 4 hours a day, 3 days a week?
9. Energy shortages mandated that, with a few designated exceptions, at least half a person's salaried work be done at home?

Student-Made Materials: Setting the Record Right

One way students—particularly motivated secondary school students—can confront bias in their books is by doing research of their own. For example, in the area of history students can turn to original written sources—diaries, letters, other correspondence—and can interview members of minority groups and women, particularly those who have lived through various recent historical episodes. Through such research, students can begin to write the stories missing from their history books. Emphasis would be on accuracy, and the supplementary work could be passed on to students in other classes. Such an exercise would not only improve the version of history that students usually receive, but would also help students develop research and writing skills.

Other texts could also be supplemented. Word problems in math texts typically have females manipulating numbers to buy sewing and cooking supplies and boys manipulating numbers to construct and build. Moreover, the reality of minority group life is frequently absent from these texts. Students could rewrite word problems in math texts eliminating the stereotypes and including more accurate portrayals of various groups.

Science texts also omit contributions of minority groups and women, and students, through research and rewriting, could correct omissions. Pictures in science texts are frequently highly biased, and student artists and photographers could create art work demonstrating that white males are not the only ones capable of working with scientific equipment.

Literature texts and basal readers do not adequately reflect the diversity in our society. Through a language experience approach, students could expand the limited nature of these readers and anthologies. Students could be asked to write stories—both autobiographical and fictional—that reflect their unique heritage. Again, student artists and photographers could illustrate the writing. These stories could be collected and the resulting book used to supplement the basal reader or literature anthology.

VALUES CLARIFICATION ACTIVITIES

Values clarification as initially developed by Raths, Harmon, and Simon [8] has provided effective strategies for helping students analyze and clarify their value perspectives. One of the key strengths of these activities is that they are often creative and even gamelike in nature, and they draw students into active classroom discussion and involvement. Values clarification activities help students:

- Communicate their feelings, ideas, beliefs, and attitudes both orally and in writing
- Empathize with other people, particularly those who come from backgrounds different from their own
- Engage in decision making and resolve problems and conflicts
- Formulate consistent beliefs and values [9]

The following values clarification activities pertain to the issue of sex-role stereotyping. When using these activities, it is important to remember that the goal of values clarification is not to inculcate values in students, but rather to help them in the process of clarification and analysis. Values clarification activities are most effective when they are integrated into lesson plans in the various content areas.

Catalog Contents [10]

- Unfinished Sentences
- Values Voting
- Rank Orders
- Personal Coat of Arms
- The "Who Am I?" Collage and "I Learned" Statements
- Autobiographical Questionnaire
- Twenty Things You Love to Do
- Diaries

Unfinished Sentences

The strategy of unfinished sentences helps students become more fully aware of emotions, attitudes, and values concerning sex roles. Give students a list of unfinished sentences such as those below. Have them complete them independently or in small groups. If you wish, hold a class discussion based on student responses.

Younger Grades

When I see a man cooking, I _____

The best toys for girls are _____

_____

A boy who wants to be a nurse _____

_____

A girl who wants to be a firefighter _____

_____

If a girl wants to play football _____

_____

If I saw a 6-year-old boy playing with a doll, I _____

_____

My best friends are (girls/boys) because _____

_____

When I see a woman changing a flat tire, I _____

_____

Middle and Upper Grades

I do/do not feel a woman should be appointed to the Supreme Court

because _____

_____

Ten women from our history who have made outstanding contributions

are _____

_____

Ten men from our history who have made outstanding contributions

are _____

_____

Ten women who are making outstanding contributions today are _____

_____

_____

I get upset when people say girls shouldn't _____

_____

I get upset when people say boys shouldn't _____

_____

I think a woman with young children who has a job outside her home

_____

_____

I think a man with young children who works outside his home _____

_____

_____

I think the phrase, "head of the house," means _____

_____

If I were a parent and my 10-year-old son asked to take ballet lessons,

I _____

_____

When I write a letter to a woman, I would/would not address her as

Ms. because _____

_____

I do/do not think that girls should play on football teams with boys

because _____

_____

Aggressive women _____

_____

Aggressive men _____

_____

To me women's liberation _____

_____

The thing that bothers me most about equal rights for women is ____

_____

If I had to have an operation, and the doctor scheduled to operate on

me was female, I _____

_____

I do/do not think a woman can be a good athlete because _____

_____

If a man has to work for a woman boss _____

_____

The major decisions in a family should be made by _____

_____

What troubles me most about women in the army _____

_____

For a boy the hardest thing about growing up is _____

_____

For a girl the hardest thing about growing up is _____

_____

If I were a parent and my 12-year-old daughter told me she wanted to be on the football team, I _____

_____

People admire girls for their _____

_____

People admire boys for their _____

_____

People respond to crying boys by _____

_____

People respond to crying girls by _____

_____

When a man and woman ride in a car together, the man usually drives because _____

_____

Something that worries me about women as police officers is _____

_____

Something that worries me about men as police officers is _____

_____

Drafting women for the armed services is _____

_____

If a woman earns more money than her husband _____

_____

When I hear someone use the word *mankind,* _____

_____

Values Voting

Values voting is a quick way for all members of a class to make a public acknowledgement of where they stand on a certain issue—in this case, sexism. The group is asked questions that begin with the phrase, "How many of you? . . ." After each question, participants indicate their position by a show of hands. They indicate an affirmative response by raising hands, a negative response by pointing thumbs down, indecision by folding their arms.

If you wish, you can ask students to offer reasons for the way they have voted on a particular question. Or, you can let each vote stand without discussion, representing a visual public opinion poll of the way the class feels on a particular issue.

Following is a list of questions that are important to the issue of sexism. The questions can be answered by elementary or by secondary school students. These are only a sample, and many more values voting questions can be developed.

Younger Grades

How many of you:

> Think that it's all right for boys to cry?
> Think that it's all right for girls to cry?
> Think that being a nurse is a good job for a woman?
> Think that being a nurse is a good job for a man?
> Think that boys can be babysitters?
> Think that women can be firefighters?
> Think that boys should play with dolls?
> Think that it's all right for girls to play football?
> Think that girls are smarter than boys?
> Think that boys are afraid of spiders?
> Think that girls are afraid of spiders?
> Like to help out cooking in the kitchen?
> Like to help out fixing things around the house?

Middle and Upper Grades

How many of you:

> Think that participating in sports is more important for boys than girls?
> Think that the father should be the "boss" of the household and should have the final word when family disputes occur?
> Would want to be friends with a boy who is a ballet dancer?
> Think that it's important for men to be emotionally stronger and tougher than women?

Think that a woman could handle being principal of a large junior high school?

Think it's all right for your father to stay home as a homemaker if that's what he wants to do?

Would like to see boys on your school's cheerleading team?

Have ever changed a baby's diaper?

Would like to see more men teaching in elementary school?

Would not like it if you saw a female business executive dictating a letter to a male secretary?

Think that men usually die younger than women?

Think that it would be more fair if a wife shared the burden of earning money for the family along with her husband?

Think that women make better elementary school teachers than men because they are more patient with children?

Think that a woman will never be truly satisfied unless she has been a wife and mother?

Think a woman's place is in the home?

Think that men don't like to work for women bosses?

Think that women don't like to work for women bosses?

Think that it's all right for a girl to ask a boy out for a date?

Think that a boy wouldn't like to go out with a girl who is smarter than he is?

Think that there should be more women included in history and social studies books?

Think that fathers should come home earlier to spend more time with their children?

Would vote for the Equal Rights Amendment?

Have ever changed a flat tire?

Have ever mended torn clothing?

Have ever cooked dinner?

Think that women are worse drivers than men?

Think that when a boy and girl go out for a date, the boy should pay?

Think that men should open doors for women?

Would think less of a man if you saw him knitting?

Think that being a boss makes a woman less feminine?

Think that men who have working wives should help around the house?

Don't like to call a woman Ms.?

Think that a woman should take her husband's last name when they get married?

Plan on working outside the home after you finish school?

Would worry if a woman mechanic was scheduled to fix your car?

Think that women have trouble telling jokes?

Would participate in a march or demonstration for women's rights?

Have ever participated in a march or demonstration for women's rights?

Think that men need to be liberated too?

Think that men and women should be paid equal wages for equal work?
Would be offended if your date opened doors for you?
Have ever wished that you had been born a member of the other sex?
Think that men dislike highly intelligent women?
Have ever belonged to a club that is for boys only or for girls only?
Think that if a choice must be made, it is more important for a boy to get a college education than for a girl?
Think that girls are more emotional than boys?
Think that boys should not hit girls, no matter what?
Think that it's all right for boys to use rough language sometimes, but never permissible for girls?
Think that athletics is more important for boys than for girls?
Think that it's more acceptable for a boy to fight than for a girl?
Think that it's more acceptable for a boy or man to be ambitious than it is for a girl or woman?
Think that there have been fewer great women writers, artists, musicians, and scientists because, on the whole, women have less creative and intellectual ability than men?
Think that a man's main responsibility is to support his family?

Rank Orders

Students continuously make decisions in relation to competing alternatives. Many of these decisions are minor, and are not given a great deal of thought. For example, "This weekend shall I go to the movies, go to a party, or stay home and work?" Yet some of these decisions are crucial ones, affecting significant directions. "Shall I get a job, travel, or go to college?" "Shall I go into teaching, or law, or business?"

Rank orders provide practice in making these decisions, and in bringing the reasons for them to the surface. They require participants to think about their decisions and to clarify their underlying values and attitudes.

Rank orders can provide students with insights into sexist behaviors and attitudes. When rank ordering various items, they are called upon to make choices. By making these decisions, students will have to think more deeply about the reasons for these choices.

A series of alternatives (usually three) is read to a group, and participants are asked to rank order their choices from the alternative they like best to the one they like least. The choices of six or eight participants are written on the board, and discussion concerning reasons for various choices follows.

A number of rank orders dealing with sexism can be developed. Following are some sample rank orders that can be used for elementary or secondary school students.

Younger Grades

When I grow up, I would like to be a

_____ doctor

_____ secretary

_____ fashion model

When I get older, I would like to earn extra money by

_____ baby sitting

_____ delivering papers

_____ mowing lawns

When I go to the toy store, I would like to buy a

_____ doll

_____ Monopoly game

_____ baseball

Something most fathers don't do very often is

_____ sew

_____ cook

_____ read newspapers

_____ play games with children

Something most mothers don't do very often is

_____ sew

_____ play games with children

_____ fix things

_____ read newspapers

Which toy would you prefer to get as a present?

_____ an electric train

_____ a Barbie doll

_____ a 1,000-piece puzzle

Which would you want most as a neighbor?

_____ a girl your age

_____ a boy your age

_____ no preference

Which chore would you most prefer to do?

_____ fix a broken doorknob

_____ mow the lawn

_____ wash dishes

_____ iron clothes

Middle and Upper Grades

When a man and woman get married

_____ the woman should take the man's last name

_____ the man should take the woman's last name

_____ they should keep their own last names

_____ they should make up a new last name

_____ they should use both last names to make a hyphenated name

When a girl and boy go out on a date

_____ the boy should pay for expenses

_____ the girl should pay for expenses

_____ they both should share expenses

_____ the one who has the most money at the time should pay

The kind of sex bias I find most disturbing is in

_____ job discrimination

_____ school texts, television, magazines, and other media

_____ religion

_____ attitudes of parents and friends

If there could be a special program for girls in my school, it would focus on

_____ special help in math and science

_____ career awareness

_____ girls in my school don't need any special program

If there could be a special program for boys in my school, it should focus on

_____ special help in reading

_____ child care skills

_____ boys in my school don't need any special program

It is most important for girls to be

_____ attractive

_____ smart

_____ polite

It is most important for boys to be

_____ attractive

_____ smart

_____ polite

In my school, most girls want to be

_____ cheerleader

_____ voted most likely to succeed

_____ top athlete

_____ valedictorian

In my school, most boys want to be

_____ cheerleader

_____ top athlete

_____ voted most likely to succeed

_____ valedictorian

When I grow up, it will be most important for me

_____ to have a good job

_____ to have a good family

_____ not to have any responsibilities

In my school, most girls are good in

_____ English (language arts)

_____ math

_____ science

_____ history (social studies)

In my school, most boys are good in

_____ English (language arts)

_____ math

_____ science

_____ history (social studies)

A woman who impresses me is

_____ Phyllis Schlafley

_____ Barbara Jordan

_____ Anita Bryant

_____ Gloria Steinem

If I could work to improve a social problem it would be

_____ drug abuse

_____ pollution

_____ sexism

_____ smoking

A job that I really don't think women can handle is

_____ military combat

_____ police officer

_____ business executive

_____ there is no job that women can't handle

Who gets called on most in your classroom?

_____ girls

_____ boys

_____ girls and boys get called on equally

In my books there are more pictures of

_____ boys

_____ girls

_____ there is approximately the same number of girls and boys

If both husband and wife work, who should stay home when young children get sick?

_____ always the mother

_____ always the father

_____ it depends on whose job is more important

_____ it depends on whose schedule is more important during that day

Would you rather marry a person with

_____ intelligence?

_____ wealth?

_____ sex appeal?

You have learned that you have gotten the best grades in your class. Do you

_____ feel proud of your accomplishment?

_____ feel a little worried that other people will consider you too brainy?

_____ tell other people that it was just luck and that it will never happen again?

_____ purposely drop your grades back so you don't get such high grades again?

You have just watched a television commercial where a woman is made fun of because she can't get the "ring" out of her husband's collar. Do you

_____ go out and buy the cleanser?

_____ grin and bear it?

_____ talk to other people about how silly and offensive this commercial is?

_____ write a letter of protest to the T.V. station?

Personal Coat of Arms

Give students a copy of this personal coat of arms or have them draw their own. They can answer the questions on the coat of arms by completing the sentence in words or by drawing a symbol or picture that represents their answer. After students have had a chance to complete the coat of arms, they can share their responses in small groups. If students are willing, you can post the coat of arms drawings on a bulletin board "gallery."

One way that I've been discriminated against on the basis of sex is

_____

_____

_____

I used to think girls_____

_____

Now I think girls_____

_____

One way that I've been biased toward other people on the basis of sex is

_____

_____

_____

I used to think boys_____

_____

Now I think boys_____

_____

Something I plan to do to expand roles for males and females is

_____

_____

_____

The "Who Am I" Collage and "I Learned" Statements

Another values strategy is the construction of a collage. The collage may consist of words, magazine photographs, and the like. Each collage would be built on the theme "What it means to me to be a (boy) (girl)." Students bring in their collages and share them.

After the sharing, the teacher can facilitate a comparison between the boys' and girls' collages. How do they differ? Why? This exercise requires students to think about the prerogatives, penalties, and social pressures accompanying sex roles.

One useful technique for clarifying sexist values after the collage discussions is to ask the students to complete the sentence "I learned that . . ." This technique can be used in conjunction with many other value clarification strategies. Not only does it provide teachers with feedback, but it also helps students crystallize their learning.

Autobiographical Questionnaire

Hand out sheets with the following questions. Students check the appropriate boxes. This can either be used as an individual activity or one that students discuss in small groups.

Have you ever:

Yes   *No*

_____   _____   Felt angry because of sexism?

Felt that you have been discriminated against on the basis of sex?

Been angry with a friend or parent because of sexist attitudes

_____   _____   or behaviors?

_____   _____   Told your friend or parent that you were angry?

Been upset with yourself because of your own sexist attitudes

_____   _____   or behaviors?

Written a letter to a newspaper, magazine, T.V. station, or

_____   _____   some other group or company because of sexism?

Taken part in a rally or demonstration concerning sex discrimination?

Given time, money, or effort in any way to combat sex discrimi-

_____   _____   nation?

Twenty Things You Love to Do

This strategy helps students consider the question: "Am I really getting what I want out of life?"; and further, "Is adherence to rigidity defined sex roles causing me to miss much of what life has to offer?" This strategy is effective in helping elementary or secondary students become more aware of the operation of sex stereotyping in their lives.

Students are asked to list 20 things that they love to do. When the lists are completed, they are coded in the following manner. An SSM (sex stereotyped male) is written beside every activity that is considered more appropriate for males than for females. As SSF (sec stereotyped female) is written beside every activity that is considered more appropriate for females. N (neutral) is written beside activities that are considered equally appropriate for either sex. The numbers 1–5 are to be placed beside the five most important items. The best loved activity should be numbered 1, the second best loved 2, etc. The approximate date indicating the last time each activity was engaged in should also be written.

A second step in the strategy includes each participant sharing his or her list with other members of the class. Some significant questions for discussion include: Are you avoiding certain activities because they are stereotyped "male" or "female"? Would your life become richer if you incorporated any of the other sex role activities into your own life style? Would you be willing to sign a contract to try out one or two activities you have avoided?

Diaries

Ask students to keep diaries for a week in which they record all thoughts, conversations, or actions related to sex-role stereotyping. When the week is over, the students should bring their diaries into class for discussion. Following are some questions that will help students focus on how sex-role stereotypes relate to their daily lives.

1. How did your behavior conform to that considered appropriate for your sex role? How did your behavior differ from that considered appropriate for your sex role?
2. What sex-stereotyped patterns did you find yourself following in your classroom? During extracurricular and athletic activities? At home? With your friends? On dates?
3. Which patterns of sex-stereotyped behavior would you like to keep? Which patterns of sex-stereotyped behavior would you like to change? How will you go about doing this?

ENDNOTES

[1] Marcia Guttentag and Helen Bray, *Undoing Sex Stereotypes* (New York: McGraw-Hill, 1976).
[2] Ibid.

[3] Ina Mullis, *Educational Achievement and Sex Discrimination* (Denver: National Assessment of Educational Progress, 1975).

[4] Adapted from "Quiz on Women in the World of Work," in Rita Bornstein, *Sexism in Education* (Washington, D.C.: U.S. Department of Education, Women's Educational Equity Act Program, 1981).

[5] Sharon Menard, *How High the Sky? How Far the Moon?* (Washington, D.C.: U.S. Department of Health, Education, and Welfare, Women's Educational Equity Act Program, 1979).

[6] Suzanne Hurwitz and Susan Shaffer, "Activities and Recommendations for Creating a Sex Fair Classroom," in Myra Sadker and David Sadker, *Between Teacher and Student: Overcoming Sex Bias in Classroom Interaction* (Washington, D.C.: U.S. Department of Education, Women's Educational Equity Act Program, 1981).

[7] Dean Corrigan, "The Future: Implications for the Preparation of Educational Personnel," *Journal of Teacher Education* 25 (1974).

[8] Louis Raths, Merrill Harmon, and Sidney Simon, *Values and Teaching* (Columbus, Ohio: Charles E. Merrill, 1966).

[9] J. Doyle Casteel and Robert Stahl, *Values Clarification in the Classroom: A Primer* (Pacific Palisades, Calif.: Goodyear, 1975).

[10] Myra and David Sadker have published articles on values clarification and sex equity in several publications including *Instructor* and *Social Education*.

6

The Two-Edged Sword: Men as Victims

Objectives

- To analyze the nature of the male sex-role stereotype
- To consider instructional activities concerning various aspects of the male sex-role stereotype
- To develop your own ideas and approaches concerning the male sex-role stereotype

Once upon a time, it was no trick at all to figure out what a "real man" or a "real woman" was supposed to be like. Cinderella, Snow White, and other damsels in distress were to be saved by the Sir Galahads and Prince Charmings of this world. Cinderella would never consider taking bold and independent action to help herself. Dauntless princes and knights would never express trepidation or sorrow; they were—literally and figuratively—encased in armor. Sensitive heroes and assertive heroines didn't fit the fairy tale motif. It was much simpler then. And more confining.

In today's society, sorting out appropriate sex roles is far more complex. Although many people are aware of changing roles for women, far less attention has focused on the male sex-role stereotype. Fewer people realize that men also are cast into traditional roles and are measured by how well they conform to these social expectations and pressures. In fact, one result of the feminist movement has been to encourage both men and women to reconsider the characteristics traditionally attributed to "real men," and to explore the cost men may be paying for adhering to their sex-role stereotype.

By promoting sex equity in schools, educators can enhance the quality of life for boys and girls, for men as well as women. This chapter analyzes the nature of the male sex-role stereotype. Then there are several classroom lessons to help students understand this stereotype and its potential costs. These lesson plans are not comprehensive, and they should be viewed only as a point of departure. They are meant to stimulate your creativity so that you can develop your own ideas and approaches on this issue.

REAL MEN

What does it mean to be a "real man"? Several years ago, *Psychology Today* asked its readers to respond to a questionnaire on this issue. Male readers were asked to answer questions about themselves, and women were asked to answer in terms of their boyfriend or spouse. Twenty-eight thousand people responded. To see where you stand on this issue, you may want to try the following survey yourself. Although this survey is somewhat different and quite a bit simpler than the one that appeared in *Psychology Today*, it will provide you with the opportunity to consider your views on what it means to be a "real man" in our society, and then to compare your responses with others. The answer key will give you the opportunity to compare your answers with both the traditional view and the responses of the *Psychology Today* readers.

Measuring Masculinity

1. (Men) I really feel masculine when I am . . .

   (Women) I feel that my spouse or boyfriend is really masculine when he is . . .

   a. _____ competing in a sport
   b. _____ succeeding at work
   c. _____ playing with children
   d. _____ socializing with other men
   e. _____ socializing with other women
   f. _____ sharing feelings and emotions

   (Check only one)

2. (Men) I feel least masculine when I am . . .
   (Women) I feel that my spouse or boyfriend is least masculine when he is . . .

   a. _____ competing in a sport
   b. _____ succeeding at work
   c. _____ playing with children
   d. _____ socializing with other men
   e. _____ socializing with other women
   f. _____ sharing feelings and emotions

   (Check only one)

3. How important are the following concepts to your perception of a "real man"?

		Not im-portant	Slightly im-portant	Some-what im-portant	Very im-portant	Crucial
a.	Competitive	1	2	3	4	5
b.	Risk taking	1	2	3	4	5
c.	Aggressive	1	2	3	4	5
d.	Strong	1	2	3	4	5
e.	Emotional	1	2	3	4	5
f.	Bright	1	2	3	4	5
g.	Confident	1	2	3	4	5
h.	Attractive	1	2	3	4	5
i.	Short	1	2	3	4	5
j.	Successful	1	2	3	4	5
k.	Romantic	1	2	3	4	5
l.	Gentle	1	2	3	4	5
m.	Good parent	1	2	3	4	5

4. Would you doubt a man's masculinity if he were employed in a nontraditional occupation such as nurse, go-go dancer, dress designer, interior decorator or kindergarten teacher?

Yes _____   No _____

5. Can you identify an occupation that should be restricted to men only?

Yes _____   No _____

Which one(s) _____
_____

6. (Men) In comparing yourself to other men, how masculine would you rate yourself?

(Women) In comparing your spouse or boyfriend to other men how masculine would you rate him?

a. _____ far more masculine than other men
b. _____ somewhat more masculine than other men
c. _____ about as masculine as other men
d. _____ somewhat less masculine than other men
e. _____ far less masculine than other men

(Check only one)

7. (Men) How many close male friends do you have?

(Women) How many close male friends does your spouse or boy-friend have?

a. _____ none
b. _____ one
c. _____ 2–9
d. _____ more than 10

(Check only one)

8. If there is a female-male partnership in your home, how is house-work done?

a. _____ always by the female partner
b. _____ mostly by the female partner
c. _____ equally by the male and female partner
d. _____ mostly by the male partner
e. _____ always by the male partner

(Check only one)

CHARACTERISTICS OF THE MALE SEX-ROLE STEREOTYPE

A Sporting Chance

Competing in sports is a traditionally masculine activity, but being suc-cessful, becoming a star athlete, is a medal of masculinity reserved only for the chosen few. Think back to your own high school or college days, and you can probably recall the accolades heaped upon the star quarterback or center fielder. Can you remember the instant status that came to the young woman who dated the school's star athlete? She was "in" and there was enough starlight emanating from her boyfriend to elevate her to a "somebody." For males, the taste of success on the athletic field was sweet indeed. Earning a letter in track or baseball was a real achievement. And wearing that lettered school sweater was a clear announcement of another kind of accomplishment.

The social importance of athletics has been verified in several studies. High school students have reported that being a star athlete was the single most important factor in a boy's popularity. Success on the athletic field was rated more important by far than scholastic achieve-ment.[1] Another study found that athletes feel better about themselves and have more group involvement than nonathletes.[2]

Why is the successful athlete, the "jock," offered such a privileged position in our society? Certainly, part of the answer can be found in the perception that success in athletics is related to success in life, and that both represent a test of one's manhood. In a recent study of middle-class fathers, 19 out of 20 fathers indicated that they wanted their sons to become good athletes. These fathers stated that "failure along these lines seems to symbolize . . . inability to be properly aggressive and competitive, now and in the future." [3]

For these fathers and for many others, the sports arena is seen as a microcosm of society. Those athletic gladiators who find victory and glory running between third base and home plate seem destined to win similar contests in later years in the corporate board room or on the sales force of multinational corporations. For the star athlete is competitive, strong, skilled, and a winner. These are the traits that are the core of the male sex-role stereotype. So it is a small jump from success on the athletic field to winning at work—another component of the male sex-role stereotype.

Our "Jock"ular Vocabulary

The relationship of success at sports to success at "being a man" is evident in our language. Consider the following:

Winners

The battle of Britain was won on the playing fields of Eton.   (Winston Churchill)

Winning is not the most important thing; it is the only thing.   (Vince Lombardi)

Except for war, there is nothing in American life—nothing—which trains a boy better for life than football.   (Robert F. Kennedy)

He took the ball and ran with it.   (Anonymous)

Losers

He's out in left field.

He took the ball and fumbled.

He struck out.

He went down for the count.

He's a lightweight.   (A!! Anonymous)

The Office Quarterback: Men at Work

Many of the masculine values from the athletic field are transferred to the world of work. The competitive instinct, strength, and skill of the athlete are applied to jobs and careers as men strive to become winners at work. The work place becomes the new arena, as men compete against each other for promotions, raises, and status.

For many men, work provides a single, intense focus for their lives. Wives and children, recreation and leisure—all are relegated to a minor corner. When asked "What do you do?" men describe their work. Few areas of life are rated, measured, labeled, and rewarded as is work.

Touchdowns at work are scored by long, taxing hours—which, it is hoped, are noticed and noted by the boss. One corporate executive tells how the system works in his company: most middle-level managers vie for offices with windows overlooking the parking lot. When they see their bosses get into their cars and drive home, they feel it is the right time for them to leave. They always avoid leaving before their superior. If their bosses stay late, or leave without their cars, the middle-level managers may find themselves trapped in their offices well past the dinner hour.[4]

If society emphasizes the masculine expectations of competition, hard work, and the need to win, it also provides a very tangible reward for those who fulfill the expectations—money. Success at work can be measured by a man's salary, and in many minds, a man's paycheck is also a measure of his masculinity. A man earning $60,000 a year is often viewed as more manly than one earning $10,000.

Many men enjoy their work, and this is a special benefit; however, it is a benefit irrelevant to the expectation that men should earn enough money to support a wife and family, and to support them as well as possible. "Keeping up with the Joneses" is important. "Beating the Joneses" is better.

While competing, winning, putting in long hours, succeeding, and earning a big salary are all components of the traditional masculine work ethos, not everything associated with work is considered masculine. In fact, openings in certain occupations might as well advertise "No *real men* need apply." For example, a male nurse is seen as unmasculine, unlikely ever to be considered tough, competitive, or manly. Men who wish to become nurses, secretaries, ballet dancers or teachers of young

---

Men as Money Objects

If women have been dehumanized by being treated as sex objects, men have gone through a similar dehumanization by being treated as money objects. The phenomenon of measuring a man's masculinity by the size of his paycheck is reflected in our language. Did you ever think of men as fish? Don't dismiss the idea too quickly. Maybe you've heard a story like this one!

Women cast their lines into the *sea of matrimony* in hopes of hooking a man. They *bait* their hooks, and at the appropriate time, they *reel* in their man. If he has a limited career goal and low economic potential, they toss him back. After all, there are *plenty of fish in the sea.* However, when they reel in a potential doctor or lawyer or tycoon, then that is a *good catch.*

children encounter social contempt or even ostracism for their career choice. Men in these occupations may be seen as stray fish swimming in a sea of women workers, and poor risks in terms of ever making a good living and supporting a family in style.

Avoiding Fears and Tears

Another traditional model of masculinity is the fearless, tearless, strong man who never loses his calm, cool, and collected demeanor. In pain he refuses to cry; in frightful predicaments he refuses to reveal fear. He is the solid oak, that piece of the rock that women are expected to rely on.

Early in life boys learn that being called a "crybaby" is only a notch or two above leprosy or related debilitating diseases. Boys are taught that they must suppress their emotions and exhibit a cool and rational demeanor whether confronting small dilemmas or major disasters. Research studies indicate that as early as 5 or 6 years of age, boys know that they are expected to show neither fears nor tears.[5] This emotionless, inexpressive characteristic continues on into adulthood. In studies of male undergraduates, Chafetz found that men are characterized as individuals who are "unemotional, stoic, and don't cry." [6]

But you needn't look only to the research to understand this characteristic. The unemotional man is also popular in the media, as exemplified by the strong cowboy (John Wayne), or the unflappable playboy spy (James Bond). How many other media characters, on television or in the films, can you think of who demonstrate, even thrive and grow rich on the portrayal of a hero who seldom reveals tenderness or fear?

Many men have become quite skilled at hiding their feelings and emotions. In some cases, it has become impossible for their wives and closest friends to know when they are anxious, frightened, or depressed. Sometimes emotions have been shackled so effectively that men themselves may be unable to discern their own feelings. These men have hidden their feelings so well that they end up fooling even themselves.

The stereotype for women is quite the reverse, for they are portrayed as being overly emotional. While the traditional male is cool, calm, and collected no matter what the predicament, the stereotyped woman is continually on the verge of emotional outburst, and even hysteria. One might gain a false sense of comfort from these opposing yet complementary stereotypes. On the one hand, we have a picture of a woman who, at the slightest problem, loses her composure and control. Yet this is balanced by the rational and emotionless man, ready to calm her down, himself fortified against and oblivious to his own feelings. These extreme stereotypes provide a sort of emotional "odd couple." But it is indeed an odd and unrealistic couple. All men are not stoic towers of strength. All women are not bundles of emotions. To cast individuals into sex-stereotyped emotional expectations is to deny the rich diversity of the human experience, and the reality of individual differences.

Healthy Tears

Research tells us that stress-related tears may actually be good for your health. William Frey has reported finding a biochemical in tears of anguish which is not present in other kinds of tears, such as those caused by eye irritation. Male-stereotyped behavior, which calls for the suppression of tears and crying, can cause the retention of stress-related biochemicals. The retention of these biochemicals may contribute to health problems, including peptic ulcers.[7]

The Homefront and Other Alien Cultures

It was only a century ago that the legal status of wives and children was virtually nonexistent; like mules and other property, women and children were owned and controlled by men.

Although this situation began to improve in the nineteenth century, vestiges of the past persist to this day. A popular T.V. commercial for a tonic to maintain youth and energy portrays a husband looking at his wife and declaring, "I think I'll keep you." In a very real sense, that attitude captures the traditional male view of family life.

The traditional male role divides the world into two spheres: work and home. The husband competes in the work place to financially support his family. In return, his wife maintains his life support systems at home. Stereotypic males have little understanding of or respect for domestic life and child rearing. Aprons and recipes represent an alien culture and are anathema to the traditional male role. After all, domestic chores are women's work.

But what happens when a wife also has a career? With a greater and greater percentage of women joining the salaried work force, one might assume that men will feel the pressure to abandon this aspect of the male stereotype and share in maintaining the household. Hardly. A survey in a 1980 edition of the *Christian Science Monitor*[8] reports that wives with full-time jobs still spend almost a quarter of their day on housework. The study said that in most families, the woman still does 80 to 90 percent of the housework, even when she takes on a job outside the home.

The male role not only relieves men of household tasks, but of child-rearing responsibilities as well. This process starts early. Boys are

---

I Forgot to Defrost the Meat

A recent study of the sharing (or nonsharing) of household chores conducted by Richard and Sarah Berk of the University of California and Catherine Berheide of Skidmore College revealed some interesting findings. A full-time female homemaker spends eight hours a day on housework, a woman employed part-time outside the home spends seven hours a day on housework and a woman employed full-time outside the home spends five hours a day on household chores.

Men, on the other hand, spend approximately two hours or less a day on these chores, and then use a variety of dodges to avoid increasing this effort. Husbands procrastinate, suffer from convenient lapses of memory, and claim total ignorance concerning such complex topics as all-temperature soaps, the best methods to defrost meat, and where anything is kept that is used for cooking or cleaning.

The study also revealed that these strategies are highly effective. Few women complained about the uneven distribution of household chores.[9]

---

told that playing with dolls, which might also be viewed as learning about being a parent, is an activity for girls only. However, there are exceptions to this prohibition. Dolls that kick footballs or shoot guns are viewed as appropriate training toys for adulthood; dolls that drink from bottles or wet diapers are viewed as inappropriate, as unmasculine.

These early lessons are reinforced in adulthood. Men are taught to compete, not nurture; to work hard, earn a sizable wage, and become successful in their careers. Arriving home at or after supper time does not allow much of an opportunity for the development of a close relationship between a father and his children. And in the traditional male role, a close relationship is not expected. Fathers are called upon to underwrite and support families, to apply discipline now and again, and to keep lawns mowed and the garbage removed on schedule. Given the time demands on the major wage earner, men simply have not been expected to share equally in keeping the homes fires burning, or in raising their children. In many ways, men have been socialized to view the home as an alien environment.

The Mechanical Man

The emotionless, competitive, and frequently workaholic male role has led several authors to draw fascinating analogies. Marc Feigen Fasteau compares traditional male characteristics to those attributed to machines. In *The Male Machine* Fasteau points out that men are socialized to side-track family and personal issues and focus on achieving success, power, and, of course, money. Like the wheels and gears of a machine, men function without emotions or intimacy. According to Fasteau, men are conditioned to become functional, well-oiled cogs in the workforce, and they are not taught to develop other interests and abilities.

   The male machine is also trained, schooled, and expected to understand and manipulate other machines; to be "mechanically inclined." While women are schooled and socialized to avoid close encounters of the mechanical kind, men are taught to engage in hand-to-hand combat with almost every specimen of the machine population, from dishwashers to automobiles. When man meets dysfunctional machine and fails to reestablish that melodious mechanical hum, he is labeled as "not handy," and expectations of manly capabilities are lowered.

   The link (or should we say linkage) between the world of machines and the male role is an interesting facet of the male stereotype. If time and space permitted, additional characteristics could be explored. But what we have attempted to do in this section is include some of the basic components of the male stereotype; to paint a portrait of traditional views of masculinity. From the evidence, it is a portrait of masculinity learned quite early in life.

   Hartley, for example, studied 41 boys ages 8–11 and reported that the boys understood clearly that a man "is supposed to be rugged, independent, able to take care of himself, and to disdain sissies. . . . They have to be able to fight in case a bully comes along; they have to be able to play rough games; they need to know how to play many games—curb ball, baseball, basketball and football." [10] From the early years forward, boys and men are taught, conditioned, reinforced, and measured in relation to traditional male-role expectations.

   So what? Isn't competition responsible for making this country great? Am I supposed to feel guilty because I enjoy watching those tough jocks on the Washington Redskins beat their opponents on Monday Night Football? What's wrong with the male-role stereotype anyway?

Paying the Masculinity Bill

The characteristics of the traditional male role are not all negative. The problem is one of universal expectation and intensity. When all men are measured by the same standards of masculinity, regardless of individual differences, then the male stereotype can become dysfunctional and even damaging. When the characteristics of the stereotype become overemphasized and are pursued with an unrelenting intensity, then the stereotype can become hazardous to the health and happiness of men. Consider the following costs for men who pursue this traditional and highly limited notion of masculinity.

Health

The life expectancy for men is approximately eight years less than for women. Men are more likely than women to succumb to heart disease, stroke, cirrhosis of the liver, and a variety of cancers. In addition, men are more likely than women to be victimized by accidents and suicides. Is this shorter male life expectancy due to pressures of the male stereotype, or a bad draw of genes?

It is unlikely that the early mortality rate among men can be attributed solely to biology or to socialization. But, it would be difficult to deny that male socialization is an important contributing factor to early death. Waldron [11] estimates that three-fourths of the difference in life expectancy between the sexes can be accounted for by sex-role related behaviors. For example, the significantly higher rate of male smoking may contribute to both heart disease and cancer. Men's aggressive, competitive characteristics are important factors in "Type A" or "Coronary Prone" behavior, a pattern of behavior closely linked to heart disease. Since men consume alcohol at a rate four times greater than do women, they can be expected to succumb to cirrhosis of the liver far more frequently. [12]

Men also die more frequently from external causes, such as suicides, homocides, accidents in general and motor vehicle accidents in particular. A good case can be made that male socialization pressures contribute to this phenomenon as well. Society pressures men into more high-risk occupations, underscores male toughness, and is more accepting of aggressive and violent behaviors, which lead to nondisease-related death.

Whether from disease or from external causes, statistics reveal that men are far more likely than women to die earlier in life; more likely to die in hospital beds; more likely to die on the highways; more likely to die on the job; and even more likely to die by suicide. Evidence currently available clearly suggests that male-role socialization contributes to the higher mortality rate of men. [13]

Male Anxiety

Men who differ from the socially prescribed norm often experience role strain and anxiety. A man who is not particularly competitive, aggressive, tough, athletic, or financially successful would be a prime candidate for this sort of role strain. But even boys and men whose individual traits and characteristics are congruent with the male-role stereotype experience role anxiety; no matter how hard they try, no matter how competitive they are, there is only one winner and frequently many losers. Most men who conform to the male stereotype live in the shadow of the super athlete or the very successful businessman or professional who monopolizes the spotlight and corners the lion's share of rewards and recognition.

But even for them, the few highly successful models of the male role, there is role strain. For instance, superstar athletes tell of the sacrifices they must make in order to achieve their success, sacrifices in time taken from other activities, as well as the high degree of energy and emotional effort that must be devoted to achieving success. Even extraordinarily effective and successful men experience anxiety as they weigh what they have been forced to sacrifice in order to achieve social and monetary recognition.[14]

Among the most recent studies of role strain among men is the investigation of college seniors by Komarovsky.[15] She reported that over 80 percent of the college men interviewed experienced some form of role anxiety, ranging from mild to severe. These college seniors reported that they felt role strain in their emotional, intellectual, and sexual relationships with women, in their relations with women, in their relationships with parents, in occupational plans and self-image. Eighty percent!

In short, conforming to the male role is stressful, and most men experience anxiety in their efforts to fulfill society's expectations.

Alienation

Given the characteristics of the male role, it is not surprising that men pay a significant cost in their willingness and even their ability to relate to others. The emphasis on competition leads to adversarial relationships, and men taught to suppress their emotions are also being taught that they should not communicate their feelings fully and share their thoughts with others. Male toughness requires the construction of a shield to hide vulnerability and block honest relationships and intimacy with others.

Research studies document this alienation. Mussen [16] found that men who were rated as more masculine as adolescents were rated 20 years later as less "sociable," less "self-assured," and less "self-accepting" than men who had been rated as less masculine in adolescence. Another study reports a negative relationship between masculinity and sensitivity.[17] Men are less likely to share their emotions [18] or reveal information about themselves.[19] Men report that they have few intimate or open relations with other men.[20] Men caught in the stereotype can fight and injure one another, but are not allowed to express affection or intimacy. For example:

> The main disadvantage of a male friend, as confidant, was his threat as competitor. A guy means competition. I have competed with guys in sports and for girls. Once you let your guard down, the guy can hurt you and take advantage of you.[21]

> Even your best (male) friend, gets a certain amount of comfort out of your difficulty. [22]

Career Lock-in

For many men adhering to their role expectation, work is not only the single greatest purpose for life; it may turn out to be a lifelong prison as well. Men caught in the breadwinner role may feel trapped in their jobs, unable to explore other career options. The husband and father tired of selling life insurance for 15 years and interested in attending law school may be forced to view a legal career as an unobtainable pipe dream. After all, who would support his family during the three years that he would be in law school, not to mention the time it might take to become established and financially secure as a lawyer? Adhering to the traditional responsibility of providing for the family's financial security costs many men their freedom to explore new careers. This may represent a 40- or even 50-year term in a specific career, with no hope for a reprieve or a parole.

Another facet of the career lock-in is the leisure and retirement lock-out. Some men are so conditioned to work, that they feel uncomfortable and purposeless without their work environment. Have you ever known a man who spent his entire vacation calling the office? Or a man who died a few months after retirement, for without work there was no purpose in life? Or men who spend their retirement in a state of suspended animation, unable to relate to their new situation? In fact, the suicide rate for retired men is several times that of retired women.[23]

Other Costs

Although we've talked about the career lock-in, financial pressure, and competition, we have not talked very much about all the careers men are locked out of, or at least taught that they ought not pursue. Traditional voices urge boys and men not to consider "unmasculine" careers such as ballet, nursing, secretarial work, or teaching young children. Men who pursue these careers are swimming upstream and in the face of social ostracism. Perhaps these careers are seen as not competitive enough for men, or not financially promising. Or perhaps the problem is that these career areas are simply populated with too many women. But whatever the reason, the effect is to limit the career options of boys and men.

Conventional views of masculinity also reduce men's options at home as well as at work. Because of their career and financial responsibilities, there is little time left to nurture relationships with wives and children. In fact, the typical father spends only a few minutes a day actively involved with his children. Columnist Ellen Goodman has characterized fathers not so much as parents, but as "trans-parents." As a result, a man may become alienated from his family. He spends his life putting in long hours at work to support the family from whom he grows more and more distant and out of touch.

The male role effects not only individuals but society as a whole. What impact has the macho image had on formulating the foreign policy of this and other nations? How might society's institutions, even institutions like the military, be altered if the male role was not so heavily imprinted on policies and practices? How would our society change if toughness was reduced through greater cooperation? From the Little League to the armed forces, from the Boy Scouts to political campaign strategies, the male role has helped to form and mold contemporary society, and in return, society's institutions have served to reinforce the male stereotype.

ANSWER KEY: Real Men

Although there are no "right" or "wrong" answers to the "real men" quiz which opens this chapter, you may wish to review your answers and see where you stand compared to the following descriptions:

Traditional and Nontraditional Views of Masculinity

If your responses to the opening quiz are congruent with the male characteristics described in this chapter, then your view of masculinity can be characterized as fairly traditional. For example, if you described the ideal man as competitive and successful at work (1a and b; 3a and j) as aggressive, strong, and confident, then you have outlined traditional perceptions of men. If you also suggested that the ideal man avoids nontraditional occupations (e.g., secretary), and is a junior or nonexistent partner in tackling housework, then you have underscored some additional traditional characteristics. Conversely, questions that referred to the ideal man playing with children, being emotional, gentle, highly sociable with both sexes, willing to explore nontraditional occupations, and sharing household responsibilities are indicative of nontraditional, nonstereotypic perceptions of the male role.

Did your responses cluster around traditional or nontraditional views of masculinity? Or did your answers represent a "mix" of both views? If you would take this quiz now, would your responses change?

Responses of *Psychology Today* Readers to the "Ideal Man"

There was no single trait that the readers applied to men, but not to women. Thirty-eight percent of the men and 27 percent of the women reported that the ideal man is competitive. About a third of the readers reported that the ideal man takes risks, is aggressive, and is successful at work. More than half the respondents reported that ideal men are gentle, warm, romantic, soft, and able to cry. And an overwhelming majority indicated that both intelligence and self-confidence were essential elements. The results indicate a mix of stereotypic and nonstereotypic characteristics.

Fewer than 10 percent said that they felt a man would lose his masculinity if he were in a traditionally female occupation, and about a third thought that the only occupation that should be limited to men is armed combat. About three out of every four respondents both supported the women's liberation movement and felt that men could use some liberating too! The results of this survey indicate that although readers of *Psychology Today* generally hold nontraditional views of masculinity, stereotypic male characteristics are not totally absent from their responses.

LESSON PLANS: The Male Sex-Role Stereotype

The following section consists of lessons concerned with sex-role stereo-typing in general, and male sex-role stereotyping in particular.[24] These lessons are designed to help students become aware of the limiting effects of sex-role stereotyping, and then to consider ways of reducing or eliminating sex-role stereotyping in their personal lives, and in society at large.

Each of the lesson plans includes objectives, concepts, required materials, and specific directions for the teacher. Following are some brief guidelines that you will want to be aware of as you teach these lessons.

1.   Although the primary focus of this unit concerns male stereotyp-ing, female stereotyping and sexism in general are also included. For practical as well as philosophical reasons, it is felt that male stereotyping cannot be treated in isolation.

2.   Several lessons incorporate the use of "support groups." Support groups enable a greater number of students to become actively involved and also encourage an open exchange of thoughts and feelings. In sup-port groups, students are asked to attend to and respect the personal positions of other students.

3.   You may wish to use these lesson plans exactly as written, adapt them to specific classroom environments and student grade levels, or use them as springboards for other lessons that you may want to develop. You are encouraged to use these materials in the ways that you believe would be most effective for reaching the objectives of the lessons and for reducing the impact of sex-role stereotyping on your students.

4.   Consideration of sex-role stereotyping in a classroom inevitably involves consideration of sex-role values that students have learned in the home or in the local community. For this reason, it is important that both students and parents recognize that the purpose of this unit is not to impose on students an uncritical rejection of any particular role or characteristic but to encourage them to evaluate role alternatives and to choose among them based on their individual interests and values. You may wish to share with parents the objectives and some of the data reflected in this unit in order to assist them in understanding their children's activities and to alleviate any concerns they may have regarding the purposes or outcomes of the unit. Sex-role norms and values may differ from community to community, and you will need to remain sensi-tive to the unique concerns of your community.

Lesson Plan 1

THE MALE-ROLE STEREOTYPE

Target Group

Grades 5–12

Objectives

- To identify the characteristics of the male-role stereotype
- To identify some of the problems and sacrifices that result from conforming to the male-role stereotype

Learning Concepts

1. The male-role stereotype includes the following elements: suppressing emotions, developing an intense commitment to competition and winning, projecting a tough image, and working in an occupation considered appropriate for men.

2. As boys and men try to fulfill these sex-role expectations, they encounter two types of problems:

   a. Some males simply are not comfortable with the characteristics that society says they should have.

   b. Some men emphasize these characteristics to such an extent that they become destructive.

3. Males who do conform to this sex-role stereotype encounter a number of problems that inhibit their personal relationships, sense of fulfillment, and physical health.

Materials

Copies of "The Male-Role Stereotype." Two versions are included. One is more appropriate for students in grades 5 through 8. The second is at a higher reading level and is more appropriate for students in grades 9 through 12.

Structuring the Learning Activity

1. Distribute and ask students to read "The Male-Role Stereotype." Before students in grades 5 through 8 read "The Male-Role Stereotype," it may be helpful if you review the following vocabulary words:

victim
discriminated
competition
competitive drive
insensitive
emphasis
conform

Be sure to discuss the following definitions with your students:

Role: The way that people who share a common characteristic are supposed to behave.

Stereotype: A belief that if a particular group shares one characteristic in common, they share several others as well. Examples: Jewish people are rich. Black people are good athletes.

Role stereotyping: The belief that all males share a common set of abilities, interests, and values. Also, all females share a different set of abilities, interests, and values. Sex-role stereotyping is oversimplified thinking. It does not pay any attention to the differences among individuals. Examples: Boys are good in math and science. Girls are good in reading and language arts.

The following definitions may be helpful for students in grades 9 through 12.

Role: A behavior pattern typically expected by our society of people sharing a common characteristic.

Stereotype: An uncritical or oversimplified belief regarding the characteristics of a particular group; this belief is based on the assumption that because members of the group share one characteristic, they are similar in many others.

Role stereotyping: The assumption that because males share a common sex, they also share one common set of abilities, interests, values, and roles, and that because females share a common sex, they share a different common set of abilities, interests, values, and roles. Sex-role stereotyping reflects oversimplified thinking, and it ignores individual differences.

2.   After the students have completed the reading, conduct a class discussion.

a.   What are the characteristics of the male sex-role stereotype? Can you think of examples of men on T.V. shows who demonstrate the characteristics of the male sex-role stereotype? Who and how?

b.   What are the costs of the male sex-role stereotype? Can you think of boys or men whom you know personally who are paying the cost of conforming to this stereotype? Give examples.

THE MALE-ROLE STEREOTYPE
(Grades 5–8)

When you first consider that many men now feel that they are victims of role stereotyping, you might say: "Are you kidding? Why should men feel discriminated against? Men have the best jobs; they are the business and political leaders. Everyone says, 'It's a man's world.' What are men worried about? What are their problems?"

It is true that men hold most of the important jobs, and it does seem that many men "have it made." The problem is that men pay a high cost for the ways that they have been stereotyped.

To understand why many men and women are concerned, we need to take a look at the male-role stereotype. Here is what this stereotype is about—and the costs that men must pay.

Code of Conduct: The Male-Role Stereotype

1.　*Act "tough":* Acting tough is an important part of the male-role stereotype. Many boys and men feel that they have to show that they are strong and tough. They act like they can "take it" and "dish it out" as well. You've probably met some boys and men who like to push people around. They use their strength and act tough. In a fight, these males would never consider giving in, even when this would be the smartest or kindest thing to do.

2.　*Hide feelings:* This part of the stereotype teaches males to hide feelings of fear or sorrow or tenderness. Even as small children, they are warned not to be "crybabies." As grown men they still hold back tears and keep a "stiff upper lip."

3.　*Earn "big bucks":* Men are taught that they must earn money for their families. So men try to choose occupations that pay well, and then they stick with those jobs, even when they might prefer to try something else. Men who do not earn a good living are often considered unsuccessful. In fact, men are often judged not on how kind or thoughtful they are, but rather on how much money they make.

4.　*Get the "right" kind of job:* If a boy decides to become a pilot, other people will approve of him. That is considered the "right" kind of a job for a man. But if a boy decides to become an airline steward, many people will think that somewhat strange. Boys can decide to be doctors, mechanics, or business executives, but if a boy wants to become a nurse, secretary, librarian, ballet dancer, or kindergarten teacher, he will have a tougher time. His friends and relatives will probably try to talk him out of his decision, because it's just not part of the male-role stereotype.

5.　*Compete—very hard:* Another part of the male-role stereotype is to be supercompetitive. This competitive drive is seen not only in athletics, but also in school and later at work. This competitive drive leads to still another part of the male stereotype: getting ahead of other people to become a winner.

6.　*Win—at almost any cost:* From the Little League baseball field to getting jobs that pay the most money, boys and men are taught to win at whatever they may try to do. They must work and compete so that they can get ahead of other people. When boys and men are taught to win at any cost, they may have to make many personal and even moral sacrifices.

Those are some of the most important parts of the male stereotype. When you first read about them, they may not seem to be harmful. Yet when you look more closely, you may find that many males who do "buy" the message of the male-role stereotype end up paying a very high price.

The Cost of the Code: What Men Give Up

1.   Men who always try to compete and win can lose their good judgment. Competition is not necessarily bad. Almost everyone has enjoyed some competitive games and activities. But when a man tries to compete and win at any cost, he runs into problems. You've probably seen sore losers (and even sore winners). These are signs of too much value placed on competition and winning. Supercompetitors have trouble making friends, because they're always trying to go "one-up" on their friends. And when cooperation is needed, true-blue competitors have a hard time getting along.

The next time you watch hockey players hitting each other with their hockey sticks or politicians or businessmen willing to do almost anything for a Senate seat or a big deal, you know that you are seeing some of the problems of the male role stereotype. These men put too much emphasis on competition and the need to win at any cost.

2.   Hiding feelings can hurt. Men who hide their feelings may seem to be rude and insensitive. They look like they don't care about other people. And men who are always hiding their feelings may find that they get "bottled up" inside. Sometimes it can make people feel better to share their feelings instead of hiding them inside.

3.   The heavy emphasis on earning a lot of money may also cause problems. Some men choose careers they really do not like, just because the job pays well. Others choose a job which at first they like, only later to find out that they would rather do something else. But they stay with their jobs anyway, because they can't afford to earn less money.

When they try to earn as much as possible, many men work long hours and weekends. Some even take second jobs. When men do this, they begin to lead one-track lives—the track that leads to the office or business door. They drop outside interests and hobbies. They have less and less time to spend with their families. That's one reason why some fathers never really get to know their own children, even though they may love them very much.

4.   Too much emphasis on competition, winning, and earning a lot of money can be unhealthy. Men who try to do these things may have little time left for hobbies and leisure. They may be likely to suffer from serious disease and illness. In fact, on the average, men die eight years sooner than women. Loss of life is a high cost to pay for following the male-role stereotype.

5.   Those boys and men who do not follow the male code of conduct may also find their lives more difficult. For example, some boys choose to become nurses rather than doctors. They decide to be kindergarten teachers rather than lawyers, and artists instead of electricians. Other people can make life very difficult for males who enter these nonstereotyped careers.

And some boys do not want to hide their feelings in order to act strong and tough. These boys may be gentle and sensitive people who do not fit the male-role stereotype. When any group is stereotyped—by race, religion, or sex—it becomes difficult for individuals to break out of the stereotype and be themselves.

Now you are aware of just what the male stereotype is. You know some of the problems it can cause. Think about the different ways that you, or boys and men you know, are taught to conform to the male sex-role stereotype. The important thing to remember is that you do not have to follow stereotypes. You can make choices about the kind of person you want to be.

THE MALE-ROLE STEREOTYPE
(Grades 9–12)

When you first consider that many men now feel that they are victims of role stereotyping, your natural response might be: "Are you kidding?" Why should men feel discriminated against? Men have the best jobs; they are the corporation presidents and the political leaders. Everyone says, 'It's a man's world.' What do men have to be concerned about? What are their problems?"

It is obvious that men hold most of the influential and important positions in society, and it does seem that many men "have it made." The problem is that men pay a high cost for the ways that they have been stereotyped and for the roles that they play.

To understand why many men and women are concerned, we need to take a look at the male-role stereotype.

Code of Conduct: The Male-Role Stereotype

1. *Act "tough"*: Acting tough is a key element of the male-role stereotype. Many boys and men feel that they have to show that they are strong and tough, that they can "take it" and "dish it out" as well. You've probably run into some boys and men who like to push people around, use their strength, and act tough. In a conflict, these males would never consider giving in, even when surrender or compromise would be the smartest or most compassionate course of action.

2. *Hide emotions:* This aspect of the male-role stereotype teaches males to suppress their emotions and to hide feelings of fear or sorrow or tenderness. Even as small children, they are warned not to be "crybabies." As grown men they show that they have learned this lesson well, and they become very efficient at holding back tears and keeping a "stiff upper lip."

3. *Earn "big bucks":* Men are trained to be the primary and often only source of income for the family. So men try to choose occupations that pay well, and then they stick with those jobs, even when they might prefer to try something else. Boys and men are taught that earning a good living is important, so important that a man who doesn't earn "big money" is considered inadequate in meeting society's expectations of what a "real man" should be. In fact, men are often evaluated not on how kind or compassionate or thoughtful they are, but rather on how much money they make.

4. *Get the "right" kind of job:* If a boy decides to become a pilot, he will receive society's stamp of approval, for that is the right kind of job for a man.

But if a boy decides to become an airline steward, many people would think that quite strange. Boys can decide to be doctors, mechanics, or business executives, but if a boy wants to become a nurse, secretary, librarian, ballet dancer, or kindergarten teacher, he will have a tough time. His friends and relatives will probably try to talk him out of his decision, because it's just not part of the male-role stereotype.

5.   *Compete—intensely:* Another aspect of the male-role stereotype is to be supercompetitive. This competitive drive is seen not only on athletic fields, but in school and later at work. This commitment to competition leads to still another part of the male stereotype: getting ahead of other people to become a winner.

6.   *Win—at almost any cost:* From the Little League baseball field to getting jobs that pay the most money, boys and men are taught to win at whatever they may try to do. They must work and strive and compete so that they can get ahead of other people, no matter how many personal, and even moral, sacrifices are made along the way to the winner's circle.

Those are some of the major features of the male stereotype. And certainly, some of them may not appear to be harmful. Yet when we look more closely, we find that many males who do "buy" the message of the male-role stereotype end up paying a very high price for their conformity.

The Cost of the Code: What Men Give Up

1.   Men who become highly involved in competition and winning can lose their perspective and good judgment. Competition by itself is not necessarily bad, and we've all enjoyed some competitive activities. But when a man tries to fulfill the male stereotype, and compete and win at any cost, he runs into problems. You've probably seen sore losers (and even sore winners)—sure signs of overcommitment to competition. Real competitors have trouble making friends, because they're always trying to go "one-up" on their friends. And when cooperation is needed, true-blue competitors have a difficult time cooperating.

The next time you see hockey players hitting each other with hockey sticks or politicians or businessmen willing to do almost anything for a Senate seat or a big deal, you know that you are seeing some of the problems of the male role stereotype: an overcommitment to competition and the need to win at any cost.

2.   Hiding emotions can hurt. For one thing, hiding emotions confuses people as to what someone's real feelings are. Men who hide their emotions can be misunderstood by others who might see them as uncaring and insensitive. And men who are always suppressing their feelings may put themselves under heavy psychological stress. This pressure can be physically unhealthy as well.

3.   The heavy emphasis that the male stereotype puts on earning big money also creates problems. Some men choose careers they really do not like, only later to find out that they would rather do something else. But they stay with their jobs anyway, because they can't afford to earn less money.

And in trying to earn as much as possible, many men work long hours and weekends. Some even take second jobs. When men do this, they begin to lead one-track lives—the track that leads to the office or business door. They drop outside interests and hobbies. They have less and less time to spend with their families. That's one reason why some fathers never really get to know their own children, even though they may love them very much.

4.   Many men who are absorbed by competition, winning, and earning big bucks pay a terrible price in terms of their physical health. With the continual pressure to compete, be tough, earn money, with little time left for recreation and other interests, men find themselves much more likely than women to fall victim to serious disease. In fact, on the average men die eight years sooner than women. Loss of life is a high cost to pay for following the code of the male-role stereotype.

5.   Those boys and men who do not follow the male code of conduct may also find their lives more difficult because of this stereotype. For example, some boys choose to become nurses rather than doctors, kindergarten teachers rather than lawyers, artists rather than electricians. Social pressure can make it terribly difficult for males who enter these nonstereotyped careers. Other boys and men feel very uncomfortable with the continual pressure to compete and win.

And some boys do not want to hide their feelings in order to project an image of being strong and tough. These males may be gentle, compassionate, sensitive human beings who are puzzled with and troubled by the male-role stereotype. When society stereotypes any group—by race, religion, or sex—it becomes difficult for individuals to break out of the stereotype and be themselves.

Now you are aware of just what the male role stereotype is, and you know some of the problems it can create. As you go through the other lessons in this unit, you will be able to understand and judge the social pressures placed on you to conform to stereotypes. And with this understanding, you will have a better chance to make your own decisions about the kind of person you want to be.

Lesson Plan 2

PRESSURE POINT—IT'S NOT ALL RIGHT TO CRY

Target Group

Grades 4–9

Objectives

- To identify different ways in which men suppress emotions
- To compare and contrast how males and females show or avoid showing emotions
- To be aware of the consequences of suppressing emotion
- To analyze personal patterns for expressing or suppressing emotions

Learning Concepts

1. Sex-role stereotyping encourages males to hide feelings associated with fear, sorrow, and tenderness, and encourages females to express such emotions.
2. Consistently suppressing one's emotions may have adverse effects on psychological health and interpersonal relations.
3. Individuals may have stereotyped behavior patterns for expressing or hiding emotions.

Materials

Copies of:
> "Observation Sheet"
> "Role-Playing Situations"
> "Pattern Detector"

Structuring the Learning Activity

1. Ask for six volunteers, three boys and three girls, to take part in the three role plays described below. Do not provide any background information concerning the purpose of the role-playing situations. Read each role-playing situation and instruct the students to improvise how they would behave in that particular situation. Distribute the "Observation Sheet." Students should perform the role plays consecutively without any class discussion between them. After each role play, however, tell the students to answer the appropriate questions on the "Observation Sheet."

2. After the three role plays are completed and the observation sheets have been filled out, tell the students that the role-playing situations were set up to bring out potential differences in the ways males and females have been taught to show or hide their feelings. Remind students that hiding emotions, particularly those emotions concerned with fear, sorrow, compassion, and tenderness, is a key element in the male-role stereotype.

3. Conduct a class discussion.

    a. Did the male and female in the role play "Bat" react differently to their unwelcome guest? Did their reactions conform to stereotyped

252 SEX EQUITY HANDBOOK FOR SCHOOLS

patterns of behavior? Did the male volunteer avoid expressing fear or worry?

b. Did the female and male in the role play "Baby" respond differently to the wide-awake infant? Did their reactions conform to stereotyped patterns of behavior? Did the male volunteer avoid treating the baby tenderly? Did he avoid playing with and caring for the child?

c. Did the female and male volunteer in the role play "Love Story" respond differently to the sad movie? Did their reactions conform to stereotyped patterns of behavior? Did the male volunteer avoid crying? Did he express his feelings in other ways?

d. What are some words or phrases that encourage you to hide your feelings? (To the teacher: Examples might be: "Keep cool"; "Keep a stiff upper lip"; "Act your age—don't cry"; "Only sissies cry.") Are these expressions used more often with boys than with girls?

e. What are some of the positive consequences of hiding your feelings? (To the teacher: Some points to bring out include: Other people will think you're in charge of the situation if you hide your feelings. People may learn to rely on you and look to you for leadership).

f. What are some of the negative consequences of hiding your feelings? (To the teacher: Some points to bring out include: When you hide your real feelings, you are not communicating openly and honestly with others. Suppressing your feelings can be a severe psychological burden. When you consistently hide your emotions, you may lose touch with how you really feel about things. Others may regard you as cold and lacking compassion.)

4. Distribute "Pattern Detector." Ask students to fill out the pattern detector as accurately and honestly as they can.

5. Divide the class into support groups of no more than five students to a group. Tell students that a support group is a place where students can express their reactions and where other members of the group show their respect for each individual by listening carefully and attentively. If a student does not want to share any of the responses, he or she always has the option to pass. After students have shared reactions in their support groups, tell students to think about their responses and to consider whether they have a pattern of hiding or expressing their feelings and whether this is a pattern they would like to keep or to change.

ROLE-PLAYING SITUATIONS

"Bat"

It is the beginning of summer, and Miguel and Sharlene take a trip to their family's summer camp. It has been unused all winter, and they begin to get it ready for the summer season. They go upstairs to the attic to air it out when something flies past them. The "something" is a large bat.

"Baby"

Kim and Paul are at home watching television when a neighbor knocks at the door holding a 6-month-old sleeping infant. The neighbor tells them that she has run out of milk for the baby and must drive to a nearby shopping center to buy the milk and other groceries. She asks Kim and Paul if they will watch the baby for a few minutes until she returns. The neighbor assures them that the baby should sleep for at least another hour, but as soon as the neighbor leaves the baby wakes up.

"Love Story"

Maria and Raymond buy tickets for the movie "Love Story." The picture starts out promisingly enough as two college students, played by Ali McGraw and Ryan O'Neal, fall in love, get married, and begin to build their life together. However, the couple learns that Ali McGraw is suffering from an incurable illness and does not have long to live.

OBSERVATION SHEET

Role Play: "Bat"

How did Miguel act when he discovered the bat? _____
_____
How do you think he felt? _____
_____
How did Sharlene behave when she discovered the bat? _____
_____
How do you think she felt? _____
_____

Role Play: "Baby"

How did Kim behave when the baby woke up? _____
_____
How do you think she felt? _____
_____
How did Paul behave when the baby woke up? _____
_____
How do you think he felt? _____
_____

Role Play: "Love Story"

How did Maria behave as she watched the movie "Love Story"? _____
_____

How do you think she felt? _____

How did Raymond behave as he watched the movie "Love Story"? _____
_____

How do you think he felt? _____
_____

PATTERN DETECTOR

Here are some questions that ask you to remember how you felt and how you behaved in various situations. Think back and try to remember each situation as vividly and as clearly as possible. Think about how you felt in the situation and how you acted. When you describe your feelings and actions, try to be as specific as you can.

Situation	I felt	I acted

1. The last time I was worried was when _____
_____
_____

2. The last time I was scared was when _____
_____
_____

3. The last time I was really proud of something I did

was when _____
_____
_____

4. The last time I felt very sad was when _____
_____
_____

5. The last time someone came to me with his or her

troubles was when _____

_____

_____

6. The last time I spent time with a small child was

when _____

_____

_____

7. The last time I was worried about my ability to ac-

complish a job or assignment was when _____

_____

_____

8. The last time I talked about my feelings with some-

one was when _____

_____

_____

Lesson Plan 3

PRESSURE POINT—WINNING

Target Group

Grades 5–10

Objectives

- To analyze ways in which there is heavy pressure on males to compete and win

●   To evaluate the positive and negative aspects of this pressure to compete and win

Learning Concepts

1.   Being a winner is a key element of the male sex-role stereotype.
2.   There are negative as well as positive aspects to competition when there is a heavy stress on winning.

Materials

Copies of "Championship Game"

Structuring the Learning Activity

1.   Remind students that "beating the other guy" and being a winner is a key element of the male sex-role stereotype. Suggest that males are pressured to be winners in athletic competitions.

2.   Distribute and read "Championship Game." Tell the students to write an ending for the story.

3.   Ask several students who completed their stories so that Jimmy won the game for the team to read their endings to the class. Ask several students who finished their stories so that Jimmy and his team lost the game to read their endings to the class. Ask any students who finished their stories so that there were no winners or losers to read their endings to the class.

4.   After several endings have been shared, conduct a class discussion.

a.   How will Jimmy feel if he wins the game for Cony High? How will he be treated by his classmates? How will members of the Monroe team feel?

b.   How will Jimmy feel if he loses the game for Cony High? How will he be treated by his classmates? How will members of the Monroe team feel?

c.   Have you ever participated in an athletic event when the outcome of the game depended on you? Did you win or lose for your team? How did you feel about it?

d.   Is being a winner in sports as important for girls as it is for boys? Why or why not?

e.   In what other areas besides sports is there pressure on boys to be winners?

f.   In what areas is there pressure on girls to be winners?

g.   Have you ever felt the pressure to win and compete in areas other than sports? When? Who put the pressure on you?

5.   Ask students to think about the class discussion on the "Championship Game" and about competing and winning in general. Write these two personal opinion statements on the board and ask students to complete them in writing:

I think the best things about competition are _____

_____

_____

_____

I think the worst things about competition are _____

_____

_____

_____

Ask several of the students to read their personal opinion statements to the class. On the board, compile two lists, one including the negative aspects of competition, the other including the positive aspects of competition.
(To the teacher: Depending on the thoughtfulness of student response, you may want to introduce or emphasize the following positive and negative points about competition in class discussion.)

  a. *Positive aspects:* Competition can encourage people to achieve to their fullest potential. It helps to identify individuals who are particularly talented and competent. Competition offers a way of rewarding people who do a particularly good job. It can also lend an element of excitement and adventure to athletics and other activities.

  b. *Negative aspects:* When someone is driven to compete intensely and to be a winner at all costs, important parts of that person's character and lifestyle may be sacrificed. This kind of competitive pressure can make people anxious and unhappy. If someone is consistently a loser rather than a winner, this person can develop bad feelings about him/herself, and may even give up trying to achieve at all. There are times when competition can get in the way of cooperation, and instead of encouraging achievement, it can hamper it.

6. Here are some other questions for class discussion:

  a. Do you want to be a person who competes intensely? Do you want to be the best at whatever you try to do? What are the good points about being this kind of competitor? What are the costs of being this kind of competitor?

  b. Is there a way of keeping the good things about competition and getting rid of the bad aspects of competition?

   c. The well-known football coach, Vince Lombardi, has said: "Winning
       is not the most important thing. It's the only thing." Do you agree
       with this statement? What would be the positive aspects of that attitude
       toward winning? What would be the negative aspects of that attitude
       toward winning? In our society, does this kind of pressure to win
       apply more to males than to females? Why or why not?
   d. For the most part, would you rather participate in activities in which
       winning is important or in activities in which winning is not important?
       Why?

Follow-up Activity

1.   Tell the students to make a list of all the games they can think of in
which winning is important. Tell them to make another list that includes all the
games they can think of in which winning is not important. Conduct a discussion
about which list is longer and why.

2.   In all likelihood, the list in which winning is important will be longer because
most of our games are structured so that there will be winners and losers. Tell
the students to work individually or get together in small groups to see if they
can develop an interesting game in which there are no winners and no losers.
Have students play some of these loserless games and discuss whether or not
they were interesting and enjoyable.

CHAMPIONSHIP GAME

Instructions: Read this story and then write an ending for it.

It is the championship basketball game between Cony High and Monroe High,
two teams who have been traditional rivals for many years. The score is 88 to
87 in favor of Monroe, when the ball is passed to Jimmy Jones, Cony's star
player. Jimmy knows that, with only a few seconds left to play, the game's outcome
rests with him. In one corner of his mind, he hears the Cony cheerleaders shouting
encouragement, and the noise from the bleachers seems to be deafening. Then
the noise and the cheering fade into the background. Jimmy takes aim and lets
the ball go. The overflow crowd is suddenly quiet as the ball hovers on the
basket and then _____

_____

_____

_____

_____

_____

_____

_____

_____

_____

_____

_____

_____

_____

_____

_____

_____

Lesson Plan 4

PRESSURE POINT—ACTING TOUGH

Target Group

Grades 5–10

Objectives

- To identify different ways in which men act tough
- To analyze personal behavior patterns for elements of this acting-tough syndrome

- To identify elements of the acting-tough syndrome in various societal institutions
- To identify some of the consequences of acting tough

Learning Concepts

1. In each individual there may be elements of the acting-tough syndrome.
2. The acting-tough syndrome affects the direction of many societal institutions.
3. Acting tough may have adverse consequences on one's personal well-being and the well-being of others.

Materials

Copies of:

> "Tough Guys"
> Several copies of newspapers or news magazines

Structuring the Learning Activity

1. Remind students that acting tough is a key element of the male-role stereotype. It involves making a big show of one's strength, toughness, and ability to dominate others. It also involves "taking it," refusing to give in even when capitulation would be the most rational and humane course of action.

2. Distribute "Tough Guys." Tell students to read the brief story and then write their answers to the questions following the story.

3. Conduct a class discussion. Ask students to share their answers to questions 1 to 5. Depending on the thoughtfulness of student response, you might want to bring out the following points when discussing question 2; key elements of "acting tough" in this story are:

a. laying claim to one's own territory or turf
b. throwing weight around; trying to boss and dominate others
c. projecting a machismo image; acting strong and tough
d. using violent means to solve a problem
e. making no attempt to resolve conflict peacefully
f. being able to "take it"; refusing to give in even when capitulation is the most rational and humane course of action
g. trying to "dish out" worse than you get; seeking revenge

4. Tell students to break up into their support groups and share their response to question 6 in these small groups. Remind the class that a support group is a place where students get a chance to share their experiences and express their reactions. It is important for support group members to listen attentively to each other and respect one another's contributions. Also, remind students that they always have the option to pass if they so wish.

5. After students have had a chance to share their experiences in their support groups, tell them to think about how female responses may have differed from male responses. Also, tell them to think about how they might want to change any elements of acting tough in their own personal behavior patterns.

6. Distribute a newspaper or news magazine to each support group. Tell students that many people who have important roles in society frequently demonstrate elements of acting tough. Ask students to skim the paper or magazine and to identify two examples of local, state, national, or world leaders acting tough. Students should clip or copy these examples.

7. Ask each group to share their examples with the class. They should discuss the following questions:

    a. In what way do these quotes demonstrate elements of acting tough?
    b. How might events have turned out differently if people had not been so concerned about acting tough?
    c. In what other areas of society do people demonstrate "acting tough"? If possible, give specific examples.

8. Ask students to collect pictures and quotes of people in politics, business, sports, the military, the media, and other areas that demonstrate elements of the acting-tough syndrome. Post these on the "Tough Guys" bulletin board.

TOUGH GUYS

Harry Conn and a group of his friends were heading to the empty lot behind the Eastern Avenue apartments for an afterschool baseball game. They were used to practicing on the field every day, so they were surprised to see that it was already occupied. Jimmy Nagel and a group of boys from a neighboring high school were already in the middle of a game.

"Hey, what are you doing on this field?" Harry shouted. "This our turf—so buzz off."

"You got a deed of ownership?" Jimmy and his friends laughed. "Anyway," Jimmy continued, "possession is nine-tenths of the law. We're here—and we're staying."

"You creeps!" Harry was getting really angry now. "You better clear out now if you know what's good for you. This is our final warning."

Jimmy, not moving from the pitcher's mound where he was stationed, called back, "Sounds to me like all bark and no bite. You want us to get off, huh? Well then, make us!"

Harry and his friends could not let that kind of challenge go by. They moved onto the baseball field, and Harry headed straight for Jimmy Nagel. Harry was a good deal taller than Jimmy, and he figured his opponent would be a pushover. Consequently he was amazed to find himself, only a few minutes later, flat on his back, Jimmy on top of him, pinning his arms to the ground.

"O.K., punk," Jimmy taunted. "I guess this proves who has the right to this field. Now be a good boy and say 'uncle,' and I might let you up."

More than anything, Harry wanted to get free of Jimmy's hold, and get him back. "Make me," he muttered.

"You asked for it." Jimmy gave a quick sharp turn to Harry's wrist. "Say 'uncle.' "

Harry shut his eyes, and said nothing. He gritted his teeth and pretended as hard as he could that he was somewhere else.

"C'mon, say 'uncle.' " Another sharp turn to the wrist.

Harry felt like he was entering a deep well of pain. "Make me."

Jimmy was getting restless. He was also getting a little worried about doing any serious damage to the boy pinned beneath him. "O.K., punk. I'm gonna let you go this time. But watch out when you see Jimmy Nagel coming because next time you may not be so lucky."

Harry, his clothes torn and his eye swollen closed, wanted nothing more than to slip into the house unnoticed that evening. As luck would have it, he almost walked smack into his father coming home late from work.

"Whew . . . ," his father gave a long, slow whistle. "Must've been some brawl. Boy, I'd sure like to see the other guy. Just as long as you gave better than you got, son. That's all that matters."

1. How do you think Harry responded to his father? Write down his answer.

_____

_____

2. There are many elements of "acting tough" in this scene. List as many of these elements as you can. _____

_____

_____

_____

3. How might this conflict have been avoided? Rewrite the dialogue at a point where the fight could have been stopped. _____

_____

_____

4. Were there positive payoffs for acting tough? _____

_____

_____

_____

5. Do girls ever act tough? If so, in what kinds of situation? _____

_____

_____

_____

6. Think back to the last time you were a "tough guy" or a "tough girl." Then complete the following sentences as honestly and as accurately as you can.
   The last time I acted tough was when _____

_____

_____

_____

   If I could live that situation over again, I would/would not act differently because _____

_____

_____

_____

Lesson Plan 5:

OPPORTUNITY KNOCKS: A GAME FOR OVERCOMING STEREOTYPES

Target Group

Grades 5–12

Objectives

- To review some examples of sex-stereotyped situations
- To consider examples of individual actions that may be taken to counteract sex-role stereotyping

Learning Concepts

(Note: In addition to the concepts listed below, this lesson is a summarizing activity and serves to review several of the concepts of previous lessons.)

1. In contemporary society, there are numerous pressures that encourage and reinforce sex-role stereotypes.

29 OPPORTUNITY KNOCKS	28 SUMMER CAMP FREE * SPACE	27 GO BACK ONE SPACE	26 PRESSURE POINT	25 SHORT CUT	24 PRESSURE POINT	23 PRESSURE POINT	22 OPPORTUNITY KNOCKS	21 GYM FREE * SPACE	20 OPPORTUNITY KNOCKS
30 PRESSURE POINT									

31 OPPORTUNITY KNOCKS
32 EARLY PROMOTION ← GO AHEAD
33 DETENTION HALL ←
34 PRESSURE POINT — GO BACK

START

35 OPPORTUNITY KNOCKS	37 AFTER SCHOOL CLUB FREE * SPACE	38 PRESSURE POINT	39 OPPORTUNITY KNOCKS	40 PRESSURE POINT	41 OPPORTUNITY KNOCKS	42 LONG CUT	43 COUN-SELOR'S OFFICE FREE * SPACE	44 PRESSURE POINT	45 OPPORTUNITY KNOCKS
36 SUMMER JOB FREE * SPACE									

2. In order to resist these numerous pressures encouraging sex-role stereo-typing, individuals have the right to make independent decisions and take positive, personal action.

Materials

Copies of the gameboard and the various sets of cards ("Free from Stereotype," "Opportunity Knocks," and "Pressure Point"). You should have one set of all game materials available for every two, three, or four students in your class (depending on how many students you want playing on each gameboard).

Assemble gameboards.

Cut out the cards and stack them in three piles: "Free from Stereotype," "Opportunity Knocks," and "Pressure Point."

Select a system for having the students move along the gameboard. Use any or all of the following suggestions:

1. Ask the students to bring the dice and/or spinners from games at home. Students can spin the spinner or roll one die to determine how many spaces to move.

2. Cut out strips of paper numbered 1 through 6 and place them in a container. Students can pick out pieces of paper with the number of spaces they should move.

3. Construct a number of spinners. This can be done with paper fasteners

19	18	17	16	15	14	13	12	11
PRESSURE POINT	PRESSURE POINT	LOSE ONE TURN	PRESSURE POINT	OPPORTUNITY KNOCKS	KINDER-GARTEN FREE • SPACE	OPPORTUNITY KNOCKS	PRESSURE POINT	GO AHEAD ONE SPACE

							10
							PRESSURE POINT

1	2	3	4	5	6	7	8	9
MATER-NITY WARD FREE • SPACE	GO AHEAD	PRESSURE POINT	PRESSURE POINT	LOSE ONE TURN	SANDBOX FREE • SPACE	OPPORTUNITY KNOCKS	GO AHEAD FOUR SPACES	PRESSURE POINT

46	47	48	49	50	51	52	53	54	OVERCOMING
PRESSURE POINT	LOSE ONE TURN	PRESSURE POINT	GO BACK ONE SPACE	PRIN-CIPAL's OFFICE FREE • SPACE	GO AGAIN	OPPORTUNITY KNOCKS	PRESSURE POINT	PRESSURE POINT	STEREOTYPES

and heavy paper or cardboard. On a sheet of paper, draw a circle and divide it into six even slices. Number them 1 to 6.

Push a paper fastener through the center and then bend the prongs.
You now have a game spinner.
You need one spinner, one die, or one set of six numbered slips of paper for each group of students.
A button, coin, paper clip, or the like, can be used by each student as his or her playing pieces.

Structuring the Learning Activity

1.   Divide the class into groups of two, three, or four players and distribute the game materials. Make certain that at least one boy and girl are in each group.

2.   Read the directions aloud. Be sure to emphasize that this game is not a competition between students. There can be several winners as well as losers. The objective is to accumulate at least five "Free from Stereotype" (FFS) cards by the game's end.

3.   The game should easily be completed within 30 minutes. Individuals who finish earlier can play a second game.

4.   During the game, you can serve as a facilitator for students with questions. You may also be asked to arbitrate the answers to questions from the "Opportunity Knocks" cards.

5.   After the game is completed, ask for student reactions. Some of the issues that should come out of the discussion are:

   a.   Traditional forces in society tend to reinforce sex-role stereotyping and reduce the ability of individuals to leave the sex-stereotyped role. Television, peers, instructional materials, and so on, often serve to reinforce sex-role stereotypes. Note that there are exceptions to this generalization.

   b.   Independent action is needed to reduce the effects of sex typing on individuals and on society.

   c.   Ask in what ways the negative social pressure cards in the game are similar to the social pressures in the real world. In what way does the game fall short of accurately describing sexist pressures? How well does the game reflect individual action students can take to eliminate sex-role stereotyping? What changes might be made to improve the game?

   d.   Ask the students to describe any actions that they could take to avoid being sex stereotyped. What independent actions could add to their real-life FFS cards?

OPPORTUNITY KNOCKS: A GAME FOR OVERCOMING STEREOTYPES

Game Instructions

"Opportunity Knocks" reflects the way social pressure is applied to promote sex-role stereotypes. The game also shows how individual decisions and actions can reduce and eliminate sex-role stereotyping. In this game you will have a chance to use the information that you have learned in previous lessons to turn off the pressure and liberate your decisions.

Objective

Many sources, such as television, friends, and school, pressure you into conforming to sex-role stereotypes. The objective of this game is for you to consider individual actions which can be taken to reduce sex-role stereotyping.

You show that you are able to recognize sex-stereotyped behaviors if, by the end of the game, you reach the "Overcoming Stereotypes" space with at least five "Free from Stereotype" (FFS) cards. You have a chance to collect these cards when you land on "Opportunity Knocks" spaces. When you land on "Pressure Point" spaces, you sometimes will gain "Free from Stereotype" cards—and sometimes you will lose them.

Remember, you need to earn five FFS cards to demonstrate that you are aware of sex-role stereotypes and the actions you can take to overcome them.

Directions

The gameboard represents the first 18 years of your life, from the hospital delivery room through high school. As you move around the board, you must follow the instructions of the space you land on. There are different kinds of spaces.

Free Spaces

When you land on a free space, you draw no cards and simply wait your next turn.

Short-Cut, Long-Cut Spaces

There is a short-cut space, which saves you time, and a long-cut space, which makes you go back several spaces. If you land on these spaces by exact count, you must take the short or long cut, as the board indicates.

Go Ahead, Go Back Spaces

Some spaces tell you to go ahead or back a specific number of spaces. Follow these directions if you land on one of these spaces by exact count.

Pressure Point Spaces

When you land on a "Pressure Point" space, you are to draw a "Pressure Point" card (PPC). Sometimes these cards describe social pressures that society may impose to reinforce sex-role stereotyping. If you draw a negative "Pressure Point" card, it will cost you one of your "Free from Stereotype" cards.

Other "Pressure Point" cards describe situations in which you avoid stereotyped course of action. In these cases, you gain a "Free from Stereotype" card.

Opportunity Knocks Spaces

When you land on an "Opportunity Knocks" space, another player will draw a card from the "Opportunity Knocks" deck, and read the question on the card to you. These questions are about male-role stereotyping and sex-role stereotyping in general. If you are able to answer the question accurately, you will gain two "Free from Stereotype" cards. These "Opportunity Knocks" spaces are very important. They give you a chance to demonstrate your knowledge about sex stereotyping and the actions you can take against sex-role stereotypes.

What Happens if More than One Player Gets Five or More "Free from Stereotype" Cards?

That's great! The more awareness of stereotyping and the actions that can be taken to overcome them the better. Remember, the goal of the game is not to beat somebody else. It is to check your own awareness. Each player with five or more FFS cards has reached his or her personal goal.

What Happens if You Give Up All Your "Free from Stereotype" Cards?

If you are unaware or if social pressures make a victim of you, you may lose all your FFS cards. If you do, you may have to go into debt and borrow five more FFS cards. Just keep score of how many you have borrowed and remember to pay back your debt at the end of the game.

Don't give up hope!

What Happens Now?

Shuffle the "Pressure Point" cards and the "Opportunity Knocks" cards and put them in two separate piles by the gameboard. Put the FFS cards in another pile. Decide who goes first. Use the spinner or dice or whatever method your teacher has provided to determine how many spaces you move. Then follow the directions on each space. See if you recognize social pressures and overcome stereotypes.

Free from Stereotype	Free from Stereotype	Free from Stereotype
Free from Stereotype	Free from Stereotype	Free from Stereotype
Free from Stereotype	Free from Stereotype	Free from Stereotype
Free from Stereotype	Free from Stereotype	Free from Stereotype
Free from Stereotype	Free from Stereotype	Free from Stereotype
Free from Stereotype	Free from Stereotype	Free from Stereotype
Free from Stereotype	Free from Stereotype	Free from Stereotype
Free from Stereotype	Free from Stereotype	Free from Stereotype
Free from Stereotype	Free from Stereotype	Free from Stereotype
Free from Stereotype	Free from Stereotype	Free from Stereotype
Free from Stereotype	Free from Stereotype	Free from Stereotype
Free from Stereotype	Free from Stereotype	Free from Stereotype

"Opportunity Knocks" Card

Question: Describe one action you could take immediately to help eliminate sex-role stereotyping. (If you have already answered this question, draw another card.)

Answer: There are many, many possible answers.

Value for correct answer: Two FFS cards.

"Opportunity Knocks" Card

Question: Name at least four ways in which girls and boys are taught to conform to sex-role stereotypes.

Answer: T.V. programs and commercials, teachers, parents, newspapers, magazines, friends, counselors, employers, etc.

Value for correct answer: Two FFS cards.

"Opportunity Knocks" Card

Question: Describe one action you could take immediately to help eliminate sex-role stereotyping. (If you have already answered this question, draw another card.)

Answer: There are many, many possible answers.

Value for correct answer: Two FFS cards.

"Opportunity Knocks" Card

Question: Describe one action you could take immediately to help eliminate sex-role stereotyping. (If you have already answered this question, draw another card.)

Answer: There are many, many possible answers.

Value for correct answer: Two FFS cards.

"Opportunity Knocks" Card

Question: Describe one way in which you have become less sex-role stereotyped since the beginning of this unit. (If you have already answered this question, draw another card.)

Answer: There are many, many possible answers.

Value for correct answer: Two FFS cards.

"Opportunity Knocks" Card

Question: Describe one way in which you have become less sex-role stereotyped since the beginning of this unit. (If you have already answered this question, draw another card.)

Answer: There are many, many possible answers.

Value for correct answer: Two FFS cards.

"Opportunity Knocks" Card

Question: Identify at least four characteristics of the male sex-role stereotype.

Answer: Many, including acting tough, competing intensely, obsession with winning, limited occupational choices, earning a big salary, hiding emotions.

Value for correct answer: Two FFS cards

"Opportunity Knocks" Card

Question: To what part of the male-role stereotype do these phrases refer: "Play it cool"; "Keep a stiff upper lip"; "Only sissies cry."

Answer: Hiding emotions.

Value for correct answer: Two FFS cards.

"Opportunity Knocks" Card

Question: Identify at least five costs that men pay for becoming sex-role stereotyped.

Answer: Many, including a loss of friendship with other males; an overcommitment to competition and difficulty in cooperating with others; the stress of hiding emotions; the feeling of being "locked in" to a particular job; a lack of time to develop noncareer hobbies and interests; a lack of time to spend with family; a proneness to certain physical diseases; earlier average age of death.

Value for correct answer: Two FFS cards.

"Opportunity Knocks" Card

Question: You are female. You tell your guidance counselor that you are considering becoming a pilot. The counselor tells you that the job of stewardess is more appropriate for women. What would be a polite but nonstereotyped response?

Answer: There are several possibilities. You could politely tell the counselor that you're following your own interests and not sex-role stereotypes.

Value for correct answer: Two FFS cards.

"Opportunity Knocks" Card

Question: Describe one way in which you have become less sex-role stereotyped since the beginning of this unit. (If you have already answered this question, draw another card.)

Answer: There are many, many possible answers.

Value for correct answer: Two FFS cards.

"Opportunity Knocks" Card

Question: Identify three ways that schools may reinforce sex-role stereotyping.

Answer: Many, including instructional materials, counseling, sex-segregated extracurricular activities, staffing policies (male principal–female teachers).

Value for correct answer: Two FFS cards.

"Opportunity Knocks" Card

Question: Which of the following words describes the male sex-role stereotype: (1) compassionate, (2) dependent, (3) competitive.

Answer: (3) Competitive

Value for correct answer: Two FFS cards.

"Opportunity Knocks" Card

Question: You and your friend are watching your younger brother who is 5 years old. He has just gotten into a squabble with some neighborhood children and comes home in tears. Your friend says to him, "Don't be a sissy. Only girls cry." What would be a polite but nonstereotyped response?

Answer: There are many possibilities. You might suggest that both boys and girls cry and that always hiding emotions can have harmful effects.

Value for correct answer: Two FFS cards.

"Opportunity Knocks" Card

Question: John Peters is a man who is driven to be the best at whatever he tries. Family, friends, hobbies, interests—all take a back seat as he strives to sell more vacuum cleaners than any other salesperson in the company. What aspect of the male-role stereotype does he demonstrate?

Answer: Winning and/or competition.

Value for correct answer: Two FFS cards.

"Opportunity Knocks" Card

Question: Briefly explain at least one way that suppressing emotions, which is part of the male sex-role stereotype, can be harmful.

Answer: Many, including: Hiding emotions presents a false image to others of what you are really like. Hiding emotions can make you lose touch with how you really feel about things. Hiding emotions causes stress and may be unhealthy.

Value for correct answer: Two FFS cards.

"Opportunity Knocks" Card

Question: Identify three occupations that are sex-role stereotyped as more appropriate for men than for women.

Answer: Many! including pilot, business executive, doctor, plumber, electrician, construction worker.

Value for correct answer: Two FFS cards.

"Opportunity Knocks" Card

Question: Identify three occupations that are sex-role stereotyped as more appropriate for women than for men.

Answer: Many, including elementary school teacher, nurse, secretary, homemaker.

Value for correct answer: Two FFS cards.

"Opportunity Knocks" Card

Question: Briefly define sex-role stereotyping.

Answer: Sex-role stereotyping is the assumption that people who share a common gender also share a common set of abilities, interests, values, and roles.

Value for correct answer: Two FFS cards.

"Opportunity Knocks" Card

Question: You are male. You tell your guidance counselor that you are thinking about teaching elementary school. The counselor suggests that you become an elementary school principal. What would be a polite but nonstereotyped response?

Answer: There are several possibilities. You could politely tell the counselor that you're following your own interests and not sex-role stereotypes.

Value for correct answer: Two FFS cards.

"Opportunity Knocks" Card

Question: Briefly explain at least three characteristics of "acting tough," which is part of the male sex-role stereotyped.

Answer: Many, including trying to dominate; acting strong; using violence; avoiding peaceful solutions; being able to "take it"; being able to "dish it out"; refusing to give in even when surrender or compromise is the most reasonable and compassionate course of action.

Value for correct answer: Two FFS cards.

"Opportunity Knocks" Card

Question: Give an example of how T.V. programs stereotype men and an example of how T.V. programs stereotype women. Be specific in explaining each one.

Answer: The answer must include specific ways the programs stereotype. Since many T.V. shows do stereotype men and women, it is important that the answers be specific as to how they are stereotyped.

Value for correct answer: Two FFS cards.

"Opportunity Knocks" Card

Question: Identify at least two ways that competition, which is part of the male sex-role stereotype, has a negative impact on individuals.

Answer: Competition can lead to anxiety, a disregard for the rules in order to win, poor self-image for someone who is constantly a loser, a lack of a cooperative spirit, insensitivity to the feelings of others.

Value for correct answer: Two FFS cards.

"Opportunity Knocks" Card

Question: Cite two T.V. commercials that use sex-role stereotypes. Describe how either men or women are stereotyped by these commercials. Be specific as to the particular commercial and the specific way that it promotes stereotypes.

Answer: Make certain that the answer is specific and describes precisely how men and women are sex-role stereotyped.

Value for correct answer: Two FFS cards.

"Pressure Point" Card

You are a male. You have a lot of school spirit and would like to try out for the cheerleading team, but you don't. You think it won't "look right" for a boy to be a cheerleader.

Lose one FFS card.

"Pressure Point" Card

You are a female. You would like to try out for the baseball team but you don't because you think that it would not be a "feminine" thing to do.

Lose one FFS card.

"Pressure Point" Card

You are a male. Your teacher disciplines the boys much more harshly than the girls, but you don't say anything because you want to show the other guys that you can take it.

Lose one FFS card.

"Pressure Point" Card

You are a female. Your teacher seems to pay more attention to boys than to girls. But you don't say anything because you don't want to take the chance of jeopardizing your grades.

Lose one FFS card.

"Pressure Point" Card

You are a male. Although you would like to teach kindergarten, your parents tell you that a boy should go to law school.

You give up your teaching goals—and one FFS card too.

"Pressure Point" Card

You are a female. Although you would like to be a lawyer, your parents tell you that you would be better off as a kindergarten teacher.

You drop your legal ambitions—and one FFS card as well.

"Pressure Point" Card

You are a male. You've just heard some terrible news and feel like crying. But you hold it in because you don't want to be called a "crybaby."

Lose one FFS card.

"Pressure Point" Card

You are a female. A boy you like asks you about politics. You know the answer but act as though you don't. You're afraid that if you're too smart, he might not ask you out.

Lose two I.Q. points and one FFS card.

"Pressure Point" Card

You are a male. You would like to take a course in cooking, but don't because you're afraid the kids will laugh at you.

Lose one FFS card.

"Pressure Point" Card

You are a female. You want to take a carpentry course, but you don't because you're afraid the kids will laugh at you.

Lose one FFS card.

"Pressure Point" Card

You are a male. Your school has just lost the big game. You congratulate the other team—and really mean it.

Help yourself to one FFS card.

"Pressure Point" Card

You are interested in women's liberation and decide to do something about it. You decide to join the National Organization for Women (NOW).

Take one FFS card.

"Pressure Point" Card

You are interested in women's liberation and want to do something about it. You decide to join the National Organization for Women (NOW).

Take one FFS card.

"Pressure Point" Card

You are a male. Your school has just lost the big game. You congratulate the other team—and really mean it.

Help yourself to one FFS card.

"Pressure Point" Card

You are a male. You are thinking about applying for a summer job as a receptionist but you don't because you think the job is for girls only.

Lose the job—and one FFS card as well.

"Pressure Point" Card

You are a female. You are thinking about applying for a summer job as a construction worker but you don't because you think the job is for boys only.

Lose the job—and one FFS card as well.

"Pressure Point" Card

You are a male. You've just watched the "Lieutenant Fred Frisbee Police Hour." Frisbee just went through six brutal murders—and never blinked. Frisbee is acting tough. He's a real male-role stereotype.

Lose one FFS card.

"Pressure Point" Card

You're a female. You've just watched the afternoon soap opera "As the Stomach Churns" and you've seen 12 dependent, sobbing women who are waiting for men to save them from their troubles.

Lose one FFS card.

"Pressure Point" Card

You are a male. Your parents tell you to stop crying and act like a man.

Lose one FFS card.

"Pressure Point" Card

You are a female. Your parents tell you to be neater and act more like a lady.

Lose one FFS card.

"Pressure Point" Card

You are a male. You want to take home economics, but you are afraid that your friends will make fun of you.

You lose many important skills—and one FFS card.

"Pressure Point" Card

You are a female. You want to take shop, but you are afraid that your friends will make fun of you.

You lose many important skills—and an FFS card.

"Pressure Point" Card

You are a male. In spite of all the suggestions from your friends, you decide to follow your own interests and become an artist instead of going into the field of business.

Take one FFS card.

"Pressure Point" Card

You are a female. In spite of all the suggestions from your friends, you decide to follow your own interests and enter the pre-med program instead of a nursing program.

Take one FFS card.

"Pressure Point" Card

You have just convinced your teacher to enroll in a Title IX workshop. Title IX is the new law prohibiting sex discrimination in education.

Take one FFS card.

"Pressure Point" Card

You've just convinced your teacher to use a new textbook that documents the contribution of both men and women in U.S. history. It also has several sections on sex-role stereotyping.

Take one FFS card.

"Pressure Point" Card

You have talked to your parents about sex bias in your school text. Your parents are concerned and arrange a conference with the principal.

Take one FFS card. (Share it with your family.)

"Pressure Point" Card

You just played this game with a friend to teach him or her about sex-role stereotyping.

Take one FFS card. (Share it with your friend.)

"Pressure Point" Card

You write a letter to the editor complaining about the newspaper's sexist articles and advertisements which stereotype men and women.

Take one FFS card.

"Pressure Point" Card

You meet with your school's Title IX coordinator and plan actions to make your school a nonsexist institution. The Title IX coordinator is the person in your school system responsible for seeing that your school complies with the law and does not discriminate on the basis of sex.

Take one FFS card.

"Pressure Point" Card

You help the librarian organize a nonsexist bookshelf in the school library.

Take one FFS card.

"Pressure Point" Card

You and your friends form a male-female group to reduce sexism in your school.

Take one FFS card.

"Pressure Point" Card

Your school system decides not to hire a female principal and a male kindergarten teacher because it "doesn't seem right."

You lose one FFS card due to these stereotyped hiring policies.

"Pressure Point" Card

Magazine advertisements and T.V. commercials limit your options.

Lose one FFS card.

"Pressure Point" Card

Your school guidance counselor hands out career guidance information that is filled with sex-role stereotypes.

Hand in one FFS card.

"Pressure Point" Card

It's time for spelling and your teacher says, "Let's have a spelling bee. Boys against the girls." You're receiving some sexist instructions, so:

Hand in one FFS card.

"Pressure Point" Card

Your school has a bulletin board that lists sex-restricted job opportunities (a delivery boy; a girl Friday).

Lose one FFS card—and a lot of job opportunities, too.

"Pressure Point" Card

Your parents have always encouraged you to be whatever you want to be and to ignore sex-role stereotypes. You're lucky.

Take one FFS card, and thank your parents.

"Pressure Point" Card

You have just bought a nonsexist book for your friend's birthday.

Take one FFS card. (Share it with your friend.)

"Pressure Point" Card

Your parents have made sure that you, your brothers, and your sisters have always had nonsexist toys to play with.

Take one FFS card, and your parents deserve a vote of thanks.

"Pressure Point" Card

You write an article for your school newspaper entitled "Our Right to a Nonsexist Education."

Take one FFS card.

"Pressure Point" Card

You organize a successful protest against dress codes that have different regulations for boys and girls.

Collect one FFS card.

"Pressure Point" Card

At the dinner table, you share your ideas about the limitations of sex-role stereotyping with your family.

Take one FFS card.

"Pressure Point" Card

You are female. You enroll in a Fundamentals of Mechanics course because you want to be able to fix your own car.

Take one FFS card.

"Pressure Point" Card

You are male. In spite of pressure from your friends, you decide to take a course in child care so that you can be a better father.

You are entitled to one FFS card.

"Pressure Point" Card

You are female. You decide to try out for the school's all-male swimming team.

Congratulations! You earn one FFS card.

"Pressure Point" Card

You are male. You have just become the first boy in the school cheerleading squad. Congratulations!

Take one FFS card.

"Pressure Point" Card

You've just organized a "Career Day" with speakers involved in nonsex-typed jobs (a female doctor, a male first-grade teacher, etc.)

Take one FFS card.

ENDNOTES

[1] James Coleman, "Athletics in High School," in D. S. David and R. Brannon (eds.), *The Forty-Nine Percent Majority: The Male Sex Role* (Reading, Mass.: Addison-Wesley, 1976).

[2] J. Lipman-Blumen, "Toward a Homosocial Theory of Sex Roles," *Signs* 2 (1975).

[3] David F. Aberle and Kaspar D. Naegel, "Middle Class Fathers Occupational Role and Attitudes Toward Children," *American Journal of Orthopsychiatry* 22 (1952).

[4] Marc Feigan Fasteau, *The Male Machine* (New York: Dell, 1975).

[5] J. Bardwick and E. Donavan, "Ambivalence: The Socialization of Women," in V. Gornick and B. Moran (eds.), *Woman in Sexist Society* (New York: American Library, 1971). *See also* D. G. Brown, "Sex Role Preference in Young Children," *Psychological Monographs* 70 (1956). L. B. Fauls and W. D. Smith, "Sex Role Learning of Five-Year-Olds," *Journal of Genetic Psychology* 93 (1958).

[6] J. Chafetz, *Masculine/Feminine or Human.* (Itasca: Ill., F. E. Peacock, 1974).

[7] W. H. Frey, "Not-So-Idle Tears," *Psychology Today* 13 (January 1980).

[8] Robert Press, "A Husband's Housework Is Never Done," *Christian Science Monitor* (August 22, 1980).

[9] Ibid.

[10] R. Hartley, "Sex Pressures in the Socialization of the Male Child," *Psychological Reports* 5 (1959).

[11] I. Waldron, "Why Do Women Live Longer than Men?" *Journal of Human Stress* 2 (1976).

[12] D. Calahan, *Problem Drinkers* (San Francisco: Jossey-Bass, 1970). *See also* D. McClelland et al. *The Drinking Man* (Riverside, N.J.: Free Press, 1972).

[13] J. Hanson, "Male Sex Role and Health," *Journal of Social Issues* 34 (1978).

[14] P. Stein and S. Hoffman, "Sports and Male Role Strain," *Journal of Social Issues* 34 (1978).

[15] Mirra Komarovsky, *Dilemmas of Masculinity* (New York: Norton, 1976).

[16] P. Mussen, "Long Term Consequences of Masculinity of Interests in Adolescence," *Journal of Consulting Psychology* 26 (1962).

[17] T. Harford, C. Willis, and H. Deabler, "Personality Correlates of Masculinity-Feminity," *Psychological Reports* 5 (1967).

[18] S. Bem, W. Martyna, and C. Watson, "Sex Typing and Androgyny: Further Exploitations of the Expressive Domain," *Journal of Personality and Social Psychology* 34 (1976).

[19] Jourard, *The Transparent Self* (New York: D. Van Nostrand, 1971).

[20] K. Olstad, "Brave New Men: A Basis for Discussion," in J. Pętras (ed.), *Sex: Male/Gender: Masculine* (Port Washington, N.Y.: Alfren, 1975). *See also* E. Powers and G. Bultena, "Sex Differences in Intimate Friendships of Old Age," *Journal of Marriage and the Family* 38 (1976).

[21] Komarovsky, *Dilemmas of Masculinity.*

[22] Ibid.

[23] Jack Nichols, *Men's Liberation* (New York: Penguin Books, 1975).

[24] These lesson plans are from David Sadker, *Being a Man: A Unit of Instructional Activities on Male Role Stereotyping* (Washington, D.C.: Resource Center on Sex Roles in Education, U.S. Department of Health, Education, and Welfare, 1977). This unit was developed by the Resource Center on Sex Roles in Education and the National Foundation for the Improvement of Education under contract to the Women's Educational Equity Act Program, HEW. Dr. Shirley McCune directed this project. No copyright is claimed for these lesson plans.

7

A Resource Directory for Sex Equity in Education *

Susan Shaffer and Barbara Gordon

What materials can you use to give students accurate and nonstereotyped portrayals of individuals and their society? What resources are available to help teachers work with girls and boys so it is the reality of their interest and aspirations that matters not the artificial limits of sex-role stereotypes?

This resource directory provides information about organizations, publishers, government agencies, and associations that you can turn to for help. The first section highlights resources for instructional materials and strategies for classroom use. The second section provides additional nonsexist resources on specific topics related to Title IX and sex equity. The final section describes the major providers of compliance information and technical assistance services to school districts in the areas of Title IX and sex equity. Descriptions note specific examples of materials, major objectives of the organizations, and additional types of assistance, such as research analysis, legal up-dates and interpretations, and on-call information services.

INSTRUCTIONAL MATERIALS AND CLASSROOM STRATEGIES

ABT BOOKS
55 Wheeler Street
Cambridge, MA 02138
(617) 492-7100

ABT conducts research and statistical analysis, and publishes social research reports on topics concerning children, minorities, and the handicapped. It also produces curriculum materials and educational planning aids. Classroom materials include games and curriculum units. For example, "Career Education Activities for Subject Area Teachers" includes

---

* The research and some of these descriptions were originally prepared for the *Resource Notebook*, by Susan Shaffer and Barbara Gordon. The *Resource Notebook* is available from the Mid-Atlantic Center for Sex Equity, The American University, 3301 New Mexico Ave., N.W., Foxhall Square Bldg., Suite 252, Washington, DC 20016

activities in social studies, English, mathematics, and science. A multimedia kit, "Sex Fairness in Career Guidance," for staff development or self-instruction is also available.

> ALPHA KAPPA ALPHA SORORITY
> 5211 South Greenwood Avenue
> Chicago, IL 60615
> (312) 684-1282

Alpha Kappa Alpha is the world's oldest college-based sorority founded by black women. Sorority members conduct workshops on subjects of general interest, such as problems of black women in the job market, and they can provide information about sex equity and minority-related topics. AKA publishes curriculum content materials, such as the *Heritage Series,* which highlights contemporary black women in the judiciary, politics, business, medicine, and dentistry.

> THE AMERICAN ASSOCIATION FOR THE ADVANCEMENT OF SCIENCE
> OFFICE OF OPPORTUNITIES IN SCIENCE
> 1776 Massachusetts Avenue, N.W.
> Washington, DC 20036
> (202) 467-5438

The Office of Opportunities in Science provides a clearinghouse for information on careers for women and minorities in science and engineering. Its publications include reports of sponsored conferences, such as *The Double Bind: The Price of Being a Minority Woman in Science, Access to Science,* a four-volume series newsletter targeted for handicapped students, and *Science for Handicapped Students in Higher Education.*

> AMERICAN FEDERATION OF TEACHERS, AFL-CIO
> HUMAN RIGHTS AND COMMUNITY RELATIONS DEPARTMENT
> 11 Dupont Circle, N.W.
> Washington, DC 20036
> (202) 797-4434

The Human Rights and Community Relations Department provides assistance for school personnel on Title IX and sex equity. The staff plans and conducts workshops on such topics as Title IX, nonsexist textbooks, and women's rights. The department publishes resources, magazines, bibliographies, books, and curriculum materials on sex equity for parents, teachers, and students.

> AMERICAN INSTITUTES FOR RESEARCH IN THE BEHAVIORAL SCIENCES
> P.O. Box 1113
> Palo Alto, CA 94302
> (415) 493-3550

AIR is an independent nonprofit institution established to provide research, development, and evaluation services to various public agencies, foundations, and industrial clients. Among recent publications of value to schools are:

- *Vocational Education Equity Study,* which includes primary data, literature, secondary data review, case studies, tested strategies, and a handbook.
- *Measures of Educational Equity for Women,* which describes 61 instruments to evaluate Women's Education Equity Act projects.

AMERICAN LIBRARY ASSOCIATION
50 East Huron Street
Chicago, IL 60611
(312) 944-6780

The American Library Association is an organization with the general goal of promoting library service and librarianship. Useful publications for school personnel in the area of sex equity are *A Bibliography of Materials Collected for Comparable Wages for Comparable Work Study, A Bibliography of Non-Sexists Booklists,* and "Role-free Fiction for Children", in March 15, 1977 *Booklist,* pp. 1099–1102. All materials are available from ALA.

ASSOCIATION FOR CHILDHOOD EDUCATION INTERNATIONAL
3615 Wisconsin Avenue, N.W.
Washington, DC 20016
(202) 363-6963

The association provides resources, advocacy, and support on children's issues. Specific examples of its nonsexist materials are *Growing Free: Ways to Help Children Overcome Sex Role Stereotypes* and *Dauntless Women in Childhood Education 1865–1931.*

COUNCIL ON INTERRACIAL BOOKS FOR CHILDREN
RACISM AND SEXISM RESOURCE CENTER FOR EDUCATORS
1841 Broadway
New York, NY 10023
(212) 757-5339

This organization publishes and produces a variety of multiethnic and nonsexist materials for elementary and secondary schools and libraries. Its publication, *The Bulletin,* comes out eight times a year and includes children's book reviews and articles dealing with sexism and special needs of children in education.

Some of the materials offered for classroom use include filmstrips such as *Identifying Sexism and Racism in Children's Books, Unlearning Indian Stereotypes,* and *From Racism to Pluralism.* Its newest curriculum for fifth and sixth grade is entitled *Winning Justice for All*. Print materials include *Fact Sheets on Institutional Sexism*, which contains statistics documenting sexism in education, employment, media, and government, and a *Checklist to Rate Your School for Racism and Sexism*. The Center also conducts workshops for teachers, parents, and administrators on topics such as "Sexism in Children's Books and School Textbooks: Criteria for Analyzing Materials" and "Constructive Use of Biased Materials." A free catalog is available upon request.

CURRICULUM PUBLICATIONS CLEARINGHOUSE
Western Illinois University
47 Horrabin Hall
Macomb, IL 61455
(309) 298-1917
(800) 322-3905 (Illinois only)

The Clearinghouse provides state-developed curriculum materials at a minimum cost. Its equity curriculum materials include a classroom kit on *Expanding Career Horizons*, which is designed to help male and female students understand the impact of sex bias on jobs, sex-discrimination legislation, and the problem of sex bias in guidance tests and counseling, and *A Teacher's Handbook on Career Development for Students with Special Needs: Grades K–12*, which includes materials in career education for handicapped students. The Clearinghouse publishes a materials catalog each year.

EDUCATION DEVELOPMENT CENTER
55 Chapel Street
Newton, MA 02160
(800) 225-3088
(617) 969-7100

The Education Development Center serves as the dissemination center for programs and products developed under the Women's Educational Equity Act Program (WEEAP). Examples of products applicable in elementary and secondary schools are: *Competence Is for Everyone, Aspire*, and *Maximizing Young Children's Potential*, projects which present equitable teaching strategies; *In Search of Our Past*, a junior high school curriculum on women's contributions to world history and United States history; *The Whole Person Book: Toward Self-Discovery and Life Options*, a manual which includes curriculum materials for increasing awareness of sex bias and nontraditional career planning; and, *Science, Sex and Society*, a collection of readings on the lives of women as scientists. A catalog describing materials can be obtained from EDC at no cost. It can assist school personnel in determining product applicability to specific program needs.

ERIC (EDUCATIONAL RESOURCES INFORMATION CENTER)
CENTRAL ERIC, NATIONAL INSTITUTE OF EDUCATION
Washington, DC 20208
(202) 254-7934 Library and Reference Center
(202) 254-5500 Chief of ERIC

The ERIC system disseminates information on equity related issues through specialized clearinghouses in various geographical areas. These clearinghouses identify, acquire, and process educational information (documentary form) in specific subject areas such as social studies, social sciences, or teacher education. The clearinghouses collect and process research reports, bibliographies, program descriptions and evaluations, curriculum materials, literature reviews, and conference papers. Specific relevant topics covered by ERIC include "Sex Role Development in Young Children," "Women's Athletics," "Counseling Women for Life Decisions," and "Counseling Women for Nontraditional Careers." The following ERIC clearinghouses are particularly useful for topics in the areas of Title IX and sex equity:

- ERIC Clearinghouse on Elementary and Early Childhood Education
  University of Illinois
  College of Education
  Urbana, IL 61801
  (217) 333-1386

- ERIC Clearinghouse for Social Studies/Social Science Education
  855 Broadway
  Boulder, CO 80302
  (303) 492-8434

- ERIC Clearinghouse on Teacher Education
  American Association of Colleges for Teacher Education
  1 Dupont Circle, N.W., Suite 616
  Washington, DC 20036
  (202) 293-7280

Duplicates are available through the ERIC Document Reproduction Service (EDRS), P.O. Box 190, Arlington, VA.

THE FEMINIST PRESS
SUNY/College at Old Westbury
Box 334
Old Westbury, NY 11568
(516) 997-7660

The Feminist Press is a nonprofit, educational organization that publishes nonsexist books, curriculum materials and outlines, resource lists, anthologies, bibliographies, biographies, children's books, and reprints of important and neglected women's writings for every educational level. Among its new publications appropriate for teachers and secondary students are: *Out of the Bleachers: Writings on Women and Sport, Rights and Wrongs: Women's Struggle for Legal Equality, Women Working, Books for Today's Children,* and *Black Foremothers.* In addition, the press sponsors a clearinghouse for information on nonsexist education and Title IX. It also conducts teacher and administrator workshops on the use of nonsexist educational materials and strategies.

FEMINISTS NORTHWEST
5038 Nicklas Place, N.E.
Seattle, WA 98105
(206) 524-4973 General Information
(206) 525-3788 Distribution Orders

The staff's main objective is to work to end sex discrimination in schools and society. It develops nonsexist curriculum, provides workshops and staff development programs, reviews textbooks for sexism, and disseminates materials to assist in presentations on nonsexist teaching strategies. Publications and audiovisual materials suitable for classroom use are also available. Resources include an awareness game about career and family choices entitled *Whatever Happened to Debbie Kraft?*, and materials about women in science, including the books *Hypatias Sisters: Biographies of Women Scientists—Past and Present, Again at the Looking Glass, Planning for Free Lives,* and *Sex Role Stereotyping in Elementary School Books: A Hidden Curriculum.*

GARRETT PARK PRESS, INC.
Garrett Park, MD 20766
(301) 946-2553

Garrett Park Press publishes books, pamphlets, bibliographies, and charts in the areas of sex equity, career education, occupational guidance, and social sciences. There are many resources appropriate for counselors, students, parents, and teachers. Some of these publications are:

- *Encyclopedia of Careers and Vocational Guidance*
- *Counseling for Careers in the 1980's*
- *Locating, Recruiting, and Employing Women: An Equal Opportunity Approach*
- *Margaret Sanger: Pioneer of the Future*
- *Minority Organizations: A National Directory*
- *Directory of Special Programs for Minority Group Members*

INFORMATION SYSTEMS DEVELOPMENT
1100 East 8th Street
Austin, TX 78702
(512) 477-1604

Information Systems Development created the materials for the Women's Multi-Cultural Resource Project. WMRP is a data base on women of all cultures, races, and ethnicities in the United States that was completed in late 1979. Major ethnic groups include Hispanic, Anglo-American, African, Afro-American, Middle Eastern, and Native American. The project maintains files on women's studies programs, minority women, and ethnic heritage programs. Its publications include:

- *Diosa y Hembra: History and Heritage of Chicanas in the U.S.*
- *The Chicana Feminist*
- *Chicana Readings: A Preliminary Bibliography*
- *Handbook on Educational Strategies and Resources for Sex Cultural Relevant Classroom Practices and Materials*
- *Sourcebook of Multicultural Resources for Women's Studies and Bilingual Multicultural Programs*

INSTRUCTO/MCGRAW-HILL PUBLISHERS, INC.
Cedar Hollow Road
Paoli, PA 19301
(215) 644-7700

Instructo's publications include learning activities and developmental materials. A number of resources for teachers are appropriate for use in developing sex-fair programs within the elementary schools. One of these is a poster and mobile set, which illustrates males and females in nonstereotyped roles and occupations. Other products include "Community Careers—Flannel Board Set"; special duplicating books, such as *Math Fun,* grades 1–6; *Practice in Thinking Skills,* grades 2 and 3, which shows individuals in nonstereotyped roles; "Career Decisions Game," grades 4–6; *Learning Units in Careers,* a resource handbook; and *Self-Awareness/Career Awareness in Your Curriculum,* grades K–6.

KNOW, INC.
P.O. Box 86031
Pittsburgh, PA 15221
(412) 241-4844

KNOW, Inc. publishes an extensive resource list, which contains reprints, bibliographies, pamphlets, and curriculum materials. Some of these publications include *The Second Sex: Junior Division,* which describes sex bias in books for young children, *Racism and Sexism: A Collective Struggle—A Minority Woman's Point of View,* and *Help Stamp out Sexism: Change the Language.*

LOLLIPOP POWER, INC.
Box 1171
Chapel Hill, NC 27514
(919) 929-4857

Lollipop Power is a feminist collective that publishes and writes nonsexist books for young children. Although its primary activity is writing, illustrating, and publishing children's books, the staff will also participate in workshops and develop multimedia presentations for parents and educators in the area of sex equity. Several books have been published for children ages 2 to 9. Examples include *Martin's Father, Amy and the Cloudbasket,* and *Grownups Cry Too.*

> MATH/SCIENCE NETWORK
> MATH/SCIENCE RESOURCE CENTER
> Mills College
> Oakland, CA 94613
> (415) 635-5074
> (415) 635-9271

The Math/Science Network was established to promote the participation of girls and women in mathematics and science and to encourage their entry into nontraditional occupations. At the Resource Center at Mills College the staff provides strategies and "how-to" materials to public school personnel for increasing the number of young women in math and science careers. They disseminate information through the local math-science network. The resource center has produced materials such as *Count Me In: Educating Women for Science and Math.* Films include *The Math-Science Connection: Educating Young Women for Today,* directed towards parents, educators, and other concerned adults; and *Sandra, Zella, Dee and Claire: Four Women in Science,* a film intended for junior and high school students. These resources can be obtained through the Education Development Center.

> NATIONAL EDUCATION ASSOCIATION
> 1201 16th Street N.W.
> Washington, DC 20036
> (202) 833-4267

The National Education Association is a major service organization for teachers. It assists other organizations through the implementation of affirmative action plans for women and minorities, workshops in the area of leadership training for women, and dissemination of resources related to the achievement of sex equity in education. Materials from the Division of Teacher Rights include *Sex Role Stereotyping,* a multimedia program dealing with sexism, racism, and classism in the schools; tapes on *Sex Equality—Athletics;* a manual developed for teachers on *Mathematics and My Career;* and a *Resource List for Nonsexist Education.* Further information on Title IX and sex equity and other educational issues is disseminated through the *DuShane Fund Report, Today's Education,* and *The NEA Reporter.*

NEW ENGLAND FREE PRESS
60 Union Square
Somerville, MA 02143
(617) 628-2450

The New England Free Press is a nonprofit cooperative print shop that publishes materials in the area of sex equity for classroom use at the secondary level. Nonsexist pamphlets, which may be obtained in quantity, include:

- "Liberating Young Children from Sex Roles"
- "Working Women's Music: The Songs and Struggles of Women in the Golden Mills, Textile Plants, and Needle Trades"
- "Women of the Telephone Company"
- "Goldflower's Story: A Peasant Woman in the Chinese Revolution"
- "Fourth Mountain . . . Women in China"

PROJECT HEAR (HUMAN EDUCATIONAL AWARENESS RESOURCE)
306 Alexander Street
Princeton, NJ 08540
(609) 921-1484

Project HEAR is one of two career education projects in the country. HEAR is a program that is concerned with the effects of sex bias on occupational choice. The project staff disseminate self-contained curriculum for grades 4–12 and serve as resources for in-service training on the use of these materials. Project HEAR's materials combine reading, writing, verbal, audiovisual, simulation gaming, and kinesthetic learning experiences. At the elementary school level, the primary goal of the program is to change students' attitudes toward the world of work and to break down occupational stereotypes. At the upper levels, the program aims to increase students' knowledge of the world of work and to align their occupational choices with their occupational interests. Awareness materials are available at no cost.

SCIENCE RESEARCH ASSOCIATES, INC.
155 North Wacker Drive
Chicago, IL 60606
(312) 984-2000

Science Research Associates, a major publisher of educational materials, has published several items that can assist school personnel in combating stereotyping. The SRA reading kit, *Our Story: Women of Today and Yesterday,* was developed to help teachers supplement existing texts that do not adequately cover contributions of women in our society. SRA also offers a booklet entitled, *Fairness in Educational Materials: Exploring the Issues,* which is designed to show educators why they should evaluate materials for bias. The SRA Educational Materials Catalog is available without charge.

> SOCIAL SCIENCE EDUCATION CONSORTIUM
> 855 Broadway
> Boulder, CO 80302
> (303) 492-8155

The major function of the consortium is to provide services and publications in K–12 social sciences. Included among its wide range of publications is *The Link,* a newsletter published during the school year, which includes current articles on social studies, curriculum projects, new publications, and descriptions of new instructional materials for teachers. The consortium also acts as a resource and demonstration center and as an Ethnic Heritage Studies Clearinghouse, offering a variety of educational materials. The consortium provides workshops and consultation assistance in equitable identification, selection, and adaptation of instructional materials. Its publications include *Teaching About Social Issues in American History: Four Demonstration Units,* which contains material on the *Bakke* case and the proposed Equal Rights Amendment.

> SYSTEMS SCIENCES, INC.
> P.O. Box 2345
> Chapel Hill, NC 27514
> (919) 929-7116

Reports, reprints, pamphlets, bibliographies, and curriculum materials are published at System Sciences, Inc. Its main focus is finding and developing strategies to overcome any form of discrimination. In the area of sex equity, its materials include *In Search of a Job: A Simulation Activity in Decision-Making,* appropriate for secondary students; *Sex Stereotyping, Bias and Discrimination in the World of Work: A Student Workbook;* and *Strategies to Eliminate Sex Stereotyping and Sex Bias: An Administrator's Manual.* Technical assistance in the area of sex equity is provided for the Southeast region at the standard Department of Education reimbursable cost rates.

> TABS: AIDS FOR ENDING SEXISM IN SCHOOL
> 744 Carroll Street
> Brooklyn, NY 11215
> (212) 788-3478

TABS is a quarterly journal that includes practical aids for equal education of the sexes. The journal has published posters and biographies of Fannie Lou Hamer and Marie Curie, lesson plans on such issues as "How should you decide who does household chores?" and feature articles such as "Girls and Science Careers: A Program for Change" and "How to Run a Susan B. Anthony Day in Your School." Besides feature articles, every issue contains display items for the classroom, ideas for nonsexist activities, lesson plans, reviews of curricula and other materials, instructional materials, evaluations, and biographies of women of achievement. Subscriptions are available, and posters may be purchased separately.

UNITED STATES DEPARTMENT OF EDUCATION
NATIONAL INSTITUTE OF EDUCATION
1200 19th Street, N.W.
Washington, DC 20208
(202) 254-6572

The National Institute of Education was created by the Congress in 1972 as the primary federal agency for educational research and development. Its mission is twofold: to promote educational equity and to improve the quality of educational practice. In the area of sex equity, NIE supports programs designed to promote the professional development of educators and sponsors educational research related to classroom management and learning effectiveness. Its newest publications in the area of sex equity can be purchased through ERIC and include:

- *Sex Equity in Education NIE-Sponsored Projects and Publications;* descriptions of the following projects and publications can be found in this document:

    — *Sex Differences in Reading Achievement*
    — *Women's Athletics: Bibliographies in Educational Topics*
    — *Multicultural Education: Teaching About Minority Women*
    — *The Effects of Sex Role Socialization on Mathematics*

UNITED STATES DEPARTMENT OF EDUCATION
YEARLY PUBLICATIONS CATALOG
400 Maryland Avenue, S.W.
Washington, DC 20202
Available from:
    Superintendent of Documents—(202) 783-3238
    National Technical Information Office—(703) 557-4650

This is an annual listing of all publications produced by the Department of Education or its contractees. It includes author, subject, title, series report, and classification number indexes. In the area of sex equity and Title IX, publications include *Programs for Educational Equity, Schools and Affirmative Action, Non-Print Resources in Women's Educational Equity,* and *Taking Sexism out of Education.* Publications are available for purchase from the Superintendent of Documents, U.S. Government Printing Office, the National Technical Information Office, and from the Department of Education. This catalog could have widespread practical use among educators.

UNITED STATES GOVERNMENT PRINTING OFFICE
SUPERINTENDENT OF DOCUMENTS
Washington, DC 20402
(202) 783-3238

There are over 24,000 publications, periodicals, and subscriptions available from the Superintendent of Documents. Over 250 subject bibliographies list publications by subject area. These bibliographies are free. Subject bibliographies of interest to administrators, teachers, and counselors include "Civil Rights and Equal Opportunity," "Women," "Teachers and Teaching Methods," and "Personnel Management, Guidance, and Counseling." A list of resources on Title IX and sex equity include *Complying with Title IX: A Resource Kit* with items such as "Title IX: The First 12 Months," "Why Title IX," "A Student Guide to Title IX," "Title IX Grievance Procedures: An Introductory Manual," and *Being A Man*, a curriculum unit on male sex-role stereotyping.

WOMEN ON WORDS AND IMAGES
P.O. Box 2163
Princeton, NJ 08540
(609) 921-8653

A group of feminists and consultants formed Women on Words and Images for the purpose of developing resources to combat the effects of sexism in education. Their resources are books, pamphlets, curriculum materials, and audiovisual resources appropriate for parents, elementary and secondary teachers, counselors, and students. These materials include *Dick and Jane as Victims,* a study on sex stereotyping in children's readers, *Help Wanted,* an analysis of sex stereotyping in career education materials, and *Sexism in Foreign Language Textbooks,* with accompanying slide-tape shows. These slide-tape shows and books may be obtained at a bulk rate. One of their newest publications, *Channeling Children,* concerns sex stereotyping in prime-time television. The staff also provides workshops on sexism in education.

WOMEN'S ACTION ALLIANCE
THE NON-SEXIST CHILD DEVELOPMENT PROJECT
370 Lexington Avenue, Room 603
New York, NY 10017
(212) 532-8330

The Women's Action Alliance maintains The Non-Sexist Child Development Project. This project is the national resource center for nonsexist early childhood education and is designed to develop parent education programs and in-service teacher training programs. The staff has developed classroom materials, educational toys, multiethnic resource photographs, books, a training manual to promote educational equity in early childhood (Project TREE), and multimedia resources. Nonsexist films include *The Sooner the Better,* designed for teachers, and *The Time Has Come,* created for parents. The packets for classroom use include a "Community Careers Flannel Board," which shows examples of men and woman dressed in nontraditional work clothes or uniforms and resource photos for mainstreaming on disabled adults and children. In addition, it publishes a quarterly newsletter, *Equal Play.*

RESOURCES FOR SPECIFIC PURPOSES

The following organizations provide information and assistance on specific topics including Title IX and related sex-equity legislation, counseling and guidance, vocational education, physical education and athletics, and community and parents group resources.

Title IX and Related Sex-Equity Laws

Administrators, supervisors, teachers, counselors, and other educational personnel should have knowledge of the legal structure and laws that are important for the conduct of their profession. This knowledge can be gained in many ways: through pre- or in-service education, professional meetings, specialized conferences, or written resource materials. In this section, consideration will be given to organizations that can assist educators in securing basic information, copies of laws and regulations, and interpretations and up-dates on laws and proposed legislation in the sex-equity area.

Suggested Resources

> AMERICAN ALLIANCE FOR HEALTH, PHYSICAL EDUCATION, RECREATION, AND DANCE
> NATIONAL ASSOCIATION FOR GIRLS AND WOMEN IN SPORT
> 1900 Association Drive
> Reston, VA 22091
> (703) 476-3400

The National Association for Girls and Women in Sport is a national professional organization devoted exclusively to providing opportunities for females in the sports area. This association, founded in 1896, provides materials on women's sports, such as *Equality in Sport for Women, Programs that Work—Title IX,* and *Women's Athletics: Coping with Controversy.* Also available is an audiovisual presentation, *An Equal Chance Through Title IX,* which can be purchased or rented. The latest AAHPERD publications catalog containing NAGWS materials can be obtained free of charge from the above address. In addition, NAGWS provides on-call consultant service for problems and issues that may develop with regard to interpretations of Title IX.

AMERICAN CIVIL LIBERTIES UNION FOUNDATION
WOMEN'S RIGHTS PROJECT
132 West 43rd Street
New York, NY 10036
(212) 944-9860

The ACLU provides litigation services and information on issues dealing with civil liberties. Some local chapters may also identify appropriate speakers for classroom discussions on various civil rights concerns. The Women's Rights Project staff has also published a booklet related to sex equity, entitled *How to Erase Sex Discrimination in Vocational Education.* Included in this booklet is information related to laws prohibiting sex discrimination in vocational education, statistical information on women workers and a chapter entitled "How to Gather Facts About Vocational Education in Your Area." This booklet is suitable for classroom use at the secondary level and as an information guide for vocational educators, counselors, sex-equity coordinators, and administrators. Inquiries about current publications should be addressed to the ACLU Literature Department.

ASSOCIATION OF AMERICAN COLLEGES
PROJECT ON THE STATUS AND EDUCATION OF WOMEN
1818 R Street, N.W.
Washington, DC 20009
(202) 387-1300

The Project on the Status and Education of Women began in 1971 and provides regular and timely information concerning women in higher education. The publications of this project provide information concerning sex equity, sex-equity laws, and judicial decisions. Its newsletter, *On Campus with Women,* is published quarterly. Other publications cover topics such as Title IX, other legal requirements (affirmative action, executive orders), recruiting students and employees, minority women, financial aid, and women in sports.

CAPITOL PUBLICATIONS, INC.
2430 Pennsylvania Avenue, N.W., Suite G-12
Washington, DC 20037
(202) 452-1600

Capitol Publications publishes a variety of biweekly and daily newsletters. Of special interest to elementary and secondary educational personnel are two daily publications, *Higher Education Daily* and *Education Daily,* and its biweekly newsletter, *Schools and Civil Rights News,* formerly known as *Title IX News.* This biweekly newsletter covers current information on enforcement, litigation, and compliance. Multiple-copy rates are available on request.

> FEDERAL EDUCATION PROJECT
> LAWYERS' COMMITTEE FOR CIVIL RIGHTS UNDER LAW
> 733 15th Street, N.W., Suite 526
> Washington, DC 20005
> (202) 628-6700

Funded by the Carnegie Corporation of New York and Ford Foundation, the Federal Education Project focuses its primary efforts on Title I of the Elementary and Secondary Education Act of 1964 and the Vocational Education Act of 1963. It provides technical assistance and interpretations of federal legal requirements in Title I and in vocational programs. Most concerned about uneven distribution of students in sex-stereotyped courses, the Federal Education Project supports Title IX. Its services include monitoring both Title I and vocational education in the Department of Education, operating as a clearinghouse for information on Title I and vocational education, and litigation in these areas. It also publishes a monthly newsletter, available free of charge, *The Federal Education Project,* which includes articles about vocational education.

> NATIONAL ORGANIZATION FOR WOMEN LEGAL DEFENSE AND EDUCATION FUND
> PROJECT ON EQUAL EDUCATION RIGHTS (PEER)
> 1112 13th Street, N.W.
> Washington, DC 20005
> (202) 332-7337

The Project on Equal Education Rights (PEER) is a project of the NOW Legal Defense and Education Fund and is one of the major national projects devoted primarily to the elimination of sex bias and discrimination in public elementary and secondary schools. One of its newest publications, *The Ties that Bind,* concerns the effects of stereotyping on men. PEER's quarterly newsletter, *PEER Perspective,* is free to those who so request and serves to update readers on Title IX and related rulings, interpretations, and activities. Also free is PEER's publications list of moderately priced materials.

> RESOURCE CENTER ON SEX EQUITY
> COUNCIL OF CHIEF STATE SCHOOL OFFICERS
> 400 North Capitol Street, N.W., Suite 379
> Washington, DC 20001
> (202) 624-7757

The Resource Center on Sex Roles in Education was established in 1973 to help elementary-secondary educators achieve sex equity in education. During the first phase of its operation, the center developed numerous technical assistance materials on Title IX compliance plus instructional resources on sex-role stereotyping. For example, it created workshop packages for the implementation of Title IX such as *The Context of Title IX, The Teachers Role, The Physical Activity Specialist's Role,* and *Planning for Change.* The center also provides sex-equity training and technical assistance services to administrators, teachers, counselors, community groups, and education associations.

> UNITED STATES COMMISSION ON CIVIL RIGHTS
> OFFICE OF INFORMATION AND PUBLICITY
> Washington, DC 20425
> (202) 254-6697

The United States Commission on Civil Rights has published several guides that address laws concerning sex discrimination in the United States: *A Guide to Federal Laws and Regulations Prohibiting Sex Discrimination, Sex Bias in the United States Code,* and *Women's Rights in the United States of America.* In addition, the commission's quarterly periodical, *Perspectives: Civil Rights Quarterly,* addresses sexism.

> UNITED STATES DEPARTMENT OF EDUCATION
> ASSISTANT SECRETARY FOR CIVIL RIGHTS
> 400 Maryland Avenue, S.W.
> Washington, DC 20202
> (202) 245-2184—Elementary and Secondary Education Division

The Office for Civil Rights (OCR) is responsible for the administration and enforcement of departmental policies under Title VI of the Civil Rights Act of 1964, which prohibits discrimination on the basis of race, color, or national origin in programs and activities receiving federal financial assistance; Title IX of the Education Amendments of 1972, which prohibits discrimination on the basis of sex in educational programs; and Section 504 of the Rehabilitation Act of 1973, which prohibits discrimination on the basis of handicapping conditions.

Copies of the rules and regulations for laws such as Title IX, Section 504, and Title VI can be obtained from public affairs at the Office for Civil Rights. In addition, policy clarifications can also be obtained at this office. The December 1979 Intercollegiate Athletics Policy Interpretation is available from OCR, as are the vocational education program guidelines for eliminating discrimination and denial of services.

OCR investigates complaints based on civil rights laws, which are forwarded directly to regional offices and the national office from students, educational personnel, or other citizens. In addition, school personnel may call or write their regional office for responses to questions about Title IX, Title VI, and Section 504.

UNITED STATES EQUAL EMPLOYMENT OPPORTUNITY
COMMISSION
2401 E Street, N.W., Rm. 4202
Washington, DC 20506
(202) 634-6930

The Equal Employment Opportunity Commission (EEOC) is the principal federal agency in fair employment enforcement. The Equal Employment Opportunity Commission was created by Title VII of the Civil Rights Act of 1964 and became operational in 1965. EEOC can provide educational personnel with copies of rules and regulations for specific equal employment laws and orders, affirmative action guidelines, and interpretive guidelines in specific areas of equal employment opportunity. For example, in the area of pregnancy discrimination, the April 20, 1979, Federal Register (available from EEOC) contains questions and answers on the Pregnancy Discrimination Act entitled "Guidelines on Sex Discrimination: Adoption of Final Interpretive Guidelines: Questions and Answers." Also available are the "Affirmative Action Guidelines: Technical Amendments to the Procedural Regulations," as well as news releases giving information about proposed guidelines or revisions, such as the February 4, 1980, release on "EEOC, Labor Proposes EEO Guidelines on Reproductive Hazards." Charges of discrimination against public and private employers and labor organizations should be sent to EEOC field offices.

WOMEN'S EQUITY ACTION LEAGUE
EDUCATIONAL AND LEGAL DEFENSE FUND
(WEAL FUND)
805 15th Street, N.W., Suite 822
Washington, DC 20005
(202) 638-1961
Toll-free hot line for sports equity only: (800) 424-5162

The WEAL fund works in a variety of ways to help eliminate sex discrimination in education and employment. It is a nonprofit organization mandated to secure and defend equal rights for everyone, by providing legal defense assistance and information on Title IX and other equal opportunity laws. Its publications include a *Higher Education Kit* which focuses on the Title IX regulations and sex equity, and a *Sports Kit* dealing with Title IX and athletics. It also includes the project SPRINT, which is a free public information service on physical education and athletics. It publishes a free newsletter quarterly in physical education and athletics called *In the Running.* SPRINT was created by Women's

Equity Action League and the Educational and Legal Defense Fund in 1972. The project also maintains a file of examples of rulings and interpretations on physical education and athletic cases which can be obtained by school personnel.

Guidance and Counseling

The world of work is changing rapidly. For example, technological knowledge and expertise in the information and computer area, once an option, is now a necessity. Counselors must be up-to-date on employment predictions for students who will be the workers of tomorrow. Schools, professional counselor associations, and colleges offering graduate work in guidance and counseling have developed sporadic pre- and in-service training for counselors in the area of sex equity. However, many counselors have not had the opportunity for such training. For counselors who need further resources to assist them in complying with Title IX and providing equitable counseling to their students, available materials often help. The resources which follow will provide this assistance. Resources in the area of sex equity in counseling tend to be diverse; therefore subcategories have been provided in this section.

Occupational Resources:

Materials addressing sex equity in specific careers can be obtained from many professional groups or information/resource centers. Examples of these follow:

> AMERICAN PERSONNEL AND GUIDANCE ASSOCIATION
> 2 Skyline Place, Suite 400
> 5203 Leesburg Pike
> Falls Church, VA 22041
> (703) 820-4700

APGA is the major organization for guidance and counseling specialists and provides programs and in-service training for guidance personnel as well as maintaining an informal exchange of information and providing more formal means of communication through publications, journals, films, tapes, newsletters, and conventions.

APGA has a bibliography on women available through its library and has several publications about the nonsexist counseling of women: *Facilitating Career Development for Girls and Women, Assertion Skill Training: A Group Procedure for High School Women,* and *Counseling Girls and Women Over the Life Span.* The APGA publications catalog is available free of charge.

AMERICAN PSYCHOLOGICAL ASSOCIATION
COMMITTEE ON WOMEN IN PSYCHOLOGY
1200 17th Street, N.W.
Washington, DC 20036
(202) 833-4908

The purpose of the American Psychological Association is to advance psychology as a science, as a profession, and as a means of promoting human welfare. It was founded in 1892, and is the major professional psychological organization in the United States. The APA's Task Force on the Status of Women in Psychology, established in 1969, evolved into the Committee on Women in Psychology (CWP) in 1974. An APA resource, stimulated by the CWP, which may be of interest to counselors is the publication *Careers for Women in Psychology: Strategies for Success.*

THE ASSOCIATION FOR WOMEN IN SCIENCE
1346 Connecticut Avenue, N.W., Suite 1122
Washington, DC 20036
(202) 833-1998

AWIS promotes equal opportunities for women to enter the science/ mathematics related fields. It supplies funding for predoctoral awards through its educational foundation and testifies on sex discrimination matters before congressional committees. Other activities include monitoring institutions and agencies for affirmative action compliance and publishing a newsletter that reports statistics on the status of women in the professions and reviews relevant civil rights issues and laws. AWIS also coordinates activities among members to provide support and assistance in career development and serves as an employment clearinghouse. Its national headquarters houses a collection of biographies of over 5,000 women scientists.

CATALYST INFORMATION CENTER
14 East 60th Street
New York, NY 10022
(212) 759-9700

The Catalyst Information Center is a major national clearinghouse for information on women and work. Currently the center has two major facilities; the Catalyst Library and the new Audio-Visual Center. Both are open to the public without charge.

The Center's professionally staffed library contains more than 4,000 catalogued items related to women in the labor force, to expanding career options for women, and to business, government, and social trends. The collection is comprehensive and is updated constantly. Individuals and groups can use the library, which offers a large number of self-guidance publications, including 60 of Catalyst's own career information and self-guidance books. The staff handles requests for information in person, by phone, or by mail.

Catalyst also publishes bibliographies in a number of areas for a minimal charge; for example, "Women: Achievement," "Black Women," "Economics of Sex Discrimination," "Women in Mathematics," and "Women in Skilled Trades." A free list of these bibliographies is available. New books on careers and employment are *What To Do With the Rest of Your Life: The Catalyst Career Guide for Women in the 80's* and *Marketing Yourself: The Catalyst Women's Guide to Successful Resumés and Interviews*. A recent Catalyst filmstrip, *Challenging Careers: New Opportunities for Women* is available from Guidance Associates (800-431-1242) and is appropriate for high school students.

THE NATIONAL CENTER FOR CAREER EDUCATION
University of Montana
P.O. Box 7815
Missoula, MT 59801
(406) 243-5262

The main mission of The National Center for Career Education is to communicate career education to the people of the United States and to improve, for youth, the orderly transition from school to work. NCCE has been designated by the United States Department of Education as the national repository for career education materials and has received the entire career education library of the United States Department of Education. In addition to collecting, storing, and sharing resource materials, NCCE provides training and technical assistance to educators in the area of career education. This organization is involved in all 50 states and has ten affiliate universities across the nation. A topic index is available on each of 40 areas of career education, and custom computer searches are also available. NCCE can also provide mini-libraries of documents on specific areas of career education.

THE NATIONAL CENTER FOR RESEARCH IN VOCATIONAL
EDUCATION
The Ohio State University
1960 Kenny Road
Columbus, OH 43210
(800) 848-4815

The center maintains a national clearinghouse on vocational education research and is a major source of materials development, dissemination, and technical assistance in vocational education. Technical assistance provided by the center staff is available nationally. Communication and dissemination are handled through *Centergram*, the center's monthly newsletter, ERIC, mailing lists, and networking. Also available are books, bibliographies, curriculum materials, training packages for sex-equity coordinators, and other resources specifically designed for parents, teachers, students, counselors, administrators, and librarians. Some examples include *Sugar and Spice Is Not the Answer,* a parent handbook on the career implications of sex stereotyping, *Sex Stereotyping and Occupational Aspirations: An Annotated Bibliography, Women in the Work Force: Follow-Up Study of Curriculum Materials for Secondary Students,* and *Preparing Women to Teach Nontraditional Vocational Education.* In addition, a training package entitled *Vocational Education Sex Equity Strategies* includes a compilation of workshop resources and materials on topics such as recruiting and retaining students in courses nontraditional to their sex, assessing and adapting materials, and strategies for interacting with the community. A catalog of materials is available on request from the center.

> SOCIETY OF WOMEN ENGINEERS
> United Engineering Center, Room 305
> 345 East 47th Street
> New York, NY 10017
> (212) 644-7855

The Society of Women Engineers promotes the interests of women engineers and encourages women to consider careers in engineering. Besides the national organization, there are 34 area sections of SWE throughout the United States, and 147 colleges and universities have student sections.

The society informs young women, their parents, counselors, and the general public about the opportunities available to women in the different engineering fields. Many area sections and individual members of SWE are willing to work with women high school students and with guidance personnel in this career guidance effort. Of interest to secondary school personnel and guidance counselors in particular is SWE's program of awards and scholarships for women who are outstanding in mathematics and science and are considering engineering as a career. SWE also has a list of publications that may be valuable additions to a collection on nontraditional careers for women (for example, *A Profile of the Woman Engineer*).

United States Department of Labor Resources

Essential for counselors who work with students in occupational and educational counseling are materials from the United States Department of Labor. Three subgroups are described below. The usual policy in this department is that single copies of publications are free and may be reproduced in quantity by school systems.

> UNITED STATES DEPARTMENT OF LABOR
> BUREAU OF LABOR STATISTICS
> 441 G Street, N.W.
> Washington, DC 20210
> (202) 523-1222

The Bureau of Labor Statistics has responsibility for the Labor Department's economic and statistical research activities; it is the principal fact-finding agency in the field of labor economics, particularly with respect to the collection and analysis of data on manpower and labor requirements, labor force, employment, unemployment, hours of work, wages and employee compensation, prices, living conditions, labor-management relations, productivity and technological developments, occupational safety and health, and structure and growth of the economy. The information collected by the Bureau is issued in monthly press releases, in special publications, and in its official publication, the *Monthly Labor Review.* Most of the statistical reports issued by BLS contain data by sex of workers. In addition, the booklet *Tomorrow's Jobs* offers predictions of types of workers who will be in demand and has a section on where to find additional information on work. Of particular interest to counselors are the *Occupational Outlook Handbook* and the *Occupational Outlook Quarterly,* which provide up-to-date information on jobs and predict future needs for specific workers.

Publications are also issued on specific topics, such as *Where to Find BLS Statistics on Women.* This guide gives sources for characteristics of working women, historical data on the increased entry of women into the labor force, where women are employed, women's earnings, characteristics of families headed by working women, educational levels of working women, and unemployment of women. BLS also does studies on the work-life expectancies of men and women.

UNITED STATES DEPARTMENT OF LABOR
EMPLOYMENT AND TRAINING ADMINISTRATION
Information Office
Patrick Henry Building
601 D Street, N.W.
Washington, DC 20013
(202) 376-6270

The Employment and Training Administration (ETA) is responsible for conducting several work-experience and work-training programs, funding and overseeing the programs conducted under the Comprehensive Employment and Training Act of 1973 (CETA), and conducting a continuing program of research, development, and evaluation.

The following services of the Employment and Training Act are of importance to school personnel, particularly counselors:

- The United States Employment Service maintains a system of nearly 2,500 public employment offices. The USES provides special assistance to youth between 16 and 24 years of age. Their Cooperative School Program is aimed at easing the transition from school to work through placement counseling and job-finding services, and the Summer Employment Program refers school youths to private and public summer job opportunities.

- The Office of National Programs is responsible for employment and training programs including the administration of the National Apprenticeship and Training Act. Field representatives from the Bureau of Apprenticeship and Training are available to work with schools in regard to apprenticeship programs. In a special effort to assist minority youth and women in the consideration of apprenticeship programs, the Apprenticeship Outreach Programs in approximately 100 cities offer counseling and preparation for required preapprenticeship tests.

ETA publications are an important resource for counselors. Examples are *Apprenticeship Now, An Equal Chance to Be an Apprentice,* and *Apprenticeship and CETA: Technical Assistance Guide.* In addition, back issues of its periodical, *Worklife,* include articles on sex equity in employment.

UNITED STATES DEPARTMENT OF LABOR
WOMEN'S BUREAU
Office of the Secretary
200 Constitution Avenue, N.W.
Washington, DC 20210
(202) 523-6653

The Women's Bureau, established in 1920, is the only federal agency devoted exclusively to the concerns of women in the labor force. Its major objectives are to improve the economic status of all women and to reduce discrimination based on sex and race. It participates in the development of government policies and programs that affect women's employment and their employability. The bureau's assistance and information should be considered a primary resource for secondary guidance departments and for elementary and secondary level educators.

Several issues of primary concern to the bureau are also priority issues for elementary and secondary educators and students: promoting nontraditional jobs for women, especially in apprenticeship and construction work, and in professional and management jobs; providing realistic educational and career counseling materials; increasing employment opportunities for young women; and assisting teenage mothers in achieving self-sufficiency. Publications from the bureau are an important resource for elementary and secondary school personnel who are working on career counseling. "Publications of the Women's Bureau" lists all available brochures and reports and indicates which ones are available in Spanish. Examples of publications are *Why Women Work, Women's Guide to Apprenticeship,* and *Young Women and Employment: What We Need to Know About the School to Work Transition.* Single copies of these publications can be obtained free from the bureau.

Science and Mathematics Career/Educational Experiences

A few organizations offer materials about specific career areas and, in addition, offer opportunities for special courses or on-the-job experience with ongoing science and mathematics projects. The National Science Foundation listing below is an example. All senior high school counselors should be aware of the resources offered by this organization.

> NATIONAL SCIENCE FOUNDATION
> SCIENCE EDUCATION DIRECTORATE
> 1800 G Street, N.W.
> Washington, DC 20550
> (202) 282-7150 Division of Scientific Personnel Improvement
> (202) 282-7786 Division of Science Education Resources Improvement

The National Science Foundation sponsors science training programs yearly for more than 3,800 high-ability junior and senior high school students. Most of these 1 to 12 week programs are in the summer. These programs offer the opportunity for outstanding students to have college-level instruction and participation in investigative laboratory work and problem-solving experiences. Although open to both female and male students, this program offers unique opportunities to female students who show ability in the scientific area but who have not considered career options in this field. Yearly directories for this program are mailed to schools throughout the United States or can be obtained from the above address.

The National Science Foundation also has publications aimed at increasing the participation of women in science careers. The *Roster of Women Scientists* provides school personnel a list of scientists and engineers who have indicated an interest in encouraging females to consider scientific careers; in addition, program ideas may be taken from the NSF report on science career workshops for high school students.

Motivational Posters

Some organizations have developed resources that are particularly appealing to students and motivate them to think of widening their career and educational options. One company which produced posters and accompanying resources is General Electric.

> GENERAL ELECTRIC COMPANY
> EDUCATIONAL COMMUNICATIONS PROGRAMS
> Fairfield, CT 06431
> (203) 373-2030

General Electric offers a "World of Work" kit, which consists of a series of eye-catching posters that invite students to correlate interests and abilities with areas of work. In addition, career education booklets, such as *Planning Your Career, So You Want to Go to Work?, What's It Like to Be an Engineer?* are available.

These world-of-work materials are nonsexist and portray many persons in nontraditional activities. Copies of these materials, which are especially useful for junior and senior high school students, have been widely distributed. If your school does not have a set, single copies are free from the above address.

Community Organization Assistance

Often counselors who work with students on exploring careers want community workers to talk with students about specific occupations. Sometimes searching for persons who are in careers nontraditional to their sex can be frustrating and time consuming. Often community groups can assist in this effort. Try seeking assistance from local parent-teacher association representatives, union groups, service organizations, and ethnic and minority organizations. In some cases national organizations may help you locate specific organizational resource personnel in your area. Two groups are given as examples.

> BUSINESS AND PROFESSIONAL WOMEN'S FOUNDATION
> 2012 Massachusetts Avenue, N.W.
> Washington, DC 20036
> (202) 293-1200

The Business and Professional Women's Foundation carries out an integrated program of research, information, and education to improve the quality of working life for women. It is a nonprofit research and educational organization started in 1956 by the National Federation of Business and Professional Women's Clubs, Inc.

Both the BPW Clubs and BPW Foundation have resources to assist high school women in assessing future occupational possibilities. Local BPW groups often can provide the services of members who can assist in career exploration. The foundation also has many resources that can assist secondary personnel and students in career development.

> NATIONAL URBAN LEAGUE, INC.
> 500 East 62nd Street
> New York, NY 10021
> (212) 644-6500

The National Urban League is an interracial, nonprofit community service organization that uses the tools and methods of social work, economics, law, business management, and other disciplines to secure equal opportunities in all sectors of society for black Americans and other minorities. Three of its main areas of interest are job placement, job training, and education. Many urban League affiliates conduct education programs in their local communities. They work with students, parents, and school systems in areas such as career counseling, tutoring, dropout prevention, and parent involvement. Beside the Urban League's national headquarters in New York City, there are four regional offices in Chicago, Los Angeles, Atlanta, and New York; a Washington, D.C., research department and bureau; and 116 affiliates in 36 states and the District of Columbia. Since the Urban League is an advocate of equal opportunity, many of the affiliates have members who can serve as valuable resource persons.

Career Audiovisual Series

Audiovisual presentations aimed specifically at the reduction of sex stereotyping in careers are not readily available. However, one series described below should be especially useful to counselors who work with students in class or group settings on occupational awareness.

> SCIENCE RESEARCH ASSOCIATES, INC.
> 155 North Wacker Drive
> Chicago, IL 60606
> (312) 984-2000

Science Research Associates, Inc. (SRA) has developed an audiovisual resource that can assist school personnel in combating stereotyping. *Freestyle,* a television series on career awareness for students ages 9–12, was funded through a grant from the National Institute of Education and has as a basic objective the reduction of sex-role and ethnic-role stereotyping. SRA has also developed materials to support this series—a teacher guide and home calendar. These reprints also include awareness activities for teachers. (Copies of the videotapes and accompanying materials for *Freestyle* are available through the Educational Media Division of the Los Angeles County Superintendent of Schools' Office, 9300 East Imperial Highway, Downey, CA 90242. Teacher guides and home calendars are available through KCET TV, 4401 Sunset Boulevard, Los Angeles, CA 90027, c/o English.)

Vocational Education

Vocational educators play a critical role because of the nature of the service they provide. More than any other group of educators they are directly responsible for providing students with the specific occupational skills they will need to survive as adults. Efforts towards eliminating sex discrimination will increase both the equality of educational opportunity for students and provide for a more equitable distribution of access and benefits within the workforce and other institutions. The following organizations can assist vocational educators in implementing Title IX and achieving sex equity in vocational education policies, practices, and programs.

Specific Resources

AMERICAN HOME ECONOMICS ASSOCIATION
2010 Massachusetts Avenue, N.W.
Washington, DC 20036
(202) 862-8300

The American Home Economics Association is an educational and scientific association for professionals. Current priorities are family research, education, day care and allied services, displaced homemaker legislation, and consumer advocacy.

The AHEA's Center for the Family directs attention and action to trends, issues, and needs related to the family. Annual public forums have centered on such topics as "Stress and the Family—Challenging Current Role Assignments," "Women Employed—Impact on Families," and "New Roles for Men—New Options for Families."

Some of AHEA's publications, such as *Adolescent Role Expectations,* and articles in the *Journal of Home Economics,* such as "Changing Roles: Implications for Home Economics" and "Strategies to Use in the Non-Sexist Classroom," can be used by elementary and secondary personnel in planning and supervising home economics curricula.

AMERICAN INSTITUTES FOR RESEARCH IN THE BEHAVIORAL SCIENCES
P.O. Box 1113
Palo Alto, CA 94302
(415) 493-3550

See description in "Instructional Materials and Classroom Strategies" section.

AMERICAN VOCATIONAL ASSOCIATION
2020 North 14th Street
Arlington, VA 22201
(703) 522-6121

The American Vocational Association publishes materials that contain sex-equity information. Included are *Voc Ed,* their official journal; *Update,* a monthly newsletter; *Special Report,* a monthly newsletter sent to the media and policy makers; and *Legislative Brief,* a weekly publication developed during congressional sessions. For example, the April 1980 *Voc Ed* concentrates on the theme, "Sex Equity: Are Students Free to Choose?" Topics include sex-fair teaching techniques and roles of sex-equity coordinators. AVA's special publication, *Pioneering Programs in Sex Equity: A Teacher's Guide,* looks at stereotyping and includes case studies, quizzes, and other techniques to assist teachers in discussing the changing workforce and family role structure. The association also produces and distributes the nonsexist poster series, "Know How," which depicts workers in nontraditional occupations.

In addition, the Vocational Education Equity Council (VEEC) is a part of the administrative division. VEEC's purpose is to bring to the attention of vocational educators and government policy makers the importance of sex equity in vocational education.

EDUCATION DEVELOPMENT CENTER
55 Chapel Street
Newton, MA 02160
(800) 225-3088
(617) 969-7100

The Education Development Center serves as the dissemination center for programs and products developed under the Women's Educational Equity Act (WEEAP). Examples of products in vocational education are: *The New Pioneers Seminar Handbook,* which provides tested strategies for the elimination of sex bias in occupation education; *It's Her Future,* a media program designed to encourage parents to support traditional and nontraditional career decisions; and *Focus on the Future,* a curriculum developed for students to test their own biases related to career choices. (See entry in the first section of this chapter for a complete description of EDC).

FEDERAL EDUCATION PROJECT
LAWYERS' COMMITTEE FOR CIVIL RIGHTS UNDER LAW
733 15th Street, N.W., Suite 526
Washington, DC 20005
(202) 628-6700

See description in "Title IX and Related Sex-Equity Laws" section.

THE NATIONAL CENTER FOR RESEARCH IN VOCATIONAL
EDUCATION
The Ohio State University
1960 Kenny Road
Columbus, OH 43210
(800) 848-4815
See description in "Guidance and Counseling" section.

NATIONAL COMMISSION ON WORKING WOMEN/CENTER FOR
WOMEN AND WORK
1211 Connecticut Avenue N.W., Suite 310
Washington, DC 20036
(202) 466-6770

The commission was established to change and effect policies and action plans concerning working women. Its focus is on women in the workforce who are employed in clerical, sales, service, factory, and plant jobs, "the 80 percent." The staff provides general information about occupational segregation of women in the workforce. Some of the commission's (center's) most recent publications appropriate for school use include

An Overview of Women in the Workforce and *News About Women at Work* in the Mid-Atlantic region. Also of interest is its report of the *Research Roundtable on Working Women,* which can be used as a model for other groups involved in discussing the problems of working women in non-professional, nontechnical occupations.

> PROJECT MOVE (MAXIMIZING OPTIONS IN VOCATIONAL
> EDUCATION)
> State University of New York (SUNY), College of Technology,
>   Division of Vocational Technical Education
> 811 Court Street
> Utica, NY 13502
> (315) 792-3535

Project MOVE was developed to provide training, workshops, and materials to school personnel working for sex equity in vocational education. Its workshops and conferences are planned for New York State participants, but the project will supply ideas and information to out-of-state educators who are interested in training for sex equity in vocational education. Among the materials available from Project MOVE are: an eight-minute filmstrip, *Expanding Roles in a Changing World,* a source book entitled, *Expanding Adolescent Role Expectations: Information, Activities, Resources for Vocational Educators,* and other print resources such as bulletins, planning kits, assessment instruments, reports, and games.

> UNITED STATES DEPARTMENT OF EDUCATION
> OFFICE OF VOCATIONAL AND ADULT EDUCATION
> 7th and D Streets, S.W., Suite 5600
> Washington, DC 20202
> (202) 245-8166

The Office of Vocational and Adult Education administers vocational education programs and funds model sex-equity projects. Specific sex-equity projects include *The Special Vocational Education Needs of Women, Sexism in Education, Reducing Vocational Education Stereotypes, Local Vocational Advisory Council Involvement in Effecting Sex Equity in Education,* and *Increasing Sex Fairness in Vocational Education.*

OVAE administers the Vocational Education Act of 1963, which provides categorical funding to state education agencies. Part of this act requires each state to assign personnel to work full-time to assist the state in eliminating sex discrimination and sex stereotyping and to submit one- and five-year plans that work toward this goal. States are also allowed to expend Vocational Education Act funds for grants to overcome sex bias. The act also requires advisory councils on the national, state, and local levels. These councils must have both sexes represented including persons who are advocates for women in vocational education.

UNITED STATES DEPARTMENT OF LABOR
EMPLOYMENT AND TRAINING ADMINISTRATION
Information Office
Patrick Henry Building
601 D Street, N.W.
Washington, DC 20013
(202) 376-6270

See description in "Guidance and Counseling" section.

UNITED STATES DEPARTMENT OF LABOR
WOMEN'S BUREAU
Office of the Secretary
Washington, DC 20210
(202) 523-6653

See description in "Guidance and Counseling" section.

Physical Education and Athletics

Many physical educators have recognized the challenges related to the implementation of Title IX. Sex equity in athletics necessitates recommendations for providing equal opportunity for both sexes in areas such as facilities, scheduling, practice time, and equipment. Legal and procedural questions have been raised about coeducational instruction, teaching and evaluation methods, and organizational alternatives. These questions will continue to confront physical educators in the eighties. The following organizations provide model programs, legal interpretations, and recommendations for the development of coeducational physical education and athletic programming.

Specific Resources

AMERICAN ALLIANCE FOR HEALTH, PHYSICAL EDUCATION, RECREATION, AND DANCE
NATIONAL ASSOCIATION FOR GIRLS AND WOMEN IN SPORT
1900 Association Drive
Reston, VA 22091
(703) 476-3400

See description in "Title IX and Related Sex-Equity Laws."

ASSOCIATION FOR INTERCOLLEGIATE ATHLETICS FOR WOMEN
1201 16th Street N.W.
Washington, DC 20036
(202) 833-5485

This association functions as the governing body for initiating and maintaining standards of excellence in women's intercollegiate athletic programs. It also conducts championships in women's sports. The AIAW staff offers on-call technical assistance on intercollegiate athletics for women.

Of special interest to high school athletic directors and counselors is the annual *AIAW Directory.* This directory lists addresses, contact names, women's sports, and financial assistance available to female athletes at AIAW's more than 900-member higher education institutions. The association also publishes the *AIAW Handbook,* which includes all rules, regulations, policies, and procedures for women's intercollegiate athletics as well as names of leadership personnel in this field. A list of publications can be obtained without charge from the association.

WOMEN'S EQUITY ACTION LEAGUE EDUCATIONAL AND LEGAL DEFENSE FUND (WEAL FUND)
805 15th Street, N.W., Suite 822
Washington, DC 20005
(202) 638-1961 SPRINT
Toll Free Hot Line for sports equity only: (800) 424-5162

See description in "Title IX and Sex-Equity Laws" section.

WOMEN'S SPORTS FOUNDATION
195 Moulton Street
San Francisco, CA 94123
(415) 563-6266

The Women's Sports Foundation was formed by top female athletes in 1974 to:

- encourage and support the participation of women in sports activities
- provide general assistance and encouragement to girls and women in sports
- educate the public about women's athletic capabilities and the value of sports for women

Several services provided by the Women's Sports Foundation are of particular use to secondary school personnel working with physical education, athletics, and scholarship programs. The foundation publishes an annual college scholarship and sport camp guide; provides sport camp scholarships for disadvantaged girls; works with other organizations to improve programming; and maintains an information and resource center on women's sports. The foundation has an extensive library on women and sport, and serves as a clearinghouse on the subject. In addition to the *Annual Scholarship Guide* (mentioned above), which lists over 10,000 athletic scholarships for women at post-secondary institutions, the Women's Sports Foundation also publishes a periodical, *Women's Sports,* and booklets such as the *Physical Conditioning Guide.*

Community and Parent Groups

Compliance with Title IX is most often found where the community and parent groups have been active in their expectations for equity among male and female students. This was one of the conclusions of a 1980 Rand Corporation report, *Mechanisms for the Implementation of Civil Rights Guarantees by Educational Institutions.*

School personnel usually have one of two perceptions of parent and community groups. They may be perceived as pressure groups that actually hinder the delivery of education to students or they may be perceived as an important part of the total school program, which they serve with advice, support, and resources.

In school systems where community and parent groups are made part of the team to provide sex equity, students usually benefit. Community and parent groups concerned about sex equity and Title IX compliance in schools often need assistance in such areas as:

- what their specific concerns should be
- how they can assist in a positive manner
- what resource materials are available
- how to evaluate progress in sex equity

Resources are as important to community members and parents as they are to school personnel. The organizations listed below have materials that can assist community groups who wish to work with the schools to bring about equity. In addition, many of these resources can also be used in nonschool settings such as scouts, recreational groups, service groups, and the like.

Specific Resources

AMERICAN ASSOCIATION OF UNIVERSITY WOMEN
2401 Virginia Avenue, N.W.
Washington, DC 20037
(202) 785-7700

The American Association of University Women is the largest and oldest national organization for the advancement of women. State divisions and local branches are involved in education and sex-equity study/action topics, and provide sources of role models for students. They can also supply resource persons for local advisory and policy committees. For the names of local and state presidents in your area, contact the national association's membership office.

AAUW also produces many publications dealing with sex equity and Title IX. Among recent publications are *Liberating Our Children, Ourselves, But We Will Persist* (concerning the status of women in higher education), *Monitoring Title IX, At Ease with ERA,* and *Job Hunter's Kit.*

ASSOCIATION FOR CHILDHOOD EDUCATION INTERNATIONAL
3615 Wisconsin Avenue, N.W.
Washington, DC 20016
(202) 363-6963

See description in "Instructional Materials and Classroom Strategies" section.

BUSINESS AND PROFESSIONAL WOMEN'S FOUNDATION
2012 Massachusetts Avenue, N.W.
Washington, DC 20036
(202) 293-1200

See description in "Guidance and Counseling" section.

COUNCIL ON INTERRACIAL BOOKS FOR CHILDREN
RACISM AND SEXISM RESOURCE CENTER FOR EDUCATORS
1841 Broadway
New York, NY 10023
(212) 757-5339

See description in "Instructional Materials and Classroom Strategies" section.

EDUCATION DEVELOPMENT CENTER
55 Chapel Street
Newton, MA 02160
(800) 225-3088
(617) 969-7100

See description in "Instructional Materials and Classroom Strategies" section.

THE FEMINIST PRESS
SUNY/College at Old Westbury
Box 334
Old Westbury, NY 11568
(516) 997-7660

See description in "Instructional Materials and Classroom Strategies" section.

FREE MEN
Box 920
Columbia, MD 21044
(202) 723-3989

Free Men is an organization that seeks to promote awareness in men and women of how gender-based roles limit men legally, socially, and psychologically, and to provide support and assistance to men who choose to break free of the limitations. It encourages discussion and study through meetings, workshops, and lectures, and disseminates information concerning resources available to men. In addition, the organization maintains a speakers bureau and encourages and undertakes research/demonstration projects to confront the impact of sexism on men and boys. Its publications include *Options,* a monthly newsletter, and pamphlets.

GIRL SCOUTS OF THE UNITED STATES OF AMERICA
830 Third Avenue
New York, NY 10022
(212) 940-7500

Girl Scouts of the United States of America, founded in 1912, provides opportunities for girls to develop their potential, make friends, and become a vital part of their community. The program offers a broad range of activities that address members' current interests and their future roles as women. The program encompasses science, the arts, and the out-of-doors.

THE LEAGUE OF UNITED LATIN AMERICAN CITIZENS (LULAC)
NATIONAL EDUCATION SERVICE CENTERS, INC.
400 First Street, N.W., Suite 716
Washington, DC 20001
(202) 374-1652/53/54

The league's main goal is to increase Hispanic access to and achievement in post-secondary education. There are four main components to this program for pre-college-level students. They are:

- bilingual/bicultural educational counseling
- research and advocacy
- employment counseling and training
- a national scholarship fund for outstanding Hispanic students

Activities include preparing students for college and careers, on-the-job training, investigating educational issues of importance to Hispanics, and impacting on national policies. The league was established in 1929 in Corpus Christi, Texas, and is the oldest and largest Hispanic organization in this country. It has 11 field offices throughout the country, with its national office in Washington, D.C.

LEAGUE OF WOMEN VOTERS OF THE UNITED STATES
1730 M Street, N.W.
Washington, DC 20036
(202) 296-1770

The league is a nonpartisan political action group that lobbies on national issues, coordinates strategies with other coalitions and organizations, and educates the public in citizen education. As a nonprofit organization, the league provides speakers to schools, distributes nonpartisan election information, conducts public forums on issues of local concern, and disseminates resource materials (e.g. books, pamphlets, bibliographies, and materials specifically suited for parents, libraries, and students). Some of its publications include *Women and Work, Education: Problems in Equity, In Pursuit of Equal Rights: Women in the Seventies,* and *ERA Means Equal Rights for Men and Women.* Discounts are given to schools for large quantities of some publications. Check league publications catalog for details. All publication orders must be prepaid.

LOLLIPOP POWER, INC.
Box 1171
Chapel Hill, NC 27514
(919) 929-4857

See description in "Instructional Materials and Classroom Strategies" section.

MEXICAN AMERICAN WOMEN'S NATIONAL ASSOCIATION
L'Enfant Plaza Station, S.W.
P.O. Box 23656
Washington, DC 20024
(202) 311-7667

This is a nonprofit organization representing the special interests and concerns of Mexican American Women. Its activities include meeting with local, state, and federal legislators in order to express the association's viewpoint; coordinating educational and cultural trips with a feminist perspective; sponsoring conferences; and publishing a monthly newsletter. Membership information is available from the association.

NATIONAL COMMITTEE FOR CITIZENS IN EDUCATION
410 Wilde Lake Village Green
Columbia, MD 21044
(301) 997-9300

The committee's goal is to train people to be more effective in working with schools. It has developed a series of handbooks for parents, some of which include "The Rights of Parents in the Education of Their Children" and "Parents Organizing to Improve Schools." There is a 24-hour toll free phone (800-NETWORK) to help parents get information and assistance. An eight-times-per-year newspaper, *NETWORK,* keeps the public informed on current education news. The committee also monitors citizens' participation in Individual Educational Plans. In addition, they conduct training sessions that teach parents and citizens how to deal more effectively with the public school system. From this work a *PARENT'S NETWORK* has been established to support positive action and local parent-citizen groups.

NATIONAL CONGRESS OF PARENTS AND TEACHERS
700 N. Rush Street
Chicago, IL 60611
(312) 787-0977

The purpose of the National Congress of Parents and Teachers is to promote the welfare of children and youth in the home, the school, and the community, and to bring into closer relation parents and teachers so they may cooperate intelligently in children's education. Sexism is one of many parent education issues that has been addressed through its monthly newsletter, *PTA Today*. Available for purchase is a special issue on Title IX and sex equity, which includes articles such as "Where You Can Obtain Information on Title IX's War Against Sexism," "Scholarships Available to Female Athletes," and "Women and Math: The Practice of Shunning." Similar issues are addressed in other PTA publications.

PTA branches are in each state and there are local units in 29,000 communities. Equal educational opportunities for all students is a major priority, not only at the national level, but also with state and local PTAs.

NATIONAL COUNCIL OF JEWISH WOMEN
15 East 26th Street
New York, NY 10010
(212) 532-1740

The National Council of Jewish Women is a multifaceted organization dedicated to improve the quality of life for individuals as well as to strengthen Jewish communities. Its main focus is to design programs based on community needs. Activities include conferences on women's roles, on justice for children, and on education of the disadvantaged. In addition, members focus on day care facilities and services for children, foster care programs, and the educational needs of the disadvantaged. The council advocates on behalf of human and constitutional rights and sex-equity related issues and participates in national and state conferences.

NATIONAL ORGANIZATION FOR WOMEN
425 13th Street, N.W., Suite 1048
Washington, DC 20004
(202) 347-2279

One of the National Organization for Women's (NOW) objectives is the elimination of sex discrimination in education. The organization, founded in 1966, has an Education Discrimination Committee and has established the Project on Equal Education Rights (PEER) under the NOW Legal Defense and Education Fund.

NOW also has state organizations and local chapters that have members, many of whom are particularly interested in working toward the elimination of sex-discrimination education. School personnel should consider contacting NOW members as resources in their sex-equity efforts.

Names of leaders of local and state NOW organizations can be obtained through local directories, Commissions for Women, or by contacting the national office of NOW.

NATIONAL ORGANIZATION FOR WOMEN LEGAL DEFENSE AND EDUCATION FUND
PROJECT ON EQUAL EDUCATION RIGHTS (PEER)
1112 13th Street, N.W.
Washington, DC 20005
(202) 332-7337

The Project on Equal Education Rights (PEER) is a project of the NOW Legal Defense and Education Fund and is one of the major national projects devoted primarily to the elimination of sex bias and discrimination in public elementary and secondary schools.

An action organization, PEER works to:

- press for stronger federal enforcement of legislation such as Title IX and Title VII
- mobilize coalitions of citizens groups to work with their school districts
- keep educators, parents, and community groups informed about progress and problems relating to sex bias and discrimination in education

One of its newest publications, *The Ties that Bind,* concerns the effects of stereotyping on men. PEER's quarterly newsletter, *PEER Perspective,* is free to those who so request and serves to update readers on Title IX and related rulings, interpretations, and activities. Also free is PEER's publications list for moderately priced materials.

In addition, PEER personnel have trained pilot community groups on how to determine and monitor local school compliance with Title IX and related sex-equity legislation.

THE PUBLIC WORKS, INC.
Putney, VT 05346
(802) 387-6682

The Public Works, Inc. develops educational materials on various social issues. For example, it publishes *The Women's Yellow Pages* sourcebook series. Sourcebooks contain information on issues concerning work, education, family life, legal rights, marriage and family life, parenting, and health. In addition, listings of agencies and programs serving women in specific communities are included.

WOMEN'S ACTION ALLIANCE
370 Lexington Avenue
New York, NY 10017
(212) 532-8330

See description in "Instructional Materials and Classroom Strategies" section.

YOUNG WOMEN'S CHRISTIAN ASSOCIATION, NATIONAL
BOARD
600 Lexington Avenue
New York, NY 10022
(212) 753-4700

The YWCA Public Affairs program operates under the following principles in the area of sex equity:

- to provide adequate guidance and counseling services and training opportunities for both women and girls in the work force
- to support equal access of women to all educational possibilities
- to require that there be no barriers based on race, sex, physical or mental handicaps, or minority status
- to develop programs to assure quality education—nonracist, nonsexist, nonageist, multilingual, and multicultural

Activities include counseling, training teachers to teach in multicultural classrooms, therapeutic programs for the handicapped, career planning, sports programs, media assistance, shelter, and meal programs. A special emphasis is placed on activities related to career readiness for teenage women and career retraining for displaced homemakers. Its publications include *Women—A Power for Change, A Job at the End, Let's Try a Workshop with Teen Women,* and *Child Care, A Plan that Works.* Local YWCA's are independent and plan activities targeted to local community needs.

STATE AND REGIONAL RESOURCES FOR TITLE IX AND SEX EQUITY

Elementary and secondary education personnel should be aware of two groups which can provide on-call assistance. These groups can help school personnel in locating resources, and in developing in-service training, workshops and conferences related to Title IX and sex equity. Regionally, educators can use the services and resources of sex-desegregation assistance centers. In their states, educational personnel should investigate pertinent resource persons in their state education department. Descriptions of both of these major resource providers follow.

Sex-Desegregation Assistance Centers

There are ten sex-desegregation assistance centers funded by the United States Department of Education under Title IV of the Civil Rights Act of 1964 to assist public school districts in meeting the requirements of Title IX and achieving sex equity. Centers provide services free upon receipt of a request from a district superintendent.

In accordance with Title IV of the Civil Rights Act of 1964, these centers have been created to help public school districts:

- increase the understanding of personnel concerning the problems of sex bias in education and help them avoid this bias
- identify sex bias and sex-role stereotypes in textbooks and other curricular materials and develop methods of countering their effect on students
- identify and resolve problems that arise in meeting the requirements of Title IX or obeying state laws that prohibit discrimination in education
- prepare and disseminate to parents and students materials explaining the requirements of Title IX
- develop methods to encourage student, parent, and community support for, and involvement in, the sex-desegregation process
- recruit women and men for employment in positions in which they are underrepresented
- develop procedures for preventing sex discrimination in employment practices
- provide nondiscriminatory counseling materials and techniques
- identify federal, state, and other resources that can assist in sex desegregation

Contact individual centers for specific information regarding assistance. In case of questions regarding which center to contact, call or write the United States Department of Education as follows:

DEPUTY ASSISTANT SECRETARY FOR EQUAL OPPORTUNITY
PROGRAMS
UNITED STATES DEPARTMENT OF EDUCATION
400 Maryland Avenue, S.W.
Washington, DC 20202
(202) 245-8465

State Education Agencies

Personnel in each state and territorial educational agency can provide resource assistance to local school districts in the areas of Title IX,

$850018433

Title II, and other sex-equity legislation. In addition, some states have major collections of nonbiased audiovisual presentations and print resources that can be used by local districts. Several state educational agencies have developed materials on Title IX and the general sex-equity area that usually can be obtained either free or for minimal charge by other SEAs or school districts in other states.

In order to determine the type of assistance a specific state can offer in the area of sex equity, contact the Title IX designee, the vocational education sex-equity coordinator, or in the case of states that have been awarded Title IV funds for sex desegregation, the coordinator of this project.

Personnel funded under Title IV for sex desegregation advise and assist local education agencies in the implementation of Title IX and the achievement of sex equity. Sex-equity coordinators are funded under the sex-equity provisions of Title II, Education Amendments of 1976, to provide a range of services including creating awareness, monitoring policies and practices, providing information on employment and labor data, reviewing vocational education programs for bias, and providing incentive systems to promote student enrollment in courses nontraditional to their sex.

8583